Social Relationships
and Peer Support

Teachers' Guides to Inclusive Practices

Social Relationships and Peer Support

Second Edition

by

Rachel Janney, Ph.D.
Radford University
Radford, Virginia

and

Martha E. Snell, Ph.D.
University of Virginia
Charlottesville

PUBLISHING CO.

Baltimore • London • Sydney

Paul H. Brookes Publishing Co.
Post Office Box 10624
Baltimore, Maryland 21285-0624

www.brookespublishing.com

Typeset by Barton Matheson Willse & Worthington, Baltimore, Maryland.
Manufactured in the United States of America by
Victor Graphics, Inc., Baltimore, Maryland.

All of the vignettes in this book are composites of the authors' actual experiences. In all instances, names have been changed; in some instances, identifying details have been altered to protect confidentiality.

Library of Congress Cataloging-in-Publication Data

Janney, Rachel.
   Social relationships and peer support / by Rachel Janney and Martha E. Snell.—2nd ed.
    p.   cm.—(Teachers' guides to inclusive practices)
   Rev. ed. of: Social relationships and peer support. / Martha E. Snell and Rachel Janney.
   Includes bibliographical references and index.
   ISBN-13: 978-1-55766-821-9 (pbk.)
   ISBN-10: 1-55766-821-3 (pbk.)
   1. Children with social disabilities—Education—United States.   2. Social skills—Study and teaching—United States.   3. Inclusive education—United States.   I. Snell, Martha E.
   II. Snell, Martha E. Social relationships and peer support.   III. Title.   IV. Series.
   LC4069.S54 2006
   371.826'94—dc22
                                                2006010955

British Library Cataloguing in Publication data are available from the British Library.

Contents

About the Authors

Rachel Janney, Ph.D., is Professor in the School of Teacher Education and Leadership at Radford University in Virginia. She has worked with, and on behalf of, children and adults with disabilities in a number of roles, including special education teacher, educational consultant, researcher, and teacher educator. She received her master's degree from Syracuse University and her doctorate from the University of Nebraska–Lincoln. Dr. Janney now teaches coursework in the special education teacher preparation program at Radford University, specializing in the area of cognitive disabilities. She also supervises student interns and student teachers in a number of schools that have a firm commitment to the inclusion of all students. Dr. Janney serves as Co-director of Radford University's Training and Technical Assistance Center, which provides a variety of services and resources to special education teams in school divisions throughout southwest Virginia.

Martha E. Snell, Ph.D., is Professor in the Curry School of Education at the University of Virginia, where she has taught since 1973. Her focus is special education and, specifically, the preparation of teachers of students with mental retardation and severe disabilities and young children with disabilities. Prior to completing her doctoral degree in special education at Michigan State University, she worked with children and adults with disabilities as a residential child care worker, a provider of technical assistance to school and residential programs, and a teacher. In addition to teaching courses at the undergraduate and graduate levels, she currently directs the graduate program in severe disabilities and coordinates the special education program, serves on the boards of several community agencies serving people with disabilities, and is an active member of the American Association on Mental Retardation and TASH.

Drs. Janney and Snell have conducted several research projects in inclusive schools and classrooms. These projects have studied the ways that special and general educators work together to design and implement modifications and accommodations for students with disabilities in inclusive settings. Both authors frequently present workshops on topics related to successful inclusive education.

Acknowledgments

Many colleagues, friends, families, and students merit recognition and deserve thanks for their contributions to our knowledge about social relationships and peer support. Some of these individuals whose work we have learned from and built on include Catherine Breen, Tom Farmer, Doug Fisher, Marsha Forest, Michael F. Giangreco, Charles Greenwood, Tom Haring, Carolyn Hughes, Pam Hunt, Deborah Kamps, Luanna Meyer, Sam Odom, Cap Peck, Bob Perske, Cynthia Pitonyak, Christine Salisbury, Debbie Staub, and Hill Walker.

Kenna M. Colley, Laura K. Vogtle, and Monica Delano deserve acknowledgment for their work on the first edition of *Social Relationships and Peer Support.*

We also would like to acknowledge our editors at Paul H. Brookes Publishing Co., Rebecca Lazo and Janet Betten, for their excellent editing and persistence in completing this and the other books in the *Teachers' Guides to Inclusive Practices* series.

*To all of the educators, parents, and students
who are working to create and maintain inclusive schools:
places where all students have membership,
enjoy social relationships with peers,
and have the needed supports to learn what is
important for them to be successful in life*

Social Relationships
and Peer Support

Chapter 1

Building Social Relationships

This book is intended for teachers and other individuals who work in inclusive schools (or who are striving to help their schools to become more inclusive) with students whose social relationships are lacking, nonsupportive, or troublesome. The focus is on the development, facilitation, and maintenance of social relationships and peer supports between students with and without disabilities. Some students who do not have disabilities also will benefit from the strategies presented in this book to facilitate social relationships.

INCLUSIVE EDUCATION

Although issues related to inclusive schooling are widely examined in professional publications, as well as the popular media, and are discussed by parents, educators, and politicians across the country, vast variations exist in the extent to which inclusive practices actually are implemented. The statistics published in the *Twenty-Fourth Annual Report to Congress on the Implementation of the Individuals with Disabilities Education Act* (U.S. Department of Education, 2002) revealed that in 1999–2000, 52.7% of all students with disabilities were served outside of the general education classroom for more than 79% of the school day. Significant disparities existed in the extent to which students with various disabilities were served in noninclusive settings (i.e., outside of the general education class for more than 79% of the school day), ranging from 52.7% of students with specific learning disabilities to 88.8% of students with multiple disabilities. In addition to these disparities across disability categories, extensive differences also existed across the states in the percentages of students with disabilities placed in less restrictive or more restrictive settings, and, even within individual states, a student with a particular disability had the opportunity to be fully included in his or her neighborhood school in one school district and yet, in a nearby school district, was automatically placed in a more restrictive environment based on less inclusive placement practices.

In this book, we use the terms *inclusive education* and *full inclusion* in a narrow sense:

- All students in the school district have the opportunity to attend the schools they would attend if they did not have disabilities.

- All students in the school district are based in general education homerooms and classes.

- General and special educators collaborate to pull services and supports into the general education setting.

- Decision making about students is flexible, individualized, and not based solely on disability categories.

- Students are taught what it is important for them to learn, which may vary from one student to another.

The students described in this book are composites of student characteristics and personalities we have encountered over the years, all of whom have been members of classes of same-age peers. The main students discussed are

Daniel, a second-grade student with severe disabilities, including cerebral palsy and intellectual disabilities

Melanie, a fourth-grade student with autism

Sam, a ninth-grade student with behavioral disorders and Asperger syndrome

Six key elements are necessary for the successful functioning of inclusive education:

1. *Inclusive program model*—staffing arrangements, service-delivery methods, and administrative support that enable

students to receive appropriate services within inclusive, age-appropriate settings

2. *Inclusive culture in the school*—a vision of a diverse community that is put into practice

3. *Collaborative teaming and problem solving*—general and special educators with skills and strategies for productive co-planning, communication, problem solving, and teaching

4. *Accommodating curricular and instructional practices in the classroom*—teaching that is known to be effective for all learners

5. *Strategies for making and evaluating individualized adaptations*—agreed-on methods for planning, implementing, and evaluating the adaptations needed by individual students

6. *Strategies to facilitate peer relationships and supports*—formal and informal ways to foster age-appropriate interactions and relationships among students with disabilities and their classmates

This book is part of a series, *Teachers' Guides to Inclusive Practices*, which addresses other key elements for inclusive education in greater detail. Like any significant, far-reaching educational change, the development of effective, inclusive schools requires focused, systematic, ongoing efforts among administrators, general and special education teachers, parents, and support personnel. Many of those involved will need professional development to become fluent in the skills required to facilitate learning for groups of students with vastly differing characteristics and abilities. Many of those involved also may need to develop different attitudes about those variations in ability and the feasibility of ensuring both academic and social inclusion for all students.

The Team Survey of Inclusive Practices (Figure 1.1) is a tool that can be used to assist in developing action plans for improving a school's inclusive programming. The survey addresses the six elements for inclusive education listed previously. Although action planning for an individual student with significant peer relationship and support needs is done by the core team that provides services and advocates for that student, this is a broader action plan that might be developed by a grade-level team or an inclusion team that includes representatives from the entire school. Most schools have some sort of school improvement plan that has been developed through a self-study process. These plans often emphasize meeting the accountability requirements of the No Child Left Behind (NCLB) Act of 2001 (PL 107-110)—high academic standards and participation in the general curriculum for all students. Before working with the Team Survey of Inclusive Practices, the members of the team should first become familiar with the current state of the school's special education practices and with any other reform or improvement efforts that are in progress as part of the school's larger improvement plan.

Completing the survey requires making judgments about the extent to which each of the six key elements for inclusive education is in place in the school. At a team meeting, team members should discuss and reach a consensus on the rating for each of the six elements on the survey. If need for improvement is indicated for more than one element, the team should then identify which element(s) should be action priorities at the present time. In the column of the survey headed action priority, the team should assign a "high" to those elements that it wants to focus its efforts on immediately and a "low" to those elements that can wait. One strategy for selecting action priorities is to begin with an element on which the team feels confident that it can have some successful impact. Another is to set a goal, such as reaching a

Team Survey of Inclusive Practices

School:_____ Team:_____ Year:_____

Team members/roles:

_____   _____

_____   _____

_____   _____

Status key: 3 = We have done it well.
               2 = We have tried, but it needs
                   improvement.
               1 = We have not done it.

Action priority: Indicate "high" or "low." Complete Issue/Action Planning Form for high-priority items.

Practice	Status (1, 2, 3)		Action priority (high/low)	
	Date:	Date:	Date:	Date:
1. **Inclusive program model:** Do all students start from a base in general classes? Do services and supports follow the students? Does the special education model facilitate teaching?				
2. **Inclusive culture in the school:** Is diversity valued? Are we a community? Do we expect excellence and equity for all of the students?				
3. **Collaborative teaming and problem solving:** Have we identified team members' roles and responsibilities? Do we have strategies for making and communicating decisions? Do we evaluate team functioning and celebrate our successes?				
4. **Accommodating curricular and instructional practices in the classroom:** Is the curriculum meaningful? Do we use active learning; multiple modalities; and small, flexible groupings?				
5. **Strategies for making and evaluating individualized adaptations:** Do we use explicit, agreed-upon strategies for planning, delivering, and evaluating adaptations? Do adaptations facilitate social and instructional participation, and are they only as special as necessary?				
6. **Strategies to facilitate peer relationships and supports:** Do we teach social interaction and problem-solving skills? Do we facilitate social and helping relationships for all students?				

Figure 1.1. Team survey of inclusive practices. (From Ford, A., Messenheimer-Young, T., Toshner, J., Fitzgerald, M.A., Dyer, C., Glodoski, J., et al. [1995, July]. *A team planning packet for inclusive education.* Milwaukee: Wisconsin School Inclusion Project; adapted by permission.)

score of 2 on all six elements. The survey includes room for the status and priority to be reevaluated later in the year.

For a school to make changes, each individual who is implementing the change must develop a new map of his or her job. Teachers, as practitioners who care deeply about students' success, can gain motivation for a new program by seeing positive results for children. Therefore, starting small with pilot success and building on success can be a very effective way to generate momentum for change. For example, fifth-grade teachers focusing on strategies to facilitate peer relationships and supports (Practice 6) might "start small" by raising several desktops to expand seating for students with wheelchairs and working to incorporate lessons on collaborative skills into classwide guidance sessions.

WHAT ARE SOCIAL RELATIONSHIPS?

Enormous variations exist in the types and intensities of social relationships that develop between and among people. Social relationships can be lasting or temporary, loving or hateful, mentoring or modeling, intimate or superficial, balanced or uneven. One prominent way positive social relationships can vary is the degree of closeness and intensity of caring that is maintained in the relationship. Friends, due to their close bonds and mutual alliance, are situated at one end of a closeness continuum; peer group members are located in the middle range; and acquaintances fall at the opposite end of the continuum. This book focuses on strengthening social relationships among children and youth, with a particular focus on those individuals with disabilities who lack close, positive peer associations.

Acquaintances are people who we know for some period of time and have a some-

what reliable connection with; however, the role of acquaintances is less defined than the role of friends. Children confide much more in peers who are friends than they do in their acquaintances. They have fewer arguments and cooperate more with friends than with acquaintances (Hartup, 1996). The line between friendship and acquaintance is fluid and can change over time. Some children who are acquaintances become friends, whereas friendships may fade and the parties may become acquaintances. Acquaintances can be members of our social networks and provide a range of social supports, even though the relationship lacks the intimacy and loyalty of a friendship. The majority of students in a classroom are more likely to be acquaintances than friends.

Friendship has been defined in many ways, most likely because of its importance in our lives. A frequently cited characteristic of a *friend* is someone who is socially important to and particularly liked by a person. Friendships develop when several conditions or processes are present:

1. Opportunities to be together

2. Desire to interact with another person

3. Basic social interaction and communication abilities

4. Organizational, emotional, and social supports to help maintain the relationship as it develops

Friendships that are not entirely mutual or reciprocal may still be supportive and valued by one or both of the individuals; however, *social reciprocity,* or the balanced exchange of interactions between two people, is a characteristic of close relationships and differentiates mutual relationships from *helping relationships,* in which one person mainly serves as teacher, helper, or assistant to the other person (Haring, 1992; Odom, McConnell, & McEvoy, 1992).

Social networks refer to a person's reliable patterns of interaction and friendship with others as well as to the individuals that a person identifies as being socially important (e.g., kids I like to play with, those who are my friends, kids I would invite to a party).

Social support behaviors are behaviors in which a person engages to aid another person, either socially or emotionally. Social support can occur among friends, social network members, and acquaintances. Within friendships, social support is two way and often reciprocal; however, support also can be one way, as in helping or teaching relationships.

Social support seems to vary both in its form (what it looks like) and its function (its purpose), depending on the supported person's age, gender, and cultural group. For example, older female friends lend emotional support to each other in ways that appear different from the support that teenage boys give to each other, but the function—giving consolation—is the same. In the broadest sense, social support behaviors can be categorized as either emotional support (e.g., consolation, appreciation, companionship) or instrumental support (e.g., help in solving a problem, advice, physical assistance).

Examining the functions of social support more closely, Fryxell and Kennedy (1995) identified five peer support behaviors that were used by 6- to 12-year-olds and that were relevant both to children and youth with severe disabilities and to their peers without disabilities:

1. Providing information, such as advice or guidance, about daily events

2. Lending emotional support (consoling another during a crisis or sharing during a happy event)

3. Giving access to others (introductions to new people)

4. Giving material assistance (physical help, lending needed items)

5. Assisting with daily choices (making decisions)

For most of us, social relationships give life meaning. Relationships are usually a motivating force of children's school attendance; adults' relationships at work usually make the week more interesting. Relationships provide opportunities to give support to others, both socially and emotionally, and to receive support in return. Our ability to build and keep relationships goes hand in hand with our social skills. We call on these skills repeatedly throughout a given day; when we forget to do so, disharmony and conflict with others can result. Over the long term, our relationships have a strong impact on our general outlook on life and on our self-concept.

EDUCATIONAL IMPORTANCE OF SOCIAL SKILLS AND PEER RELATIONSHIPS

Social skills and peer support are not tested by state assessments, and their impact on student learning is not measured on typical achievement tests. Many school curricula do not place the achievement of stable, positive social networks on par with reading, mathematics, and geography; however, for children with disabilities, as for most of us, good social relations are an essential indication of quality of life (Strain, Storey, & Smith, 1991). Children who are not accepted by their peers often do not like school, do not achieve well academically, and are more prone to emotional disorders than their peers who are well liked (Hymel, Rubin, Rowden, & LeMare, 1990; Ladd, 1990). Young adults who are lacking in social skills and who have minimal social supports are far more at risk for job loss than are those lacking in basic academic and production skills (Chadsey-Rusch, 1992). Poor social relations in childhood are a relatively reliable predictor of poor adult outcomes, including decreased likelihood of independent living, decreased life expectancy, and severe mental health problems (Strain, 1991).

These theories about the importance and impact of social relationships are even stronger with regard to students with disabilities. Literature on social relationships suggests that students with disabilities encounter a number of social difficulties, many of which are due to their lack of effective social behavior, but some of which are due to a lack of opportunities for social activity:

- The social opportunities of students with disabilities are often more limited than those of their typically developing peers (Farmer, Pearl, & Van Acker, 1996).

- Students who participate in general education classes and are currently eligible (or likely candidates) for special education, but who are not yet receiving special education services, are perceived negatively by their typically developing peers (Sale & Carey, 1995).

- Eight- to thirteen-year-old boys with intellectual disabilities requiring intermittent support experience significantly more loneliness and social isolation than their peers without intellectual disabilities (Williams & Asher, 1992), as do students with learning disabilities in inclusive classrooms (Pavri & Monda-Amaya, 2001).

- Children with autism are less likely to respond to social initiations from peers and spend more free play time engaged in solitary or nonsocial play than their typically developing peers or other children with developmental delays (Sigman & Ruskin, 1999).

- Students with disabilities often are vulnerable to social networks that support or maintain their problematic social behaviors (Farmer et al., 1996).

- Elementary and high school students with disabilities rate themselves significantly lower than their peers without disabilities on the quality-of-life variables of satisfaction, well-being, and social participation (Watson & Keith, 2002).

- More than 20% of students with multiple disabilities and about 33% of students with autism or deafblindness are reported by their parents to engage virtually never in social activities with friends (e.g., visits to one another's homes, telephone calls, recreational activities) outside of school (Wagner et al., 2002).

- Fifth- and sixth-grade students with disabilities have greater dissatisfaction with their relationships with teachers, poorer bonds with school, and perceived higher school danger than their peers without disabilities (Murray & Greenberg, 2001).

In contrast to these negative experiences, students with disabilities who have effective social skills along with the necessary social supports from peers and adults do experience a sense of belonging and self-esteem. Rothman and Cosden (1995) found that students who are socially competent and have adequate social supports report feeling included in their community and have a positive self-concept. Students with learning disabilities in inclusive educational settings have reciprocal relationships with their classmates and report feeling satisfied with their social life at school (Vaughn, Elbaum, & Schumm, 1996).

Strain and Schwartz (2001) asserted that these and other studies of the impact of positive and negative social relations on students' lives point out four primary functions of social relations:

1. A *natural support* function—social relations provide noncontingent support for completing various tasks and for gaining entrance into social groups.

2. An *advocacy* function—positive social relations promote a sense of value and self-worth.

3. An *informational or social learning* function—social relations teach us about appropriate behavior and social conventions.

4. An *affirming* function—social relations aid the development of a sense of belonging and support.

Clearly, strong justifications exist for including the development of social skills and relationships in the school curriculum: In addition to enhancing quality of life, social skills are required in many daily routines at home, at school, and in the community, and a positive relationship exists between social competence and an absence of problem behavior. General and special education teachers alike believe that fostering their students' social development is an important aspect of their role (Bradley & West, 1994) and that providing social support for students with learning disabilities in their inclusive classrooms is part of their job (Pavri & Monda-Amaya, 2001); however, the third- through fifth-grade teachers in Pavri and Monda-Amaya's study "viewed themselves as facilitators of social relations rather than as instructors of social skills," and the special education teachers said that they "did not have either the time or the training to work on social skills" (2001, p. 406). In addition, when Furman and Buhrmester (1992) investigated students' perspectives on teachers' roles, they discovered that many students see their teachers solely as sources of academic support and turn to their families and friends for social support. Pavri and Monda-Amaya (2001) reported discrepancies between the choices of teachers and students with learning disabilities for interventions to support students socially, with special education teachers tending to select teacher-initiated interventions to

certain problem situations (e.g., a student's being made fun of for physical appearance) and students with learning disabilities tending to select student-initiated or peer-initiated interventions.

One further rationale for including social goals in the education provided for many students with disabilities is, simply, that these students were *identified* as having disabilities on the basis of their social and behavioral problems. The qualifying characteristics for autism spectrum disorders, emotional/behavioral disorders, and intellectual disabilities include the presence of impairments in social and behavioral functioning. Special education services that do not address this critical domain cannot, by definition, be meeting the identified needs of these students.

Schools take an important first step in the process of making a difference in students' social lives, adult outcomes, and quality of life when they recognize the value of positive social relationships among students and their ability to affect those relationships. The critical next step is for educators to gain the skills and knowledge needed to practice those beliefs.

UNDERSTANDING DIFFERENCES IN SOCIAL RELATIONSHIPS

The nature of social relationships changes as individuals mature. Sharing common interests, enjoying the same activities, and having mutual affection form much of the basis for friendships during the elementary school years (Hartup, 1996; Rizzo, 1989). Particularly when children are young, their relationships change from year to year and even within a given school year. Some children may have acquaintances they speak to on the bus and in passing but do not play with or seek out for other social occasions. Other children may have friends from other grade levels, especially if they live in the same neighborhood or if their parents are friends. Although friends and specific peer group members may change from year to year, children establish patterns of association early on that tend to be maintained; students of all ages tend to affiliate with other students who share their behavior characteristics (Neckerman, 1996).

In middle school, friendships begin to focus on sharing secrets, gossip, mutual admiration, and support; children become better at cooperating, communicating, and resolving disagreements than younger friends (Hartup, 1996; Rizzo, 1989). In high school, young people more often mention qualities such as loyalty, trust, and intimacy as the basis for friendship (Williams & Asher, 1992). The array of high school peer subcultures is broader than those in middle school or junior high, and peer groups are less rigidly defined, giving students potentially greater access to opportunities for affiliation and friendship (Kinney, 1993).

Gender differences also occur in social relationships. Girls tend to have close friendships with two or three friends; boys have more casual exchanges within larger groups (Maccoby, 1990). Consequently, having one good friend may prevent feelings of loneliness in girls but not in boys. Group membership of one's friends can further complicate relationships, especially for children with disabilities who are part of a special education classroom (Walker, Ramsey, & Gresham, 2004).

Some of the difficulties that inhibit successful social exchanges and gatherings between students with disabilities and their typically developing peers are not unique to individuals with disabilities. There is, however, ample evidence to indicate that these behavior difficulties are more prevalent among children with disabilities, particularly when there is no focus on social skills intervention and when achievement in school has been poor. The major categories of behavior difficulties include the following (Brady & McEvoy, 1989):

1. *Aggression* (both physical and verbal)

2. *Withdrawal* from or *avoidance* of interactions with others during structured times (class) and unstructured times (recess)

3. *Nonresponsiveness* to peers or inappropriate responses to peers

4. *Interactions* with peers that are *of poor quality or immature*

5. A *failure to generalize or transfer* social skills across situations and people

It is important to consider these differences in age, gender, and ability when developing plans to build and support students' social relationships. Cultural norms and values may also bear on the selection of strategies chosen for a student's plan for social support. For example, an investigation of the sources of social support preferred by Hispanic adolescent males with and without mild disabilities revealed differentiation according to disability, gender, migrant status, and the specific support need in question; students with disabilities were more likely to choose no sources of support at all (Morrison, Laughlin, Smith, Ollansky, & Moore, 1992).

ESTABLISHING THE CONDITIONS FOR SOCIAL PARTICIPATION AND RELATIONSHIPS

Because the traditional business of schools is to teach academics, not to build social relationships, many barriers to social interaction may exist within schools. These barriers can be traced to a number of sources (see Figure 1.2) and can hinder teachers from creating conditions that are favorable to social relationships.

Six major factors influence students' social participation: 1) opportunity, 2) atmosphere, 3) social support and motivation, 4) academic achievement, 5) social

Physical and contextual barriers to social interaction: Building, scheduling, and staff issues that prevent opportunities for interacting with peers	Student barriers to social interactions: Student characteristics that get in the way of learning social skills or attaining social acceptance

• Students with disabilities are separated from peers (e.g., bus, classroom, daily schedule).
 	
• Few opportunities exist for social interactions.
 	
• Architectural barriers are present (e.g., no ramps, elevators, or curb cuts).
 	
• Adults encourage primarily helping or teaching interactions rather than social interactions.
 	
• Inappropriate contexts and activities exist:
   Age or culturally inappropriate
   Not amusing or interesting
   Nonreciprocal
 	
• Adults interfere with interaction:
   Hovering
   Interrupting interactions
 	
• Staff fear or misunderstand disabilities.
 	
• Staff do not value interactions between students with and without disabilities.
 	
• Staff models for positive interactions with students who have disabilities are lacking.
 	
• The school atmosphere is competitive or uncooperative; most students with disabilities never "make the grade."
	Students who are isolated socially may exhibit:
	
	• Antisocial behaviors (e.g., aggression, withdrawal, nonresponsiveness)
	
	• Age-inappropriate interests and behavior
	
	• Grooming problems
	
	• Communication difficulties
	
	• Challenging learning characteristics:
	   Few learned skills
	   Poor retention of learned skills
	   Poor generalization of skills
	   Physical, sensory, or health difficulties
	
	Students who are socially competent but not socially isolated may exhibit:
	
	• Negative attitudes (e.g., pity, fear, aversion) toward human differences in ability, culture, and appearance
	
	• Inexperience with others who have disabilities or differences
	
	• An inability to interact in positive ways with students who have disabilities

Figure 1.2.   Barriers to social relationships.

competence and interaction skills, and 6) maintenance and generalization of relationships (Breen, Haring, Weiner, Laitinen, & Bernstein, 1991) (see Figure 1.3). Teachers should determine whether their schools, classrooms, and individual students have shortcomings in any of these six areas. In order to build supportive social relationships between students with disabilities and their peers, teachers need to work collaboratively among themselves and with others (i.e., administrators, other school staff, students, parents) and

set goals and take actions regarding one or more of these six influencing factors. The Social Relationship Worksheet provided in Chapter 6 (Figure 6.1) is a tool that a collaborative team can use to assess needs and plan school and classroom improvements in these six areas.

Opportunity

Although it seems obvious—even trite—to say it, students with disabilities cannot

Opportunity—being physically present around typically developing peers on a regular basis with routine and spontaneous occasions to interact

Atmosphere—staff and student attitudes toward human differences and related values about social relationships, peer support, competition versus cooperation, and student involvement in resolving social concerns

Social support and motivation—having the needed supports and encouragement from adults and peers to interact socially and build relationships

Academic achievement—possessing needed academic skills and the confidence that comes from having and using these skills

Social competence and interaction skills—being able to initiate interactions with peers, respond to peers' initiations, and elaborate on the initiations or responses of peers at a typical rate

Maintenance and generalization of relationships—keeping and extending social relationships as well as remembering and transferring known social skills across different people and school and nonschool settings

Figure 1.3. Six factors that influence social relationships.

develop social relationships with their peers if they are not present in places where there are opportunities to interact. Often, interactions between students with disabilities and their peers are limited by using separate classrooms; special education wings; frequent "pull-out" sessions for special services; different lunch periods from peers; separate buses; different arrival and departure times and bus locations; cafeteria seating arranged by classroom; and rules to reduce talking and social interaction among students in the halls, cafeteria, or classrooms. Students with physical disabilities may be further isolated by architectural barriers that hinder or prevent them from having access to certain parts of the classroom or school. Moreover, when students with disabilities do not attend their neighborhood school, but are bused to a centralized location, both in-school and after-school connections with peers may be affected negatively (McDonnell, Hardman, Hightower, & Kiefer-O'Donnell, 1991).

Some of these practices are a result of special education's being "a location that one goes to" rather than "a portable set of supports." The other practices are meant to diminish peer interaction in general; these practices are based on the philoso-

phy that schools are for learning and that socializing "gets in the way." History, however, has taught us that if students with and without disabilities do not spend time together during their school years, they are less likely to develop meaningful relationships. Some administrative actions, such as the elimination of separate bus schedules for students with disabilities, the use of lift-equipped buses for all students, and the replacement of pull-out special education with classroom-based support, abolish the isolation that many children with disabilities experience during their school years.

Atmosphere

We all have been in schools that feel welcoming, that take pride in having a diverse student body, and that value all students as part of their community. Positive school atmospheres often are a product of the leadership of school administrators and certain teachers. In addition, students with disabilities are sometimes largely responsible for transforming attitudes toward disability and the value of including all students with their peers (Giangreco, Dennis, Cloninger, Edelman, & Schattman, 1993). A number of specific staff and student characteristics contribute to an atmosphere in which disabilities and other human differences (e.g., racial, ethnic, cultural, ability) are less visible. These characteristics are interrelated and include one's personal attitudes toward human differences, one's prejudices, and one's knowledge of and experiences with people and cultures different from one's own.

Student Snapshot

 Daniel is a second-grade student with cerebral palsy, visual impairment, and a seizure disorder. He uses a wheelchair and assistance with feeding and dressing. To communicate with others, Daniel is learning to use a communication device that speaks for him. When Daniel first attended the preschool special education program at age 3, several staff members who did not work with Daniel wondered why he was in school. Older pupils attending the school stared at Daniel while he was being fed in the lunchroom and even imitated the way food dribbled from his mouth. Now, in a school that values diversity and practices inclusion, Daniel is an appreciated member of Ms. James's second-grade class. Students in Daniel's school have learned to look beyond Daniel's differences and instead focus on his similarities to them.

Social Support and Motivation

Although proximity and positive attitudes strongly promote the development of peer relationships, they may not be sufficient to create friendships and other supportive relationships between students with disabilities and their typically developing classmates or even to lead to successful, positive interactions. It may be appropriate to organize *social support* strategies such as peer networks, peer problem-solving groups, or friendship pairs to encourage the focus student's

typically developing classmates to involve themselves as models, social partners, and problem solvers in the focus student's school routines. Less formal, unstructured methods for facilitating positive interactions—such as incidental cuing or modeling of ways to interact with the focus student—often also are necessary. Adults should initiate these support strategies until the focus student's peers take over and the focus student becomes comfortable with them.

The *motivational* factor concerns all of the reasons why students seek to interact socially or to avoid interaction. These motivational factors affect not only students who exhibit interaction difficulties but also students without disabilities who may be skilled at social interaction. Usually, within groups of peers who know one another, no coaxing is needed to initiate social interaction; however, depending on the age of the students, if one or more of the following circumstances is added to a social situation, the motivation for interaction may be reduced or threatened:

- Students do not know one another.

- Students are of different ages or genders.

- Students have few common interests or experiences.

- One or more of the students cannot be understood or cannot understand others.

- Students are fearful of an individual in the group.

- Students are not given a choice about whether they want to be in the group.

In addition to these inhibitors of social interaction, when students lack experience with interacting with their peers, they and their peers have little motivation for socializing. Their interaction rates are low, their initiations and responses to peers are inconsistent, and their social skills, in general, are poor. The motivational factor is addressed by strategies that teachers can use to teach and encourage positive social interactions among peers when one or more peers in the group exhibit social difficulties. Sometimes, however, adults may discourage social interaction simply by being insensitive to peer group norms and preferences.

Academic Achievement

Poor academic achievement can contribute to a student's lack of social relationships. Although a student may be fairly skilled socially, he or she may lack the confidence that arises from having and using skills in academic areas such as reading, writing, math, science, and social studies. More often, however, antisocial behavior contributes to the student's lack of friends and companions and to the student's poor academic record.

Sam is a ninth-grade student who attends general education classes and also receives individualized support from special education staff in a resource room. Although he is highly articulate, Sam has been diagnosed with obsessive-compulsive disorder and Tourette syndrome; he uses extensive behavioral support throughout the day, and his social skills are immature. When Sam's academic engagement is low (e.g., when he is upset, needs to leave class, or worries about mistakes), his learning is poor.

Frustration that arises from a student's inability to meet academic demands can spiral quickly into out-of-control behavior. Antisocial behavior patterns are closely related to school academic failure (Walker et al., 2004). Underachieving students' reactions to failure in school can change their existing reputation with peers and jeopardize their social relationships. In schools where the atmosphere is highly competitive and there are few nonacademic outlets for achievement (e.g., chorus, volunteer groups, auto or shop clubs),

only the top percentage of students will feel successful. Conditions fostering the development of antisocial behavior exist for a large number of students (Walker et al., 2004).

Because academic achievement can have a positive influence on a student's self-concept, his or her acceptance by others, and his or her success in forming social relationships, individualized educational supports may be one component of a program that is designed to build social relationships. Individualized academic support may require skill assessment, focused and effective instruction, modifications in schoolwork, and the identification and use of specific accommodations for some students. Some students need a combination of individualized academic instruction and social skills training.

Social Competence and Interaction Skills

Many researchers who have studied peer support methods have found that the incidental modeling and teaching of social skills during school routines such as lunch, between-class breaks, and in-class cooperative groups is effective enough for students with disabilities to better their social interaction skills. For some students, however, these naturalistic opportunities may be inadequate; these students may require more structured and systematic development of their social skills. The social skills that a student needs can vary widely and are related in part to the student's age and other demographic characteristics, cognitive ability, and the amount and type of the student's communication. Some students need instruction in the basics: initiating interactions with peers, responding to peers' initiations, participating in an interactive conversation, and taking turns. For other students, teams need to address reliable communication methods that the student can use with his or her peers at typical rates. Some students need to learn methods to control their anger, to monitor interfering behavior, and to self-prompt an alternate and appropriate way to react to peers.

For Sam, the-ninth grade student with a history of acting-out behavior, the transitions between classes and activities are particularly challenging, and he often reacts with confusion, anger, and aggression. At times, Sam makes comments about his own and others' biological functions, which often make peers laugh but decrease their regard for him. Both of these difficulties in social competence have motivated his team to develop teaching plans to build appropriate skills.

Age-appropriate social skills are essential to an individual's social acceptance; however, whether these skills are acquired naturalistically; through intentional, structured teaching by adults and/or peers; or through some combination of these means varies from student to student.

Maintenance and Generalization of Relationships

Some children have trouble keeping and extending their social relationships; other students, especially those with intellectual disabilities, may find it hard to remember and to carry their known social skills across different people and environments. For many students, teachers need to be alert to the frequently documented learning difficulties of skill maintenance and generalization.

Sam, who has learned to control his angry outbursts at school through a combination of self-management methods, is still verbally aggressive on the bus and at home; consequently, Sam's teachers are working with the bus driver and with Sam's family members to adjust the methods that work for Sam at school so that they are successful on the bus and at home.

STEPS FOR BUILDING SOCIAL RELATIONSHIPS

Several steps are involved in building the social relationships of students. These steps include setting goals and engaging in collaborative teaming.

Setting Goals

Students who have been placed in a general education class but have not had adequate support experience various challenges to improving their social relationships, including learning social skills and overcoming negative reputations with their classmates. Their teachers may need to adjust to modifying classwork for these students and also may be challenged to conquer their own lowered expectations for these students' academic achievement and behavior. Even in schools that have a history of inclusive practices, some students with disabilities may not be experiencing the frequency of positive social interactions and quality of relationships that their teachers and families hope for them to have.

Student Snapshot

 Paul is a sixth-grade student with a seizure disorder, learning disabilities, and a history of exclusion by peers. The following accommodations were written into Paul's individualized education program (IEP):

1. *Peer planning sessions will be conducted with Paul's classmates to brainstorm issues and to provide Paul with needed support. With some assistance from the special education teacher, Paul's peers also will learn to conduct their own planning sessions for Paul.*

2. *Peers will be taught how to increase Paul's conversational skills in planned lessons and during informal conversations with him.*

3. *Paul will learn to self-manage (i.e., identify, keep track of, control) the behaviors that are annoying to his peers (repeating topics, touching others).*

How do teachers assess a student's social relationships to determine whether supports are necessary and, if so, what form these supports should take? A variety of approaches can help the team determine this need:

- Informal conversations with those who know the focus student, including the student's peers (see Figure 1.4)

- Observations gathered by team members of a particular student

- Use of various rating scales and checklists to judge the adequacy of inclusion efforts and to pinpoint any difficulties that a student may be experiencing with social relationships

---

What the Research Says

A number of researchers have studied the attitudes and perspectives of middle and high school students without disabilities on the inclusion of students with disabilities in their schools, classes, and social networks (Fisher, 1999; Fisher, Pumpian, & Sax, 1998).

Several researchers (Hendrickson, Shokoohi-Yekta, Hamre-Nietupski, & Gable, 1996) asked more than 1,000 middle school and high school students from three states about their friendships with students who have extensive disabilities. The majority of students interviewed agreed on the following:

- These friendships were not only possible but also yielded benefits for themselves and for the students with disabilities.

- Adolescents should try to make friends with peers who have disabilities.

- Relationships were more likely to develop if students with disabilities were placed in general education classes for part or all of the day; they thought that placements in special education classes in a general education school were less facilitative but that placements in special education classes in a special education school were least likely to facilitate such friendships.

- The most effective strategies teachers and schools might use to facilitate friendships are, in order of importance: 1) use teaching approaches that allow students to work together; 2) present information on disabilities to students, teachers, and parents; 3) arrange social activities for all students; 4) teach students without disabilities to be tutors; and 5) organize a circle of friends around the student.

- The primary responsibility for facilitating such friendships should be on the students themselves; however, the students also listed others who should promote these relationships, including special education teachers; youth clubs and organizations; parents of students with disabilities; and guidance counselors, school psychologists, and social workers.

In interviews with 12 focus groups of 11–35 participants, students without disabilities in an inclusive high school in California were asked how, in general, students with disabilities could be more involved in classes, extracurricular activities, and other happenings in the school (Fisher, 1999). These students made the following recommendations:

- Some students and teachers in the school need to develop more positive attitudes toward students with disabilities.

- Administrators should work to improve teachers' attitudes.

- Students without disabilities should take some responsibility for helping their peers with disabilities to gain access to more school events by inviting them to sports events and parties, sitting with them at lunch, and so forth.

Figure 1.4. Strategies adolescents think facilitate social relationships and school inclusion. (*Sources:* Fisher, 1999; Fisher, Pumpian, & Sax, 1998; Hendrickson, Shokoohi-Yekta, Hamre-Nietupski, & Gable, 1996.)

1. Does the focus child frequently get "passed over" as if he or she were not there (ghost)? Do staff members talk about another placement as soon as there is a problem (guest)?

2. Does the teacher say, "I have 27 students plus 2 included students"?

3. Do classmates use the words *work with* or *help* whenever they refer to times spent with the focus child?

4. Is the focus child expected to participate in class activities along with everyone else?

5. Has the focus child ever been invited to a party by a classmate?

6. Does the focus child have one or more friends who call him or her on the telephone at home and/or who visit him or her after school or on weekends?

Figure 1.5. Six key questions to assess a student's social relationships. (*Source:* Meyer et al., 1998.)

For example, Meyer and colleagues (1998) found that the answers to six key questions (see Figure 1.5) about a particular student's relationships in school could be used both to target needed improvements and to informally evaluate outcomes. These questions address the ways in which staff, classmates, and the focus student behave and are listed in the left-hand column of the Rating Scale to Assess a Student's Relationships in Appendix A.

Chapter 6 discusses another rating scale, the Social Relationship Worksheet (Figure 6.1), designed around the six previously discussed factors that influence social relationships at school: opportunity, atmosphere, social support and motivation, academic achievement, social competence and interaction skills, and maintenance and generalization of relationships. This worksheet evaluates both the environmental factors that indirectly affect the conditions for social interactions among peers and the extent to which a student or students are included socially. Improvements in these factors can directly or indirectly affect the conditions for social interactions among peers.

Other teams may find that comparing their school's practices to a list of barriers to social relationships (Figure 1.2) will assist them in targeting areas for improve-

ment. Goals can be set to make general improvements in schools and classrooms so that they are conducive to the development of social relationships, but goals also may be targeted for developing and improving programs (strengthening cooperative learning groups, building a cross-age tutoring program, or organizing a Best Buddies high school chapter), staff development, peer support skills, and individual students' needs.

As adults work to understand the social limitations that a focus student experiences, set goals, and draw up support plans, it is important that they do the following:

1. Listen to the student's own expectations, hopes, and preferences

2. Recruit the viewpoints and ideas of the student's peers (using the guidelines that are established in Chapter 3)

3. Familiarize themselves with the developmental and group expectations for students of different genders, chronological ages, and cultures

Engaging in Collaborative Teaming

By its nature, inclusive education obligates teachers to collaborate as a team.

This means that the core team (general and special education teachers along with the student and the student's family) plans, selects, and implements various actions to improve the student's social relationships and peer supports. Members of the focus student's extended team may also be involved. These members may include additional teachers, therapists and other specialists, administrators, and peers. Collaborative teams are necessary: Working alone will not do the trick! Ideas that are generated individually may be off base or incomplete in some way, especially if two or more teachers share responsibility for students with disabilities. The implementation tasks are too taxing for one person to undertake and oversee. (For more information, refer to *Collaborative Teaming* [Snell & Janney, 2005], a companion book in this series.)

The following guidelines, which are discussed in more depth in the upcoming chapters, address ways in which teams should work together to plan, select, and implement actions that have been designed to improve a student's social relationships:

1. Use a collaborative teaming process to make decisions and to implement actions.

2. Examine the student's social relationships as the "yardstick" for measuring the need for or success of a social support plan.

3. Involve the focus student and his or her peers in the process: All can contribute to planning, problem solving, implementing a plan, and evaluating the focus student's progress.

4. Seek team consensus about what is the most efficient, yet most effective, initial action to take: This often translates into increasing the student's social opportunities before undertaking more complex actions.

5. Contextualize instruction: Embed teaching of social skills and peer support strategies in daily routines and in natural social contexts.

6. Don't let the implemented supports become barriers to social interaction: Hovering adults, overzealous "helpers," stigmatizing support or instruction, and a failure to fade assistance hinder natural peer-to-peer contact.

GUIDELINES AND STRATEGIES TO ENHANCE RELATIONSHIPS

Building social relationships in a classroom or school requires teachers and administrators to employ a variety of strategies. The process is not a "one-shot approach" but an evolving one. The choice of strategies differs depending on the focus student's social competence and other developmental characteristics and the school's prevailing atmosphere. In addition, the current extent of opportunity for interaction among peers with and without disabilities will influence the selected strategies. For example, the goals and action steps necessary when students with disabilities are first included in general education classes as part of a school- or districtwide improvement effort are quite different from those required to maintain and enhance social relationships in a school that has well-established inclusive practices.

The strategies must be *efficient* with respect to the amount of structure and effort required to implement them and *normalized* with respect to the student's age, culture, and gender. Two guidelines should be used to select these strategies.

1. Use adequate, but not excessive, structure and effort.

2. Design support that is only as special as necessary.

Use Adequate, But Not Excessive, Structure and Effort

As the amount of structure required for a social support strategy increases, so does the effort required of adults and/or peers. The peer support strategies described in this book vary widely in their degree of complexity and requirements of effort. Structure and effort encompass the degree of organization, the amount of planning time and teaming, whether a naturally occurring or a new peer activity is used, and the amount and type of adult involvement needed to implement the strategy (e.g., presence, instruction, feedback, data collection). For example, some strategies for building peer support build on existing scheduled school activities, such as lunch, and other strategies require the creation of activities, such as Best Buddy events. Similarly, ability-awareness activities to improve the school environment could be planned for an entire school and could extend across several weeks; however, this strategy requires a major time commitment by a planning group, in contrast with the effort required to embed ability-awareness content into a classroom unit on environmental adaptation or civil rights. Teachers may use the low-effort intervention of incidental teaching to prompt and reinforce the use of appropriate social skills, but some students may need explicit social skills training, which requires careful planning and scheduled instructional sessions in addition to incidental teaching during the course of the day.

In developing plans for building social support and peer relationships, it is necessary to consider the feasibility of implementing the plan. This does not mean that educators should not expect to experience some challenge in acquiring new skills (e.g., the skills needed to implement a formal social skills training program), or that the effort to build social relationships is not always worth it; however,

it is important to be able to see demonstrable progress on the goals that have been set and for students and teachers to experience the benefits and rewards of these changes.

Design Support that Is Only as Special as Necessary

Like instructional adaptations for students with disabilities, interventions to enhance social interactions and relationships should be normalized. A holistic plan to improve peer interactions in a school or classroom should adhere to this same only-as-special-as-necessary guideline. Figure 1.6 depicts a model for describing the intrusiveness or "specialness" of an intervention that is applied in all volumes of the *Teachers' Guides to Inclusive Practices* series. The foundational interventions to improve social relationships (those at the base of the triangle in Figure 1.6) are schoolwide or classwide interventions to create an atmosphere of community, acceptance, and understanding. Next, general curricular and instructional practices that promote achievement along with the development of positive relationships and constructive social behaviors (e.g., sharing, assisting, resolving conflicts) should be implemented. Classwide interventions such as social skill programs, buddy systems, peer tutoring, and cooperative learning fall into this category.

Finally, the most specialized interventions (at the top of the triangle in Figure 1.6) are the child-specific adaptations, such as explicit training of targeted social skills or peer support plans, which are typically developed only for students with extensive social and behavior support needs. A premise of the model is that an inclusive culture in the school and the use of accommodating instructional practices in the classroom reduces the effort required for making more individualized adaptations, whether those adaptations

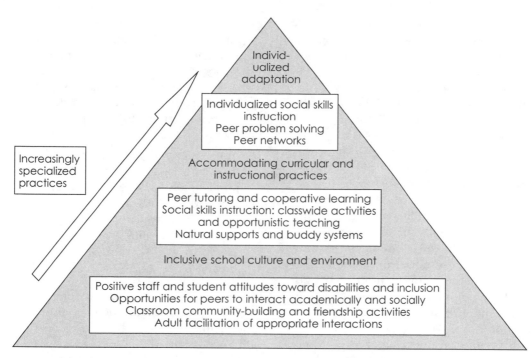

Figure 1.6. Model of "only-as-special-as-necessary" inclusive practices that build social competence and foster peer relationships.

are social or academic. (Brown, Odom, and Conroy [2001] described a similar intervention hierarchy for promoting peer interactions among young children in inclusive early childhood settings.) The four types of strategies to build social relationships are described next.

Improvement of the School Environment

Strategies for improving the school environment address the school's attitudes, its atmosphere, and its understanding and appreciation of human differences. Many researchers and practitioners have found that these indirect strategies strengthen the school's attitudinal base to allow peer support and positive social relationships to flourish. For example, ability/disability-awareness programs can help people without disabilities—including both staff and students—to understand how particular disabilities affect learning, perception, or communication,

thereby increasing their sensitivity toward and appreciation of students with disabilities. Other strategies are geared toward

1. Increasing acceptance (training in conflict resolution methods, use of classroom community groups to discuss and resolve interaction problems)

2. Accommodating human differences (learning about other cultures through social studies and reading projects, inviting speakers from other countries and cultures to address the class)

3. Creating cooperative and safe school environments (student problem solving concerning schoolwide problems, use of students as conflict mediators)

4. Teaching active participation and responsibility in society (school cleanup and recycling projects, community volunteering and sharing programs, school citizenship and Key Club groups)

In addition to schoolwide environmental improvements, teachers in individual classrooms can improve the classroom environment through ongoing adult facilitation of appropriate interactions among their students. One primary method teachers use to build camaraderie among their students is to model their acceptance of each student by demonstrating their approval and recognition of each individual student in age- and culture-appropriate ways (e.g., standing nearby and smiling at the student, using the student's preferred name, interacting with the student in natural ways). Teachers also can demonstrate how to interact with an individual who may have unique ways of communicating (e.g., using the student's picture communication board, waiting for the student to look up first, using manual signs while speaking). Other methods that teachers report using are

1. Actively promoting interactions between focus students and peers, followed by "backing off" and allowing the interaction to proceed without adult interference

2. Similar treatment of each student

3. Teaching peers to lend support to a classmate who might need it without hindering the student's independence (Janney & Snell, 1996; Salisbury, Gallucci, Palombaro, & Peck, 1995; Snell & Raynes, 1995)

Support Through Peer Groups and Pairs

Social support methods were developed in the 1980s and 1990s that encourage peers to foster social relationships and membership within stable social groups. These methods may include the following:

1. Promoting planned peer support activities and programs such as peer planning, friendship pairs or groups, and lunch partners

2. Focusing on typical environments and activities in addition to natural strategies kids use to "get connected" to social groups, and, at the same time, providing "access and support to ensure that students with disabilities can participate in similar ways" (Schnorr, 1997, p. 1)

3. Answering students' questions about disabilities while teaching them to problem-solve ways to get along and interact with others in school who may be different from them, such as students with disabilities

Social Skills Instruction

Researchers, working in tandem with teachers, have learned much about intervention approaches that can be successful with social skills difficulties such as aggression, withdrawal, nonresponsiveness, poor quality of interactions, and failure to generalize social skills across daily routines. Frequently, a combination of proven techniques rather than a single, narrow approach is used. The combination is individualized to suit the student, his or her particular behavior difficulty, and the circumstances. The emphasis has shifted from eliminating undesirable behavior to building appropriate replacement skills, or positive behavior support. Most successful approaches used in schools include the teaching of alternate, appropriate behavior as a means for reducing problem behavior. Often, these alternate behaviors include social and communication skills.

Functional assessment of problem behavior plays an important role in the design of social skills programs. This method involves studying the triggers for a particular behavior difficulty and the purpose the behavior seems to serve for a student. This information is a necessary component of many combined approaches, regardless of the social skill difficulty (Horner & Carr, 1997). Functional assessment, which is recognized in special education law as a valuable teaching tool, is discussed briefly in Chapter 4 and more thoroughly in the book *Behavioral Support* (Janney & Snell, 2000).

Peer Supports in Instruction

Student-to-student teaching can be beneficial in tutoring programs and cooperative learning groups; both strategies can produce gains in academic, language, or social skills. *Peer-mediated instruction* involves peers in cooperative learning groups, peer tutoring, and peer networking interventions with their classmates with disabilities. *Peer networks* often focus on teaching social and communication skills in natural settings, such as when typically developing youngsters are taught to initiate interactions with their classmates who have disabilities and to prompt their responses during playtime. Several peer-tutoring models exist. In *peer tutoring*, teaching is one-way and students are the same age. *Cross-age tutoring* involves an older student teaching, interacting with, or reading to a younger student. Another approach is *classwide tutoring*, which incorporates *reciprocal peer tutoring*, during which each student alternates between the tutor and tutee roles; this classwide tutoring can lead to academic improvements and can also teach cooperative interdependence among students of the same age but differing abilities.

Cooperative learning entails restructuring learning and leisure activities to promote interdependence among students. Group members learn several messages:

- "We sink or swim together."
- "Do your work—we're counting on you."
- "How can I help you to do better?" (Nevin, Thousand, & Villa, 2002)

Cooperative groups are not ability groups; group members have multiple talents and a variety of abilities and needs. The group's work tasks, activities, or games are planned to achieve academic and/or social objectives, which may vary for different group members. Students assume different responsibilities, but they make decisions as a group in order to achieve the stated group objective. For example, groups of fifth- and sixth-grade students might be given math story problems that require reasoning and basic computational math skills and can be solved in several ways. Group tasks might be to build structures from toothpicks and marshmallows or to create a video clip or poster that illustrates the group's solution. Teachers provide the structure, monitor in ways that encourage learning and group interdependence, and evaluate academic and social learning.

Tutoring, cooperative groups, and peer networks promote peer support during instruction and can lead to cooperative behaviors, social skills, and academic improvements. Depending on the approach used, peers with and without disabilities may fill equitable roles in cooperative learning groups and in reciprocal peer tutoring.

ORGANIZATION OF THIS BOOK

The rest of this book elaborates on these four types of strategies and provides tools and guidelines for using these strategies in schools with students of different ages and disabilities. Chapter 2 discusses strategies to make school environments conducive to the development of social relationships. Chapters 3 and 4 offer strategies to assess, plan for, and teach skills that bolster positive ties among peers, particularly for students with disabilities. Chapter 5 examines models of peer support in instruction, including peer tutoring and cooperative learning.

Finally, Chapter 6 provides guidelines for initiating and/or improving programs and strategies that build positive social relationships in schools and classrooms.

As stated previously, many of the strategies described in this book are most easily applied in schools where a range of inclusive practices are already in place. If students with disabilities are not full members of their schools and classroom groups, interventions to develop positive social relationships between students with and without disabilities will be different from those used in schools where there is already a shared expectation that all students will interact in positive ways and learn together. For schools that are in the process of moving from separate special education programming toward a more inclusive approach, the tactics described in Chapters 2 and 6 will be particularly helpful.

Chapter 2

Preparing the School Environment

Classroom community [is] a sense that everyone belongs, is valued, has something to contribute, and has rights but also responsibilities for the welfare or others in the class and school. . . . If students feel disconnected, disenfranchised, unwelcome, or unsafe in school, they will have great difficulty changing their behaviors or benefiting from instruction. (Korinek, Walther-Thomas, McLaughlin, & Williams, 1999, pp. 3–4)

In many school districts, meaningful inclusion of students with disabilities is limited, and these students do not belong to classes or social networks that include their typically developing peers. When students with and without disabilities have few opportunities for meaningful interaction, efforts to develop supportive relationships among them must address both creating the conditions for interaction and teaching students how to interact. When teachers and staff are themselves unfamiliar with the characteristics and needs of students with disabilities and are unaccustomed to facilitating instructional and social inclusion, they, too, will need support in acquiring new skills and different ways of thinking.

Developing positive social relationships and peer supports for students with disabilities requires the use of direct approaches to facilitate interactions and create supportive relationships between students with and without disabilities, along with indirect approaches to cultivate an inclusive school environment. Indirect approaches address the "opportunity and atmosphere" aspects of social participation (Breen et al., 1991) that were discussed in Chapter 1 (see Figure 1.3). Indirect approaches to fostering social relationships among students with and without disabilities include activities to increase understanding and acceptance of disabilities, in-services to increase teachers' skills in collaborative teaming, and efforts to ensure that students with and without disabilities have opportunities to interact. In contrast, direct approaches to increasing the social partici-

pation of students with disabilities include instructing peers in ways to communicate with, befriend, and assist their classmates with disabilities; adult facilitation of student interactions; and teaching social skills to students who need them.

Typically, both an *indirect*, or preparatory, approach and a *direct* approach are used in concert, with indirect, environmental improvements strengthening the groundwork so that schools are more receptive to direct, student-centered efforts to build peer relationships. When teachers and administrators first work to improve the atmosphere of the school and the attitudes of its staff and students by extending knowledge about disability and challenging prejudices or negative attitudes, these indirect approaches, having established an accepting, caring community, make direct efforts to creating mechanisms for peer support easier. Even in schools with a solid community culture and a history of inclusive practices, it is wise to pay ongoing attention to sustaining that culture and its values.

This chapter describes a number of helpful strategies for improving the school environment so that all students will be fully included, both instructionally and socially. Incorporating a selected array of these indirect strategies into a buildingwide plan for becoming more inclusive will help to set the stage for the use of direct, student-to-student strategies for developing supportive relationships that are described in Chapters 3 and 4. As mentioned in Chapter 1 and illustrated in Figure 1.6, this book encourages the use of broad, preparatory approaches to create an inclusive community, along with the implementation of accommodating curricular and instructional practices, as the foundation for individualized adaptations for students with the most unique learning, behavior, and social needs. Implementing these foundational practices not only establishes an environment that is conducive to genuine inclusion of all students, but it also may reduce the need for more individualized supports.

STRATEGIES FOR PREPARING STAFF

In many states, classroom teachers and general education administrators are required to complete an introductory course in special education and to learn about various disabilities; however, most school staff members and students still could benefit from learning some basic information about disabilities and from some firsthand, positive experience with individuals who have disabilities. If staff members are to model ways to effectively interact, communicate with, and provide support for students with disabilities, they will need both information and opportunities to observe and practice these behaviors themselves. Some staff members may not understand why a reform that is as challenging as inclusion is warranted; they may not know what will be required of them, may not be optimistic about the outcome, or may have misconceptions about the potential of some students with disabilities to benefit from inclusion.

Before a school can become more inclusive, its staff members often need assistance in examining their own values and mission regarding teaching and learning and also in acquiring information and guidance about 1) the potential benefits of inclusive education, 2) characteristics and needs of individuals with various disabilities, 3) collaborative teaming as a means of planning and problem solving, and 4) curricular and instructional accommodations and modifications to individualize learning experiences. As plans to include students with disabilities are being designed and implemented, staff members will continue to need regular in-service sessions and updates on topics related to inclusion. These in-services,

along with supported experiences with students with disabilities, can aid first in quelling apprehensions and, second, in developing the skills and knowledge needed to feel competent to collaboratively deliver inclusive services. It is essential to recognize that attitude change can occur incidentally, through increased exposure to individuals with disabilities, and through the acquisition of accurate information and other indirect experiences such as disability awareness activities; however, increasing peer interactions and building social relationships tend to require strategically facilitated, extended contact with individuals who have disabilities (see Figure 2.1).

Social Benefits of Inclusive Education

When teachers, parents, and administrators who are not among the original proponents of inclusive education encounter increasingly inclusive programming in their school or district, they will want to know: Why are we doing this, and what are the benefits? (Janney, Snell, Beers, & Raynes, 1995). There are several possible rationales for inclusive education (see Janney & Snell, 2004, for further discussion). For many educators and parents, the social benefits are among the most compelling. Figure 2.2 presents major themes discovered by McGregor and Vogelsberg (1998) from their synthesis of the literature on inclusive schooling practices.

Figure 2.3 provides a list of some of the social benefits associated with inclusive schooling that have been validated through research in schools. In addition, educators and parents who have had experience with inclusion will have stories to share about the mutually enjoyable, caring, and supportive relationships that they have witnessed among students in inclusive classrooms and the transformations that they themselves have gone through as they learned about inclusion.

What the Research Says

Teachers' attitudes: Feelings of anxiety, ambivalence, or even resistance toward proposed school reforms are not uncommon; however, research shows time and time again that teachers' negative or uncertain attitudes toward the inclusion of students with disabilities are reduced and even changed to attitudes of acceptance and support once teachers have acquired knowledge and skill in implementing inclusive practices. Moreover, contact with students who have disabilities is consistently reported to be a more compelling factor in attitude change than simply receiving information or hearing persuasive arguments (Giangreco et al., 1993; Janney et al., 1995).

Attitudes of students without disabilities: Research also has documented positive alterations in the attitudes of students without disabilities following participation in activities providing information about and/or contact with peers with disabilities. Studies involving young children and elementary school students (Favazza & Odom, 1997; Hestenes & Carroll, 2000; Odom et al., 1999); adolescents (Burns, Storey, & Certo, 1999; Carter, Hughes, Copeland, & Breen, 2001; Clemenz, 2002); and also college students (Curran, 1999; Eichinger, Rizzo, & Sirotnik, 1991; Hastings, 1996; Rimmerman, Hozmi, & Duvdevany, 2000; Shade & Stewart, 2001) have confirmed the positive impact of awareness programs, reading and discussions, structured play activities, peer tutoring programs, service learning projects, and adventure programming on the attitudes of peers without disabilities.

The differences among the effects of these various types of activities on peers is significant. Although attitudinal improvements result quite reliably from awareness activities (Favazza & Odom, 1997), behavior change may not (Hestenes & Carroll, 2000), but even incidental contact with peers with disabilities improves attitudes and increases the likelihood of further contact. For example, simply having had contact with students who have disabilities made high school students more likely to volunteer for peer buddy or tutoring programs (Carter et al., 2001).

When information is followed by facilitated, extended contact, however, and/or involves joint participation in activities with peers who have disabilities, attitudes become even more positive, peer interactions increase, and more enduring relationships are developed. For instance, Burns and colleagues (1999) found that when students with disabilities contributed equally to a service project, rather than being the recipient of service from a peer without disabilities, the typically developing peers acquired more positive attitudes.

Figure 2.1.   Improving teacher and peer attitudes toward students who have disabilities.

What the Research Says

In their monograph, *Inclusive Schooling Practices: Pedagogical and Research Foundations*, McGregor and Vogelsberg (1998) summarized the literature base on the best approaches to supporting students with disabilities in inclusive settings. The monograph gives the background and history of the inclusive schooling movement, provides descriptions of instructional practices that are effective for diverse students, and summarizes the research about inclusive education. Some of the key findings from the research: 1) students with disabilities demonstrate high levels of social interaction in inclusive settings; however, physical presence alone does not guarantee positive social outcomes; 2) interactive, small-group contexts facilitate skill acquisition and social acceptance; 3) friendships do develop between students with disabilities and typically developing peers; 4) teachers play an important role in facilitating the development of friendships; 5) the performance of typically developing students is not compromised by the inclusion of students with disabilities; 6) parent support for inclusion is positively affected by actual experience; and 7) although many teachers are initially reluctant about inclusive education, support and experience make them more confident in their abilities. McGregor and Vogelsberg's monograph is useful to those who want advice about how to implement inclusive programs and to those who want to be more knowledgeable about the research on the outcomes of inclusive schooling.

Figure 2.2.   What do we know about best practices in inclusive education? (*Source:* McGregor & Vogelsberg, 1998.)

What the Research Says

Social benefits for students with disabilities
- Increased social initiations
- Increased social bids from typically developing peers
- Improvements in social competence
- More varied types of social contacts in a broader range of environments
- Receipt and offering of more social support to others
- Larger friendship networks

Social benefits for students without disabilities
- Greater acceptance of students with disabilities
- Greater tolerance of other people
- Knowledge of how not to "feel sorry" for students with disabilities
- Improved self-concept
- More awareness of other people's prejudices
- Development of new personal principles
- Knowledge of how to care about other people who are different
- Improved ability to self-reflect and evaluate their own actions

Figure 2.3. Social benefits of integrated and inclusive education. (*Sources:* Biklen, Corrigan, & Quick, 1989; Cole & Meyer, 1991; Fisher, 1999; Fisher, Pumpian, & Sax, 1998; Fryxell & Kennedy, 1995; Helmstetter, Peck, & Giangreco, 1994; Jenkins, Odom, & Speltz, 1989; Kennedy, Cushing, & Itkonen, 1997; Kennedy, Shukla, & Fryxell, 1997; Kishi & Meyer, 1994; Murray-Seegert, 1989; Peck, Donaldson, & Pezzoli, 1990; Vogtle, 1996.)

Information About Disabilities and Special Education Law

In some cases, staff attitudes may include fear and uncertainty rather than acceptance and comfort in the company of individuals who have disabilities. Sometimes staff members may be critical of the differences certain students with disabilities have in their daily school routines, treatment, and educational services. Criticism often occurs when 1) the services provided to the students are extensive in contrast to those provided to other students who may need similar services but do not qualify, and 2) the service provision itself upsets classroom rules and privileges. Because these attitudes and behaviors have a strong impact on the atmosphere of the school and its classrooms, they should be addressed by the faculty at large or within a particular team or classroom.

Staff members should have opportunities to air their concerns about fairness and special services with the team of staff involved. In some cases, team problem solving can generate a plan to deliver a student's services or supports in more normalized, efficient, or less intrusive ways so as not to upset the norms of the classroom. Another useful strategy is to build all staff members' general areas of knowledge about students' abilities and disabilities and the requirements of special education law. A special education teacher, possibly with the assistance of a school district administrator or outside consultant, might conduct mini inservices at faculty and staff meetings. Copies of fact sheets or briefing papers from a source such as the National Information Center for Children and Youth with Disabilities (NICHCY) can be provided, along with a brief overview of some of the most important identifying characteristics and educational needs of students with a particular disability. An introduction to special education law,

including topics such as the requirements regarding the necessary relationships between the disability and IEP
accommodations and modifications can
allay staff concerns about the fairness of
special services and accommodations.
(Information about obtaining resources
such as those produced by NICHCY is
given in Appendix B.)

Respectful, Person-First Language

Emphasizing the person, not the disability, is one way adults can communicate respect for students with disabilities. *Person-
first* language does not equate people with
their condition (*the disabled*); it simply
means that you put the person, not the
disability, first. Therefore, you name the
person first, and then, if necessary, name
the disability: a teenager who is blind, an
infant with Down syndrome, a child with
autism. Although this way of speaking and
writing about disabilities is not new, it is
not consistently practiced in the media
and is often absent from many individuals' everyday language. The accusation of
being too "politically correct" has led to
some mockery of this practice; however,
person-first language communicates respect for the human being while noting
that the disability is just one of the individual's attributes. When adults consistently model person-first language and include it in their guidelines of proper ways
to write and converse, children will adopt
person-first language and teach it to others outside the school.

There are numerous other commonly
used words and phrases that refer to disabilities that are inaccurate, patronizing,
pity evoking, or simply negative. For example, to say that a person is *wheelchair
bound* is inaccurate. A person who uses a
wheelchair is not actually bound to the
chair—he or she *uses* it—therefore, *wheelchair user* is a more appropriate term. Like-
wise, the term *mongoloid* has long since
been replaced by *Down syndrome*. Adults

and students should be instructed to use
emotionally neutral expressions:

- "She has cerebral palsy." NOT "She is
  a victim of cerebral palsy."
- "He has autism." NOT "He suffers
  from autism."

Acronyms such as CP, LD, BD, MR, and
TMR are also not necessary in discussions
about students with disabilities with their
typically developing peers (e.g., "She's BD
and ADHD"). At times, it might be necessary to use and explain the actual term
(e.g., cerebral palsy, learning disabilities)
to typically developing students; however,
once the term has been explained, it can
simply be omitted, and the child can be referred to by name alone (see http://
www.disabilityisnatural.com/peoplefirst
language.htm). Particularly with older students (beyond second grade) and adults, it
is valuable to teach the rules and the rationale behind person- first language.

Collaborative Teaming

Genuine collaboration means working together on shared goals, not simply being
cooperative or collegial. In order to engage in productive collaborative work,
team members need defined roles and efficient strategies for communicating and
problem solving. All team members who
will be in contact with a student with disabilities need information about the student's behavioral, physical, and social
characteristics. Those who actually work
with the student also should have knowledge of his or her IEP goals and accom
modations. Schools experienced with inclusion typically have an agreed-on
schoolwide approach for sharing this information. For example, when a student
enters a school or makes the transition
from one grade level to the next, the special education teacher organizes a team
planning session and shares the student's
Program-at-a-Glance (see Figure 2.4).
The provision of information about the

Program-at-a-Glance

Student: *Daniel* **Date:** *2005–2006* **Grade:** *2*

IEP goals

Social/communication

- *Use simple switches and picture symbols to make choices among 2–3 items or activities*
- *Attend to classmates' initiations during small-group lessons and nonacademic activities*
- *Initiate, respond, make choices, and reject recognizable communication cues (yes = move head up; no = head dropped to side) and simple switches*

Functional skills

- *Recognize visual, tactile, and auditory cues (e.g., picture-object schedule) to assist in anticipating events*
- *Maintain range of motion in upper extremities through daily activity and stretching*
- *Improve visual gaze and attention*
- *Perform school/classroom jobs with peer partner*

- *Increase independence in school arrival, departure, and lunch routines as per program plans*

Academic skills

- *Identify numbers 0–10*
- *Count objects to 10 in math activities and in functional contexts throughout the day*
- *Recognize name in print*
- *Cut/color/paste pictures and words for language and vocabulary activities*

Classroom participation

- *Participate in selected steps of small-group reading, writing, and word study projects/activities*
- *Participate partially in grade-level whole class and cooperative group lessons, with objectives related to motor skills, communication, alertness, and attention*

IEP accommodations

- *Receive special education assistance/ instruction with academics, daily routines, transitions, support for communication techniques, and peer interactions*
- *PT, OT, speech-language pull-in and consultation with team regarding issues/ techniques; pull-out PT for 30 minutes once per 6 weeks to evaluate movement and equipment*
- *Separate changing area provided*
- *Peer support program*
- *Home/school communication log*

- *Educational team instructed in positioning equipment, feeding and drinking techniques, toileting, dispensing medication, lifting and positioning in/out of wheelchair, and other personal care needs*
- *Educational team familiar with and uses all augmentative communication methods*
- *Variety of manipulatives for math activities*
- *Weekly co-planning to determine adaptations for participation in language arts, math, and cooperative group activities*

Academic/physical/social management needs

- *Peer planning and problem solving at beginning of year and as needed*
- *Special education aide support for physical/health management needs*
- *Position close to classmates in variety of suitable positions as per PT/OT plans*

Comments/other special needs

- *Anecdotal records and skill acquisition data for IEP progress*
- *Core team meetings weekly; whole team meetings monthly*
- *New staff trained by experienced staff or parents in specialized routines (e.g., feeding, toileting, handling, positioning)*

Figure 2.4. Program-at-a-Glance for Daniel. (Key: IEP, individualized education program; OT, occupational therapy; PT, physical therapy.)

student's disability and abilities to staff, in-service sessions on matters such as the use of the student's assistive technology or adaptive equipment, and also the peer support approaches to be used with the student all may appear on the Program-at-a-Glance as accommodations that are required by the student's IEP.

Systems Change Efforts

When a school is still in the early stages of changing from separate to integrated or inclusive programming, a series of in-service sessions for faculty will not be adequate to facilitate the desired systemic change; a more far-reaching approach to professional development and action planning is needed. Guidelines for early steps in a system's change to inclusion are addressed in two of the other books in this series—*Modifying Schoolwork* (Janney & Snell, 2004) and *Collaborative Teaming* (Snell & Janney, 2005)—and in several other helpful references (e.g., Davern, Ford, Erwin, Schnorr, & Rogan, 1993; McGregor & Vogelsberg, 1998; Knoster, Villa, & Thousand, 2000; Roach, 1995; Villa & Thousand, 2005; York-Barr, Doyle, & Kronberg, 1996).

Teachers and others who work in schools need to have exposure to this basic information on disabilities, special education law, person-first language, collaborative teaming, and systems-change processes in ways that are suited to their existing knowledge and roles. Teaching staff should become involved in the planning and provision of information and experiences to their students only after this exposure.

STRATEGIES FOR PREPARING PEERS

Many inclusive schools apply environmental strategies on an ongoing basis to build and periodically update students' understanding of and appreciation for human diversity and their skills in being members of a diverse learning community. Other strategies to prepare peers for inclusive classrooms include adult modeling of ways to interact with students who have disabilities, ability-awareness activities, strategies to foster a sense of community in the school and classroom, and sensitively addressing students' questions about fairness.

Modeling

Modeling is a key element adults use in most approaches that are designed to promote social relationships. It involves both incidental and explicit teaching of appropriate ways to assist, relate to, and interact with students who have disabilities. Modeling can be used by adults (and by peers) and includes one's actions as well as one's attitudes as expressed in conversations and verbal remarks made about students with disabilities. When a student with disabilities is new to a school or a classroom, students without disabilities, who may feel uneasy, often look to their teachers for guidance on how to interact with the new student. The special education teacher, in cooperation with the student's family members, may be the best initial model for other staff and students; however, when other school staff members such as librarians, guidance counselors, principals, paraprofessionals, therapists, school nurses, secretaries, cafeteria staff, bus drivers, and custodians are comfortable and appropriate in their interactions with students who have disabilities and are familiar with the child and his or her capabilities and needs, positive modeling permeates the school. Two important functions these adults can serve are to 1) model appropriate interactions by using age-appropriate language, voice tone, and interaction style and adjusting the complexity and modality to suit the student's communication methods; and 2) answer peers' questions in an honest, but sensitive, manner, using explanations suited to the students' level of understanding and not providing more information than necessary.

Modeling includes both actions and words; it is a powerful teaching strategy for all ages. Adults' words and gestures can communicate respect and comfort or avoidance and uncertainty. Adults' comments about students with disabilities may be fair or unfair and may focus on positive or negative aspects of the students' abilities and personalities. Students also learn from watching the way in which others react to their ways of interacting with students who have disabilities and from the reaction of the individual with disabilities. Do teachers (or students' peers) approve or disapprove? Are students successful in their efforts to assist and communicate with their classmate or to defuse potentially disruptive behavior?

To be effective models, adults should have positive attitudes about human diversity and some awareness of the focus students' abilities (e.g., mode of communication, knowledge level, visual and auditory capabilities, mobility) and personalities. If teachers and staff are uncomfortable around students with disabilities and show outward signs of uneasiness or fear, other students usually detect their discomfort and feel uncomfortable themselves.

Another powerful point of view that bears on the ways adults include a student is the philosophy that the included student is "just another student." That is, the student is generally expected to follow the same school rules as others for lining up, taking turns, listening, being in his or her place on time, and putting his or her head down when it gets noisy (Janney & Snell, 1996). Teachers who model these expectations teach their students to treat their classmate with disabilities as they would treat each other—not to coddle, patronize, treat as if much younger, or address using "baby talk." If classmates hear adults speaking in a childish voice or otherwise treating a student with disabilities in ways that are not age-appropriate, they will imitate this behavior. Instead, typically developing students should clearly see that the student with disabilities is their peer and should be treated as such.

When a particular student with disabilities enters a new school or a class, it is appropriate to share helpful information with the staff who will be involved with the student. Early in-service sessions organized by the school's special education teachers should be held to address the general areas of knowledge about the student's abilities and disabilities that influence adult modeling. For typically developing students to be accepting of the student with diverse learning styles and needs, teachers must teach through their actions, not merely by instructing and advising (Goodman, 1994).

Student Snapshot

Before Daniel arrived for second grade at Mountain View Elementary, his special education teacher organized a team planning session and shared his Program-at-a-Glance (Figure 2.4). Daniel, who was new to the school district, had multiple disabilities (cerebral palsy, vision impairments, and a seizure disorder) and, therefore, a large educational team. Along with Daniel's mom and brother, the special education teacher and Daniel's therapists (speech-language, vision, physical, and occupational) organized two short in-service sessions for Daniel's second-grade teacher; several paraprofessionals; the principal; the guidance counselor; and the music, physical education, and library teachers. Daniel arrived for the last part of both sessions to meet everyone.

Before he arrived, those attendees who knew Daniel well gave the group some general guidelines about how to interact with him (e.g., look at Daniel when you talk, not at his teacher or mother; use a normal voice as his hearing is fine; talk to him as a second-grade student but use simpler vocabulary—he understands a lot; know that Daniel indicates "yes" by lifting his head). By discussing these guidelines before he arrived, the group did not have to talk about Daniel in front of him.

During Daniel's visit, teachers had an opportunity to see Daniel interact with his mom, his brother, and the special education teacher, who knew him well already. The guidelines and models gave Daniel's teachers confidence to try interacting with Daniel during his visits.

Infusing Diversity-Related Topics into the Curriculum

Children are aware at a very young age that color, language, gender, and physical ability differences are connected with privilege and power. They learn by observing the differences and similarities among people and by absorbing the spoken and unspoken message about those differences. Racism, sexism, and handicapism have a profound influence on their developing sense of self and others (Derman-Sparks & The Anti-Bias Curriculum Task Force, 1989).

Children and adolescents value the similarities they have with certain peers, and it is often these similarities that bring peers together into social networks and that launch friendships. Thus, teachers often will work to identify and build on the commonalities that exist among all students. An accepting atmosphere that provides information on differences while also emphasizing similarities makes it easier to build tolerance, trust, mutual support, and respect. From these interpersonal characteristics, individuals develop a sense of belonging, and, from this base, positive social relationships often result. However, human differences—and the personal, social, and political forces that both influence and reflect attitudes and behavior toward those differences—

also should be explored. A genuinely inclusive community does not deny disability or other human differences but emphasizes the value of diversity and helps to "make difference ordinary" (Biklen et al., 1989).

The most comprehensive and normalized approach to topics related to diversity, disability, and interpersonal and group relations is to make them part of the curriculum (e.g., Derman-Sparks & The Anti-Bias Curriculum Task Force, 1989; Hamre-Nietupski et al., 1989; Sax, Fisher, Chappell, & Pratt, 1999). Some examples of activities that infuse knowledge and understanding of disability into the curriculum follow.

- Include disability and diversity-related information into the social sciences curriculum, such as by examining handicapism along with racism, gender discrimination, and other prejudices; studying the history of civil rights legislation, including the Americans with Disabilities Act (ADA) of 1990 (PL 101-336); and examining the principle of universal design and the adaptive technology that we all use in everyday life.

- Conduct a lesson on stereotyping in which students wear adhesive labels on their backs that identify them as a person who is often stereotyped in a negative way (e.g., homeless person, person who is blind, new immigrant, person with HIV/AIDS, cheerleader) and mingle as they would at a community event, with the instruction to address one another as if they were talking to a person with that characteristic. Afterward, discussion can focus on how stereotypes are related to prejudice and how they are perpetuated in our society (Sax et al., 1999).

- Read and discuss literature about differences and similarities and the experiences of people and groups who have encountered stereotyping and prejudice.

- Conduct a school or community accessibility survey (Figure 2.5) to sensitize students to architectural barriers and the need for laws such as ADA, which requires accessibility.

- View demonstrations of ways to interact with someone who uses augmentative or assistive communication devices, and experiment with using these systems and devices.

- Study the concept of environmental adaptations and assistive devices and the ways we use them in everyday tasks such as buying groceries, mowing the yard, writing a check, or getting an item from a high cupboard; compare the adaptations that people with disabilities use to perform these and other daily tasks (e.g., wheelchairs, captioned television, ramps) with those that people typically use to perform the task more efficiently (e.g., eyeglasses, ladders, power rider mowers).

- Define and give examples of person-first language and other respectful ways of describing or addressing individuals or groups; discuss the emotional, social, and political reasons for using respectful terms.

Increasing Student Understanding and Appreciation

Schools that have not reached the point in their pursuit of inclusion where disability awareness can be embedded in the ways just described may need to begin with periodic lessons, activities, and events to explore concepts related to diversity. Although students without disabilities have more opportunities than in the past to know individuals who have disabilities, exploring disabilities in sensitive ways still

can be beneficial. In these cases, it is effective to have all students participate in awareness activities during which they

- Experience simulations of physical, sensory, or learning disabilities

- Learn about different disabilities and facilitative technology by using electronic communication devices and Braille

- Talk to productive adults with disabilities

- Use wheelchairs and evaluate the accessibility of a school building or part of the surrounding community

For elementary and middle school students, it is useful to plan initial activities on diversity and disability awareness on a widespread basis, with some schoolwide activities, some activities for multiple-grade clusters (fourth- and fifth-grade classrooms), and others for single-grade levels (all eighth-grade students). Later in the process, when inclusion has become more systematized, activities can be organized and implemented for individual classrooms or for each entering class of students. In high schools, the coverage of information and activities on diversity and disability are often more naturally integrated into classes on health, family life, history, and social sciences. Sometimes, middle and high school service clubs or Key Clubs may sponsor a day, or several days, of activities during which they promote understanding of differences, diversity, and positive attitudes. Planning groups should attempt to involve many different people: student leaders and representatives from all age groups, special educators, adults with disabilities from the community, staff with inclusion experience, teachers who have seniority and respect, parents of children with and without disabilities, some nonteaching and nonprofessional staff, and the principal or a key administrator.

School Accessibility Survey

Directions: Study your school to see whether it is accessible to a person who uses a wheelchair or has a disability. Put an X in the appropriate column, and answer the questions at the end.

Are these parts of your school accessible for everyone, including people who use a wheelchair or have physical disabilities?	Yes	No
1. Parking spaces (Are extra-wide spaces reserved and marked with the handicapped access symbol?)		
2. The main door (Is there a ramp? A doorway at least 32" wide? A door that opens with a single push or by pushing a button? Does the button work?)		
3. All other public entrances (same questions as above)		
4. All classrooms (Are doorways at least 32" wide? Can someone who uses a wheelchair sit in every area of the classroom [a wheelchair needs a 60" in diameter space for turning around]?)		
5. Cafeteria		
6. Gym and locker room		
7. Library		
8. Main office		
9. Auditorium (Are there spaces for wheelchairs so that a person using a wheelchair does not have to sit in the aisle?)		
10. Restrooms (Are sinks 29" to 43" from the floor? Do faucets have lever-type controls? Is there an extra-wide toilet stall?)		
11. Water fountains		
12. Hallways (Are they at least 48" wide?)		
13. All outside areas (Do ramps, curb cuts, and wheelchair-accessible paths allow access to playing fields, courtyards, and so forth?)		
14. All floors of the school (Are there ramps or elevators?)		

Overall, how would you rate your school's accessibility?

___ *Fully accessible:* Every person has equal access to every part of the school and all school activities.

___ *Mostly accessible:* Every person can use most areas of the school, but access for some people with disabilities is inconvenient, or the person might not be able to fully participate in every activity that takes place in some areas.

___ *Mostly inaccessible:* Some people would not be able to use several parts of the school.

___ *Completely inaccessible:* Environmental barriers would make it impossible for a person with a disability to be a student here.

Justify your rating. _____

_____

Figure 2.5.   School accessibility survey.

Smaller-Scale Simulations

Teaching children about disabilities through respectful classroom simulations allows students to try out being in the shoes of their classmate with disabilities. Simulations should also be suited to the ability of typically developing classmates to understand.

Student Snapshot

On a day when Nate was absent, kindergartners in Ms. Hill's classroom spent their free time "being Nate." After a discussion about how Nate talks and moves about (i.e., in his wheelchair, with his walker, on the floor), the teachers and assistants helped the students figure out ways to express themselves without words, to move around the room, and to use a drinking fountain without standing upright. Nate's classmates limited their communication to several vocalizations and facial expressions, and, instead of walking, they moved about on their knees and pulled themselves partially up with the support of a table.

They talked and moved in these ways as they used the centers, interacted with each other, and engaged in play activities.

Teachers were surprised by the students' familiarity with Nate's ways of doing things. The class discussion that followed allowed the children to process their experiences. They said things such as, "It's hard to be Nate," and "I like to say words." One perceptive student asked, "Is this why Nate yells a lot?" Then, the kindergarten students generated a list of ways in which they might get Nate to interact and play with them during class choice time and at recess. Over the next few weeks, the students' ideas were tried, revised, and expanded, and Nate's involvement with class activities and interaction with his classmates increased (see Figure 2.6).

Another way to provide simulations is to allow typically developing classmates to try using some of the adapted equipment that their peer with disabilities uses (but *only* with student, parental, and therapist approval). If this is not feasible, adults should try to address students' natural curiosity by providing simple explanations for

---

One day in October when Nate was absent, his teacher asked his classmates to think about how they could get Nate to play with them more during center time. As they sat on the blue rug and shared their ideas, she wrote them on a big piece of paper and drew small pictures by each idea. The following are some of the creative ideas they brainstormed:

1. Build things that are okay to knock down.
2. Use small blocks to make towers.
3. Help with pictures.
4. Read him a story.
5. Invite him to play in the house.
6. Help him build something with soft blocks.
7. Play ball with him.
8. Help him climb.
9. Sing him a song.
10. Encourage him to come with you.
11. Tell him what you are doing.
12. Use the WOLF (his talking communication device) to pick songs.

Ms. Hill and Nate's other teachers helped his classmates implement these ideas during the weeks that followed.

Figure 2.6. Kindergarten peers' ideas for getting Nate to play with them.

- Equipment used for mobility (e.g., wheelchairs, walkers, canes, plastic splints) and positioning (e.g., standing tables, prone boards, floor sitters, sidelyers)

- Equipment, materials, and methods used for communication (e.g., electronic systems, picture communication books, signing, picture exchange systems)

- Special procedures that might be observed (e.g., eating with specialized equipment, suctioning, tube feeding, grinding food, breathing through a tracheostomy)

- Adapted or specialized learning materials (e.g., Braille books, calculators, adapted writing implements, prostheses)

Regardless of whether there are students with IEPs in a classroom, it is meaningful for educators to address the issue of respecting diversity and understanding that, although they are not all alike, each student has unique gifts and skills.

Grade-Level or Schoolwide Ability/Disability-Awareness Programs

The general purposes of ability/disability-awareness programs often are broad. For example, one or more of the following purposes might be targeted:

- To educate a group of students about people with disabilities

- To replace stereotyped and negative views with accurate information

- To answer students' questions

- To emphasize abilities and similarities between people with disabilities and those without disabilities

- To provide a combination of experiences by using carefully planned simulations of one or several disabilities

and inviting guest speakers who have disabilities to speak to the students

- To promote positive attitudes toward individuals with disabilities

Ultimately, the school planning group must identify its own purposes for awareness activities and design them to match the school's specific needs and age range. The group will plan the activities to be carried out within or across classrooms and often will spread them out across a period of time. Devoting a small period of time each day to different activities during a disability-awareness week (or two), while also following the typical school schedule and routine, allows for better learning than does replacing an entire day's schedule with activities devoted entirely to disability awareness. Activities must be interesting to the age group as well as informative and accurate; they should be neither condescending nor pitying but should emphasize ability and the tenet that *people with disabilities are people (first) who have a disability (second)*. Examples of strategies to support this tenet include 1) studying famous people with disabilities in music, sports, writing, politics, or other careers that the students admire; and 2) interacting with people who have disabilities and who fill roles that the students respect.

Activities that involve simulating disabilities must be conducted with particular care and sensitivity so that peers achieve the desired goals of learning about disabilities, focusing on what people with disabilities can do rather than on their limitations, and experiencing challenges posed by certain disabilities. Planning teams should determine a set of dos and don'ts to follow when simulating disabilities with typically developing students (Figure 2.7). A key guideline is that the activities should generate awareness of ways to cope with exceptional needs rather than feelings of frustration and pity.

Educational teams should apply several rules of caution when planning for the use of simulations in inclusive classrooms or on a larger scale:

1. Simulations should be planned by the educational team, including students' parents; the right to veto any ideas should always exist.

2. Simulations should always focus on the positive and unique characteristics of the student or disability; they should never take on a pitying or superhuman tone and should address strategies used to cope rather than focus on frustration.

3. Simulations should be used only to help students understand an aspect of a person or a disability that is difficult to explain.

4. Simulations should always be preceded with an explanation of why they are occurring and followed by a discussion.

5. Simulations should never depict a student with a disability as the class "mascot" or pet. They should always aim to explain differences by emphasizing unique characteristics or similarities.

Figure 2.7. Rules of caution with disability simulations.

In the upper elementary grades, middle school, or high school, students might participate in a classwide or grade-level disability simulation experience in which they actually utilize equipment such as wheelchairs, walkers, crutches, eye covers, and handmade leg braces to experience simulating physical disabilities for a day. Students also could simulate "invisible disabilities" including hearing loss (students wear earplugs) and dyslexia/dysgraphia (students write by looking in a small mirror and not directly at the paper). Schedules must be established for use of the equipment, and participating students should be given clear guidelines for what is required of them (e.g., take the disability seriously; this is not a game but a learning experience), how to use the equipment (e.g., the wheelchairs and other equipment are borrowed and cost a lot of money; report any damage to your teacher as soon as possible and explain how it happened), and so forth.

Even simple activities will require careful planning (e.g., teachers will need to preview books, stories, or films; locate or construct simulation materials; and identify appropriate guests). It also is important to hold discussions after each activity in order to answer students' questions and assess their understanding and attitudes. Older students might write essays or journals or complete feedback surveys about their experience.

Parents of children with disabilities and individuals who themselves have disabilities are often the best assistants for implementing disability-awareness activities and discussions. Classroom teachers often seek the support and assistance of the special education teacher, school counselor, or a particular therapist who knows more about certain disabilities.

As described in Figure 2.1, researchers have documented the positive effects that simulations and other disability-awareness experiences can have on the attitudes of typically developing students toward their peers with disabilities. Sources of information on these and other strategies to improve the school environment through awareness and information about disabilities are provided in Appendix B.

Building Classroom Community

Included in the indirect methods that make the school environment more inclusive are activities to promote friendly, supportive relationships and prosocial behavior and to foster a sense of community.

Classroom Management

Adults set the tone for the social interactions in classrooms in direct and also subtle ways. Classroom rules expressed as long lists of don'ts, caustic remarks, punitive behavior management systems, and ignored bullying or teasing create a negative, even threatening, environment that is not conducive to positive social relationships and acceptance of diversity. Even in elementary school, a classroom's social structure can be dominated by popular or aggressive cliques, peer groups can ostracize or manipulate members of other peer groups, and group conflict can become the norm (Adler & Adler, 1996). Farmer and Cadwallader (2000) recommended that teachers assess the social structure of their classroom and seek to establish classroom routines and management systems that promote positive behavior and social acceptance for all. They suggest that teachers consider the following as they develop classroom management procedures (Farmer & Cadwallader, 2000):

- Are the interests and activities of some groups given more social prominence and support from adults than the interests and activities of other groups?

- Is social aggression or bullying by good students overlooked because it is being directed toward problem students?

- Do instructional or disciplinary practices group together students who are likely to support or complement each other's problem behavior?

- Is the social structure within the school or classroom highly stratified in ways that promote animosity and interpersonal conflict among distinct peer groups?

- Are there clearly identifiable "elite" peer groups?

- Are there clearly identifiable "outcast" or "counter-culture" groups?

- Does the general social context support aggressive and disruptive behavior?

- Are there antisocial peer groups or groups of bullies who control the social climate?

- Do nonparticipants support bullying by indicating their approval, acquiescing, looking the other way, or protecting bullies from teacher detection?

Class Meetings

In schools where inclusive practices are well instituted, teachers, sometimes with the collaboration of school psychologists or counselors, organize daily or weekly class meetings that address topics related to classroom rights, responsibilities, and relationships (Developmental Studies Center, 1996; Vance & Weaver, 2002). Class meetings can be used proactively to examine respectful, compassionate, and supportive ways to interact with other members of the classroom and school community and also in response to a particular social interaction problem that one or more class members may be experiencing. For example, one student, discouraged about his grandfather's illness and death, shared his feelings during peer planning; students later found ways to lend their support to him. In another case, fifth-grade students used some of their peer planning time to talk about the changes they feared would occur in middle school. Class meetings also could be used to

- Discuss a generally accepted virtue such as compassion. (What does *compassion* mean? What does a compassionate person do and say?)

- Discuss the results of using a Record of Friendly Deeds on which students have jotted down the things that they did during the week to demonstrate their friendship skills.

- Teach or reinforce classroom expectations for behavior by discussing reasons for having codes of conduct; make a T-chart to contrast examples and non-examples of approved behavior.

- Create a "perfect day" for one student each week. List the focus person's strengths and likes and things that could be done to make the person feel special. Students make a commitment to do one thing the following day that will help create a perfect day for the person (Janney & Snell, 2004).

Circles of Friends

The Circles of Friends (also called Circles of Support or simply Circles) exercise is a friendship awareness activity often used to introduce students and adults to the universal need for social support and relationships (Falvey, Forest, Pearpoint, & Rosenberg, 1997). It can be used with an entire class during a class meeting or social studies lesson, or as an initial strategy in the process of building a social support network for a focus student at risk for loneliness.

First, students are shown an example of a Circles worksheet (Figure 2.8) and asked to draw four concentric circles on a piece

Directions: Think about the people you spend time with in your life. Put their names or the group's names in circles that best describe their relationship with you.

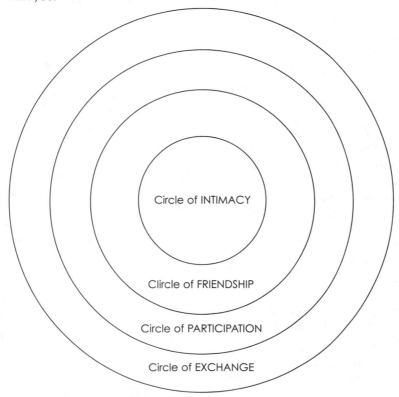

Figure 2.8. Circles of Friends (or Circles of Supports) exercise. (From Falvey, M.A., Forest, M., Pearpoint, J., & Rosenberg, R.L. [1997]. *All my life's a circle: Using the tools: Circles, MAPS & PATHs* [2nd ed.]. Toronto: Inclusion Press; http://www.inclusion.com. Reprinted by permission.)

of paper (or, students may be provided with a prepared worksheet). Then, they write their name in the middle of the circle and are asked to put names of people and groups they know into four concentric circles that describe the relationship:

- The inner circle, the Circle of Intimacy, reflects those family members and friends who are closest to the student and who the student really cares for and couldn't imagine living without.

- The second circle, the Circle of Friendship, lists the student's good friends—those who are friends but not as close as those in the first circle.

- The third circle, the Circle of Participation, lists the people, organizations, and networks the student is involved with (e.g., baseball team, choir, reading group, scouts, people at work, swimming team).

- The fourth circle, the Circle of Exchange, contains people who provide services for the student for money (e.g., the dentist, hairstylist/barber, doctor, teacher, therapist).

The general discussion that follows does not involve sharing specific numbers or names of those placed in the students' circles; students keep their circle information private because it is personal to them. Instead, the discussion is focused on why students put the people they did into the different circles. The teacher could ask the students questions such as the following:

- Think about the people in the inner circle and the second circle. Why did you put them there?

- How would you feel if you had very few people in your first and second circles?

- How would you feel if you had very few individuals or groups in the third circle?

- Do you have any circles in which you would like to have more people? What could you do to make that happen?

- What are some of the reasons why a person could have few people in their circles?

Discussing the answers to these questions can lead the way to a comparison of the circles of typically developing peers to the circles of students with disabilities. This comparison may reveal several differences: People with disabilities often have 1) fewer individuals in the first two circles, 2) fewer groups in the third circle, and 3) either as many, though often more, paid people in the outer circle. The Circles exercise can be a potent way to increase awareness of these differences and to emphasize the value that friends have in our lives. The often stark contrast between the circles of typically developing peers and the circles of a classmate who has disabilities can be used as a springboard to introduce the value of peer support and to initiate recruitment of members into a focus student's Circle of Friendship (Fisher & Snell, 1999), as is discussed in Chapter 3. Keep in mind, however, that this exercise used alone and not accompanied by any other planned activities may not result in any changes in rates or types of social interactions between students and their classmates who have disabilities (Fritz, 1990); however, Circles of Friends interventions that involve regular meetings over the course of at least 6 weeks have been shown to have a positive impact on the focus student's social acceptance by peers (though not on the focus student's social competence or on the general ethos of the classroom) (Frederickson & Turner, 2003).

Addressing Students' Perceptions of Fairness

Issues of fairness are commonly addressed in most schools and homes as children are growing up and may also influence a child's social environment. Both adults and students have their own perceptions of fairness. Although teachers adjust some standards for behavior, they should expect students with disabilities to follow classroom rules as much as possible. Generally, teachers should encourage typically developing peers to view their classmates with disabilities as class members who are to be "treated the same," regardless of whether the supports they require are extensive or minimal.

Tony goes to the office every afternoon to take medication for his hyperactivity. Usually, before lunch, it is harder for Tony to sit and work at his desk. At these times, he might be given responsibilities that let him move around, he might move his work to the floor, or he may just take a break from sitting. Do peers notice or care that he goes to the office every lunch period? Will peers think his activity breaks are unfair?

Bethany's reading has always been exceptional. In eighth grade, she reads high school– and college-level materials. For special projects, her teachers provide her with books from the nearby high school and college libraries on interlibrary loan. Lately, Bethany has received permission to use the school's connection to the Internet to seek information for school assignments. Although peers know she is a "super reader," will they view Bethany's book and computer privileges as unfair?

Fairness issues may be raised by students, sometimes in the context of a class meeting or discussion during which issues of concern are discussed and problem-solved. Students might comment about things they believe to be unfair. "How come Tony can stop his work and we can't?" "I want the good books like Bethany gets." Try to address these questions directly with students but with great care. Many times, our answers address the issues of a reasonable accommodation. "Because that is how Tony learns best." "Because these books are ones that Bethany understands." When such ques-

tions repeatedly arise, they probably should be addressed through disability-awareness activities such as those described previously and through class discussions about individual differences. Students could examine questions such as Does equality require that everyone be treated exactly the same way? If questions about fairness repeatedly arise from multiple classmates regarding a particular student, that student's educational team needs to discuss these concerns and search for solutions. The solutions may involve improvements in the accommodation itself, in the workloads and activities of students who do not have accommodations, or in the ways that teachers treat students' differences in learning and accomplishment.

It seems easier for peers to understand treatment differences as being fair accommodations under certain classroom and school conditions:

1. The student's disability is reasonably understood by classmates; however, for less visible disabilities or when students choose not to disclose their disabilities, this understanding may not be directly associated with the student who has the disability.

2. Peers are accustomed to having their teachers treat differences in student ability as ordinary and are taught to applaud individual accomplishments, even when a classmate's disabilities are subtle and not recognized by peers.

3. The student's accommodations or modifications are appropriate, "match" his or her needs, and are non-stigmatizing.

4. Teachers and classmates routinely share, discuss, and problem-solve classroom concerns such as fairness.

5. Teachers place more emphasis on students' similarities than on their differences.

6. The classroom culture is cooperative, and competition is applied only by students to themselves: "improving my own performance" or "improving our team's record."

To the extent that accommodations are appropriate and fit students' needs and that class members are used to being in heterogeneous groups and working together cooperatively, students will be more accepting of differences in ability, workload, ways of responding, and accomplishments.

Teaching in ways that enable students to accept differences among classmates is rather different from teaching by the pro-claimed standard of "We are all the same," particularly when it is obvious that we are not! Students in inclusive classrooms often recognize differences among themselves; denial of these differences may only further emphasize them for some students.

The strategies and programs that have been described in this chapter will help create a school environment that is receptive to the inclusion of students with disabilities. A culture in which disabilities are understood, all students are equal members, and the expectations for achievement are high for everyone greatly eases the way for establishing friendships and other supportive relationships among students.

Chapter 3

Building Support Through Peer Groups

Although adults cannot manufacture or mandate friendships among children with diverse abilities, they can assist in the creation of a variety of positive relationships. This chapter describes some proven methods for direct, student-to-student facilitation of social relationships. Many of the structured approaches for building social relationships that are described in this chapter involve carefully planned, age-appropriate disclosure of a student's disability to classmates. An individual's disability is private information that must be handled with care. As with any other confidential student information, staff must be certain about the wishes of students and their families regarding the sharing of such information. Selecting students for peer support, identifying objectives, and planning the approach is a team process that involves general and special educators, family members, the student, and often the student's peers.

AGE AND PEER SUPPORT STRATEGY

Facilitating relationships among young children with and without disabilities is often easier than it is with older children and teenagers. Some disabilities are less apparent when children are young, and disparities in academic ability are less pronounced. In addition, there are more opportunities in preschool and elementary school for teachers to emphasize social interactions both in the classroom and during recess, snack breaks, and so forth. If typically developing students experience positive interactions and relationships with peers with disabilities when they are young, some of these relationships continue through the years; also, peers without disabilities are more likely

to continue to be more accepting of individual differences as they grow older when such values are instilled early.

In elementary school, the development of peer relationships is facilitated by the group membership that is established by the classroom as a unit, by students' engagement in shared activities throughout the day, and by teachers' expectations that students of this age require social and emotional support. As children age, their feelings, beliefs, expectations, and attitudes can change, and friendships can grow and change accordingly.

After the move from elementary school to middle or junior high school, the maintenance of old relationships and the development of new ones can be made more difficult, as several elementary schools feed into a single middle school, and students who were friends or acquaintances in elementary school may no longer share classes. The cliques and crowds that often characterize the social networks of preteens and adolescents can create social edifices that are difficult for students with poor social skills to join.

In high school, students attend classes in a larger building with more students, more teachers, and greater differentiation of curricula, which make both instructional and social inclusion of students with disabilities more challenging. Academic demands accelerate, and some students with disabilities need modified curricular goals and more extensive social and academic supports in order to experience success. The physical and organizational structure of high schools also can present challenges to the facilitation of social relationships. Therefore, in secondary schools, peer support approaches focus on using natural opportunities to foster interactions and on devising ways for students with and without disabilities to become members of activity groups.

APPROACHES FOR
BUILDING PEER SUPPORT

The goal of peer support strategies is to facilitate the development of a normalized range of positive and age-appropriate social relationships, including acquaintances, friends of varying degrees, and membership in various groups and subgroups. Support and assistance should be nonstigmatizing and aid a student in achieving independence. Strategies used to build peer support vary in their degree of structure, and, accordingly, in the amount of adult effort and involvement required for implementation, as illustrated in Figure 3.1.

Reciprocity occurs in peer relationships when turns are balanced, when partners understand one another, when both people are actively involved, and when the involvement of each person influences the other. It is characteristic of *most* close friendships involving children of the same age. Unlike friendships, support relationships are not always reciprocal or balanced. Many educators and parents fear that when relationships are *limited* to one-way helping, the quality of the relationship between the partners is lessened (e.g., Van der Klift & Kunc, 1994). Staub, Schwartz, Gallucci, and Peck (1994) found that teachers relied heavily on the friends of children with extensive support needs to assist in classroom management and to serve as instructional resources. In several cases, this reliance appeared to change the nature of the relationship from a friendship that was more balanced to one in which the peer without disabilities took on a caregiving role.

Several obvious solutions to this dilemma exist:

1. Teams can define guidelines for peers who help and teach other peers.

2. Teachers can encourage and facilitate a cooperative culture in the class-

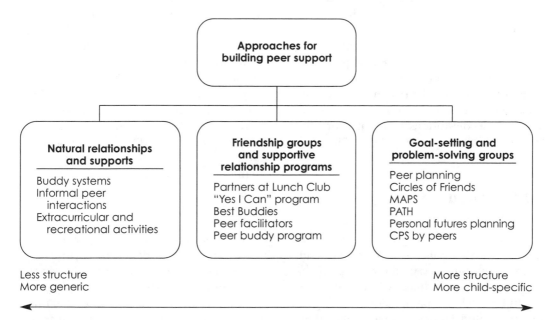

Figure 3.1. Approaches for building peer support. (Key: CPS, collaborative problem solving; PATH, Planning Alternative Tomorrows with Hope.)

room, making appropriate helping an acceptable and normal aspect of peer interactions among all students.

3. Teachers can design and implement more cooperative activities in which peers learn to take (or share) the lead and to alternate turns.

4. Teams can carefully monitor their reliance on peers for providing care to classmates with disabilities.

5. Teams can look to themselves and to their supervisors for the needed classroom supports.

Nonreciprocal relationships may indeed be positive and enjoyable; however, it is unlikely that anyone would be satisfied with a relationship circle primarily composed of nonreciprocal, helping relationships. The ideal that teachers and other school staff members should aim for is to even the score: Students should not always be the recipients of help or always be the givers of help. Instead, they should experience both getting and giving help, with help based on need. Cooperative interactions and interdependence should replace one-way helping. Also, help should be provided on an as-needed basis: "The roles of helper and helpee are defined situationally, rather than being based on the immutable definitions of ability and disability" (Janney & Snell, 1996, p. 79).

ADULT FACILITATION

One key to building positive peer relationships in schools for students with and without disabilities is guidance, assistance, and teaching by adults. Adult facilitators include teachers, paraprofessionals, parents, related-services personnel, other school staff, and volunteers. Adult facilitation may be indirect and incidental, such as when teachers serve as models for students or other adults or consciously re-

frain from allowing adult presence to interfere with peer interaction, or it may be direct and explicit, such as when teachers teach structured lessons on how to interact with, relate to, and lend support to peers with disabilities. Both types of facilitation are part of the general support plan for a student and will be listed on the IEP as accommodations.

Modeling and role playing are two important methods that adults use to facilitate peer relationships. For example, a teacher might use modeling and/or role playing to demonstrate how to 1) ask a student where he or she wants to sit, then help the student navigate his or her wheelchair to that table in the cafeteria; 2) offer a toy to a classmate with autism and ask, "Do you want to play?"; 3) remind a classmate who pushes and grabs to use words to ask for something; 4) react when a classmate starts to get angry or has a tantrum; and 5) pose a question to a student who uses a yes/no system of communicating.

Adult demonstrations may be accompanied by a simple explanation for the actions that are being role played. Negative and positive examples of the interaction in question might also be demonstrated by adults, with students then giving a critique. Next, students may imitate the model or role play and be given feedback by the adults and/or peers. Finally, students can be coached in planned or incidental contexts in which they use the method with their peer with disabilities.

When a student needs ongoing support to be successful in an inclusive classroom, adults often have to counteract the tendency to help *too much*. This may be due to fear that the student will get hurt or will not complete an activity successfully. When adults are assigned to work one-to-one with a student, they may feel that others will think they are not fulfilling their responsibilities if they do not stay close by; however, adults can inhibit interactions between students with and without disabilities in several ways.

Giangreco and his colleagues (1997) found that typically developing peers, when given a choice, often left groups involving a student with support needs who was supervised by a paraprofessional. Peers left because their offers of assistance were refused by the adult, they were "rebuffed" by the adult, or their initiations were interrupted by the adult. When Broer, Doyle, and Giangreco (2005) interviewed students with disabilities about their experiences with paraprofessional support, they found that four roles emerged describing students' relationships with paraprofessionals: mother, friend, protector, and primary teacher. Broer's research team found cause for concern in each of these roles and urged educational teams to carefully consider the social validity of the supports provided as well as students' preferences regarding ways to meet their own support needs.

Other research on this topic examined teacher–child and child–child interactions in an inclusive preschool (Harper & McCluskey, 2003). Videotapes of children during free play revealed that, after an adult had initiated an interaction with a child with disabilities, that child was less likely to initiate an interaction with a peer and more likely to initiate another interaction with an adult. In addition to stifling peer interactions in these ways, adult proximity does not always increase student engagement: In one study, elementary-age students with autism who had been assigned full-time paraprofessionals were on task most often when working with their peers (Young, Simpson, Smith-Myles, & Kamps, 1996). These findings suggest the possibility that carefully limiting adult interaction could enhance social integration more easily than more structured, higher-energy interventions.

Awareness of the extent and effects of hovering by adults can be increased by videotaping peer interactions and small-group instruction and critiquing one's teaching. Another strategy is to assign two paraprofessionals rather than just one to students who require extensive support; these staff members alternate part way through the day and follow the practice of assisting all students, not simply a student with disabilities. Staff members also can learn effective ways to teach pairs or small groups of students without dominating group members' interactions and to provide prompts or physical assistance to children in the least intrusive way.

Teachers in inclusive classrooms describe "backing off" as a successful strategy (Janney & Snell, 1996). One teacher will set up activities and interactions with clear explanations to all students regarding what their roles and responsibilities are for the activity. Then, he or she will physically pull back from the activity and move on to assist another student or group. The teacher will maintain visual supervision of the students' interactions, and, if students appear to be floundering or are at a standstill, he or she will reenter the group and provide some direct assistance Once the students are "back on track," the teacher retreats again.

NATURAL RELATIONSHIPS AND SUPPORTS

The least structured ways of facilitating social relationships involve methods that simply encourage natural peer supports and relationships during school activities and routines. There are many options, including buddy systems, informal peer interactions, and extracurricular and recreational activities. As valuable as peer buddies and "friendship" approaches can be, students with significant learning or behavior problems may not necessarily make noticeable gains in social competence or meaningfully expand their social network until they actually participate in instructional activities in general education classes with their typically developing

1. Adult facilitators and/or experienced peers need to teach others to communicate with the focus student; they should be taught to both understand and use the student's communication system (e.g., facial expressions, picture pointing).

2. Adult facilitators should share and practice ways to amend conversations or interactions that are not working.

3. If the focus student is not able to get around without assistance, peers need to be taught respectful ways to assist and to encourage the student's participation while also promoting independence and choice. Peers also should be taught basic information about the equipment or procedures the person routinely uses.

4. Adult facilitators should teach peers the importance of balanced turn-taking, mutual enjoyment, and reciprocity in interactions.

5. Adult facilitators should determine and use or identify and try out preferred activities and materials that the focus student has in common with peers. These activities and materials should be age appropriate, nonstigmatizing, safe, and fun.

6. Adult monitoring of interactive activities should be kept unobtrusive while enabling the adult to collect information about activity or program outcomes and participants' level of satisfaction.

7. Adults should schedule regular times to meet with the focus student's peers so that buddies, partners, or group members can problem-solve, plan, and discuss success stories, challenges, and things about which they are unsure (with the focus student present and participating if possible).

8. Adult facilitators should encourage and promote responsible peer control of the support activities.

9. Participation in the support activities should be fun, voluntary, and age appropriate.

Figure 3.2.   General guidelines for using natural peer supports.

peers (Carter, Cushing, Clark, & Kennedy, 2005; Kennedy & Itkonen, 1994; Myles, Simpson, Ormsbee, & Erickson, 1993). Therefore, in addition to structured and natural approaches for facilitating social interactions between students with disabilities and their peers, it continues to be important for educators to 1) teach student-specific social skills if necessary, and 2) work toward social and instructional inclusion in general education settings for students of all ages and disabilities.

Jorgensen defined *natural supports* for school-age students with disabilities as

> Those components of an educational program—philosophy, policies, people, materials and technology, and curricula—that are used to enable all students to be fully participating members of regular classroom, school, and community life. Natural supports bring children closer together as friends and learning partners rather than isolating them. (1992, p. 183)

When harnessing natural or less structured supports to promote social relationships, educators will find it helpful to develop and follow some general program guidelines that emphasize the importance of sensitivity toward peer preferences, existing networks, and chronological age; show respect for social exchanges between peers; and provide minimal but thoughtful assistance (see Figure 3.2).

Buddy Systems

There are many different versions of buddy systems. Some buddy programs have goals of simply having fun or of providing assistance to a given individual. Most buddy systems are based within a classroom and involve incidental teaching during nonstructured, routine activities. Incidental support and teaching by peer buddies can address many types of skills, including social skills and any other skills that the specific activity requires (e.g., independent travel in the school, behavior in public).

For young children, learning to be a buddy focuses on playing together, eating snacks, and interacting during table activities (English, Shafer, Goldstein, & Kazmarek, 1997). In elementary schools, buddy systems often concentrate on social interactions during arrival and departure, recess, lunch, learning centers, and cooperative group activities (Kamps et al., 2002). In middle school or high school, peer buddies may provide instructional support during inclusive classes and/or lend social support, such as assisting their peers in getting to class or to the bus (Hughes & Carter, 2006; Hughes, Carter, Brown, & Washington, 2004). (The more formal, structured buddy programs that focus on instructional support for secondary students during inclusive classes are discussed in the peer buddy program section later in the chapter. Individually crafted peer-mediated instruction strategies are addressed in Chapter 5).

Because successful communication is central to any social interaction, many buddy systems emphasize increasing and improving a focus student's communication with his or her peers. Teachers can teach social interactions naturalistically, but they can also provide some simple training for peers on ways to initiate, prompt, and sustain social-communicative interactions. One relatively easy-to-use and effective way to promote social communication is a *communication book* (Hughes et al., 2000; Hunt, Alwell, & Goetz, 1991; see Figure 3.3). Teachers and peers can assist a student with severe disabilities to create a personalized communication book that serves as a focal point for social exchanges with peers. The focus student and peers are then taught how to initiate and maintain an interaction using the communication book (see Chapter 5).

Figure 3.3. A page from a communication book.

An important function that all peer buddies (and their classmates) can serve is to advocate on behalf of their friends and classmates with disabilities. When students without disabilities have gained awareness and understanding of prejudice and discrimination and have learned basic assertiveness skills, they may intervene as advocates whenever another student requires assistance to complete natural routines or navigate a social encounter. Care must be taken so advocates are not viewed by peers as "tattlers" or as violating the practice of "not telling on peers" (Schnorr, 1997, p. 8).

At recess, Marci observed a student with intellectual disabilities being asked to do something inappropriate by a group of her peers. Marci approached the student and told her that she did not need to do what the other students said; Marci then asked the student to play a ball game with her and her friends.

Before starting a buddy system, teachers should ask the focus student about his or her desire to interact more with peers and should discuss how peer buddies will be selected. Buddies may be asked to help or may volunteer and be given specific roles. The natural affinities that develop between certain students with and without disabilities can at times create self-selected buddies. Buddy activities should not be required or graded and should not be associated with any sort of incentive system (i.e., rewards, negative consequences) for either the focus student or the peer buddies. It is not recommended that buddy duties be assigned as a classroom job—unless every student in the class has a buddy.

Cameron, who knows Jared from middle school and his ninth-grade physical education class, is asked to be Jared's physical education buddy. He willingly agrees to the position for the month of October. Cameron helps Jared open his locker, reminds him to "stay cool," and helps him follow the teacher's directions when needed.

Peers can learn buddy skills through incidental teaching, following the model–prompt–reinforce method. Peers may sometimes need to know specific ways to interact with the focus student, such as ways to help without helping too much. If peers have primarily observed adults interacting with the focus student, they may need some assistance in helping like a peer. Younger students are often eager to assist their peers; however, caution should be taken to teach them not to over-help or baby the focus student. Assistance should be presented in the context of *we all need help sometimes.* Peer buddies should allow their peer partners to ask for help, refuse help, accept help, and give help, and they should also assist in teaching their peer partners to engage in the full range of helping behaviors (Janney, Snell, & Fisher, 2004). Buddies may meet periodically with an adult facilitator for a discussion of concerns and successes and for progress updates.

Informal Peer Interactions

Middle and high school students often need adult facilitation of informal peer relationships and interactions. Of course,

the strategies and appearances of this facilitation should suit the age and environment. Secondary school educators need to focus on using natural opportunities to promote interactions and on creating other opportunities by engineering times and places for various subgroups of students to interact with each other. Educators should focus on the following elements when brainstorming ways to increase interactions:

1. Inclusive and social nature of each class

2. Activities that occur after and outside of school

3. Reputation of the educators who facilitate the experience with the secondary students (e.g., well-respected, aware, daily exposure to students)

4. Other locations in a secondary school outside of classes (e.g., hallways, cafeteria, school store)

5. Preferred activities at the secondary level that draw kids together (e.g., music, Hacky Sack, computer games)

6. Effect that socialization outside of school has on secondary student relationships in the particular school and community

These six informational elements can be used to design in- and out-of-class activities that are appealing to secondary students and that will provide a context for social interactions between students with disabilities and their peers.

Schnorr's (1997) study of high school classrooms and student membership reveals some findings that are relevant to social relationships. One of the most noteworthy conclusions was that by itself, participation in informal and class-related interactions did not seem to influence membership in a class. Instead, student membership in a class depended on one's affiliation with a subgroup of

What the Research Says

Schnorr's (1997) findings regarding high school social relationships suggest that

- *Those who participated in the common types of class interactions* (e.g., greeting one another, loaning pencils/paper, and imitating others) were more likely to be connected to peer subgroups and viewed favorably.

- *Peer network strategies*, in which peers are connected to existing social networks or subgroups, seem to offer a more powerful means to expand a student's social membership in secondary schools than other strategies.

- *Getting connected* (i.e., developing relationships and achieving membership) was reported as the first priority by typically developing students new to a high school. This included *learning classmates' names, avoiding conflicts, "fitting in," "getting along," and taking the initiative early in the school year,* or it didn't happen.

Support staff could help this process by

- Assisting teachers and peers in seeing the focus student as someone who is capable of understanding

- Sensitively providing any needed interpretations of the focus student's efforts to interact

- Tuning into the individual's efforts to interact with peers, providing support if and when necessary

Figure 3.4. Findings regarding high school social relationships. (*Source:* Schnorr, 1997.)

peers (a small group or a partner) in that class. Of the six students with severe or multiple disabilities who were included in general education classes in the high school where Schnorr (1997) observed, only two students seemed to have affiliations with a peer subgroup; the other four students were "outsiders." Schnorr's findings regarding high school relationships are discussed in Figure 3.4.

Extracurricular and Recreational Activities

Regardless of the age group, games can be an enjoyable way to create opportunities for students to interact with peers who have disabilities. The game design (e.g., interesting to all) and when the game is scheduled to take place (e.g., during physical education, after school) are key elements. Participation will vary depending on the student's disability, but planners need to aim for active participation that every student can enjoy.

Teachers may need to work on improving the focus student's communication skills and game skills apart from typically developing peers; however, these skills should also be taught naturalistically—as a game gets underway and during the game. Some facilitators have found it helpful to figure out any necessary game adaptations ahead of time and to teach the required game skills to the focus student before he or she joins peers. Peer planning sessions also can be used to engage typically developing peers in problem-solving adaptations to increase the focus student's participation.

Student Snapshot

During indoor recess on rainy days, Daniel's classmates liked to play "basketball" by standing at a free-throw line several yards from the trashcan and tossing in a foam basketball. When it was Daniel's turn, one of his peer buddies would push Daniel's wheelchair up to the trashcan and assist Daniel to drop the basketball in. But

Daniel's peer buddies were not satisfied with this adaptation and problem-solved during their next peer planning meeting about ways to enable Daniel to "throw" the basketball. They decided to rig a catapult made of wire coat hangers and a bungee cord to Daniel's wheelchair. The next time the group played indoor basketball, Daniel's wheelchair was placed at the free-throw line and a peer helped Daniel to launch the basketball from the catapult.

Figure 3.5 shows two simple games that a teacher adapted so that middle school students could play and have fun with three of their peers who had fairly exten-

---

Balloon Volley

Materials: Heavy balloon, chairs placed in a circle

Participants: At least four peers (eight works best)

Procedure:

Players are seated on the chairs. One student "serves" (tosses the balloon up and hits it). The group volleys the balloon for as long as possible (when it hits the floor, is double-hit by one person, is caught, or someone stands up, the volley is over). After each volley, a different student serves. The group counts hits to identify which was their best volley.

Adaptations:

One person sits next to the focus student and assists him or her by holding/tossing the balloon when it's the student's turn to serve or by guiding the student's arm to help him or her hit the balloon. If the focus student is unable to volley, he or she could serve on every other volley (or more frequently as the group will tolerate it).

Positive outcomes:

Each person has equal control/turns; everyone participates.

The pace is suitable for a group of students with mixed disabilities.

Students receive counting practice.

Contributor: Deb   **Tested:**   Yes

Adapted Uno

Materials: Uno cards with "reverse" and "skip" cards removed. Cheap Talk communication device (Enabling Devices) on which the messages "Reverse" and "Skip" are recorded.

Participants: Focus student and at least two peers

Procedures:

Players sit at a table. The focus student has access to two switches connected to Cheap Talk; each switch activates one of the messages. After the cards are dealt, the dealer says "Go!" The game proceeds according to Uno's rules (but players hurry!). The focus student is instructed to use the switch every 15 seconds (or an appropriate interval for that student). The Cheap Talk message applies to whoever is taking a turn when the message is heard.

Adaptations:

One student assists the focus student with prompts to hit a switch at regular intervals (or variable intervals for more excitement).

Positive outcomes:

The focus student controls an important component of the game.

Switch activation results in immediate reinforcement (excitement from other players).

The focus student receives one-step switch activation practice.

Contributors: Dee, Cassandra, Deb   **Tested:**   Yes

Figure 3.5.   Simple adapted games for middle school students with and without disabilities. (From Morris, D. [1997, Fall]. *Invented and adapted games that allow active participation by students with severe disabilities and their peers.* Unpublished manuscript, University of Virginia, Charlottesville; adapted by permission.)

sive support needs. Teachers will find the manual by Heyne and colleagues (1994) very helpful in planning recreation activities to promote friendships between students with and without disabilities.

In order to transform its segregated recreation programs for young people with disabilities into more normalized recreational opportunities, the Special Olympics organization developed the Unified Sports program (see http://www. specialolympics.org). The program provides opportunities for athletes to improve their sports skills and to experience a new level of competition, as athletes with and without disabilities are mingled together on teams. Unified Sports programs give athletes with disabilities additional recreational choices outside of Special Olympics; the programs often are co-sponsored by community parks and recreation departments, schools, or other community sports organizations.

FRIENDSHIP GROUPS

Supportive relationships and friendship groups are programs that are more structured than natural relationships and supports. The primary goals are to bring together students with disabilities and their peers for socialization and fun, to create informal support channels for students with disabilities, and to build social relationships and peer support. Although the idea of setting up friendship groups or partners may seem somewhat artificial, these arrangements can provide a good opportunity to get students with and without disabilities to interact around a common theme. Friendship groups work particularly well when inclusion is minimal in school, as often happens during the high school years (Carter et al., 2001). They are also especially crucial if a student with disabilities is new to a school

and peers without disabilities have been together for many years.

A friendship group may be organized by the educational team, special education or general education teacher, or guidance counselor. Sometimes, these groups are coupled with a student club (Best Buddies or Key Club). Clubs can be formed to provide specific types of support to students—a Signing Club for students who want to learn signs to communicate with a classmate or a Recess Club to help students learn to use playground equipment and play games (Hunt, Alwell, Farron-Davis, & Goetz, 1996). Friendship groups may meet weekly around specific, longer-lasting themes, such as the homecoming dance or school grounds improvement. During these meetings, the students can brainstorm ways that their classmate with disabilities can be integrated into cooperative group activities. Some schools have organized these groups to meet during lunchtime, recess, at the end of the day, or after school.

Once a group is established, most facilitators find that regularly seeking information on the "health" of the group, such as the following, is valuable:

- *Peer opinion of the group's success with focus students*—Opinions can be collected through group discussion and short, anonymous questionnaires.

- *Peer satisfaction with, and duration of, their membership*—Satisfaction ratings can be collected through discussion or short, anonymous questionnaires. Facilitators can examine whether participants reaffirm, change, or end their voluntary participation.

- *Behavior changes made by the focus student*—Data can be obtained by peers or facilitators and may be anecdotal, involve direct observation of behavior (Haring & Breen, 1992), or include self-report by focus students.

Partners at Lunch Club

The cafeteria is a social setting in which students with disabilities can have difficulty navigating, even in a school that seeks to be guided by inclusive practices (Hughes et al., 2001). Having a small group of peers regularly eat lunch with a student who has disabilities is an excellent way to foster peer support and relationships. The Partners at Lunch (PAL) Club is one example of an extensively tested, somewhat structured approach that has been used in several California middle schools. The PAL Club (Breen & Lovinger, 1991) began with pairs of students (one with disabilities and one without) and evolved into small peer networks in which a single student with disabilities was included. Student pairs were based on age, gender, and interests, along with the consideration of student preferences. After a PAL Club orientation meeting (What do we do? Why? Who? How? When? What is my commitment?), students who signed up recruited two to four of the friends they hung out with to join the PAL Club, as in social networks. At the next club meeting, in addition to voting on a name for the club, the group generated activities to do and organized themselves by deciding which lunch periods they would share with the focus student (one to four times a week) and determining how they would get together (which teacher and room they would go to and at what time), and where they would eat. Focus students were changed if there was a "mismatch in personalities between students" (Breen & Lovinger, 1991, p. 115).

During lunch, adult facilitators unobtrusively wandered by all the groups, intervening with their interactions as little as possible; they found that when they prompted, corrected, or even modeled for group members, they stifled interactions and stigmatized the student and even the group itself. Therefore, adults intervened only if the focus student's behaviors or interactions were not being handled by peers and threatened social acceptance. Adults taught the focus students any needed social interaction skills outside the lunch period and reinforced any appropriate interactions among the lunch group.

Once a week, all groups (including focus students) met together for a school-wide PAL Club meeting, during which they ate pizza or ice cream, watched videotapes, listened to music, played games, or just interacted with one another. As described by Breen and Lovinger (1991), weekly club meetings involved age-appropriate fun and interaction between peers and focus students. Adult facilitators circulated and sought unobtrusive comments from each group about their interactions during the previous week. Facilitators provided suggestions, on-the-spot problem solving, and feedback on ways to improve group interactions. The PAL Club concept provides a tested model for loosely organized friendship groups that have worked well with middle school students.

"Yes I Can" Program

The Institute on Community Integration at the University of Minnesota (http://www.ici.umn.edu) developed the "Yes I Can" program to facilitate the inclusion of students with disabilities in recreational and social activities in their communities (Abrey, Schoeller, Simunds, Gaylord, & Fahnestock, 1997). The program, which is designed for middle and high school students and is currently being implemented in 13 states, is coordinated by local school staff who may obtain training and technical assistance from personnel at the Institute on Community Integration if desired. Student volunteers with and without disabilities who participate in the program attend instructional meetings guided by the "Yes I Can" curriculum.

The year-long curriculum includes 20 lessons that help students to gain cooperative teamwork skills and increase their understanding of ways to remove or reduce the barriers to community participation that often are experienced by individuals with disabilities (Abrey et al., 1997). Students with and without disabilities are then paired based on personal interests and spend the rest of an academic year exploring and enjoying weekly recreation and leisure activities in the community and developing social relationships. The student who is identified as the *inclusion facilitator* assists his or her partner in increasing access to these recreation and leisure activities. Peer inclusion facilitators may also fill an advocacy role for focus students in the program in situations of harassment, gossip, or teasing in school.

The instructor's manual for the "Yes I Can" curriculum includes lesson plans, master copies for handouts, and other materials to assist teachers and staff in implementing the program. Lesson topics include how we're alike, myths and misconceptions, being an advocate, and person-centered social inclusion planning (Abrey et al., 1997). School districts that implement the "Yes I Can" program may offer academic credit for participation and/or make the program part of their service learning curriculum.

Best Buddies

The international organization Best Buddies (http://www.bestbuddies.org) was started by Anthony Kennedy Shriver in 1987, when he was a senior at Georgetown University. The organization's mission is to match students with people who have intellectual disabilities for the purpose of friendship. The single chapter at Georgetown expanded into Best Buddies Colleges in 1994, and there are now more than 1,000 Best Buddies chapters in colleges, high schools, and middle schools in all 50 states and on six continents. Best Buddies programs, involving more than 250,000 individuals, now include Best Buddies High Schools, Colleges, Citizens, Jobs, and e-Buddies, each with the interrelated purpose of providing support and companionship and involving teens with intellectual disabilities in ongoing social activities with their peers.

The Best Buddies organization uses a process similar to other support programs with one exception: Best Buddies is an actual international nonprofit organization with its main office located in Washington, D.C. The organization's services include guidance in organizing Best Buddies groups; training officers; selecting faculty advisors (adult facilitators); recruiting volunteers (members and buddies); and recommending processes for member application and commitment, buddy matching, and chapter activities (regular buddy contacts and activities, chapter meetings, group outings, and fundraising).

SUPPORTIVE RELATIONSHIP PROGRAMS

Peer support and student aide programs (also sometimes called *peer buddy programs,* although they are more structured than the buddy systems described previously) pair peer volunteers without disabilities and focus students with disabilities for various sorts of support, including serving as a monitor, helper, friend, advocate, and teacher (Hughes & Carter, 2006; Rodifer, Castagnera, Fisher, & Sax, 1999). These moderately structured peer support approaches are often implemented in middle schools, junior high schools, and high schools and typically involve focus students with moderate to severe disabilities. Depending on the focus student's needs and preferences, peers' responsibilities might include assistance in moving more quickly through crowded halls to get to classes, using adapted classroom materials, and getting involved in social interactions at lunch and during class transitions.

Especially at the high school level, the typical student's day tends to be very structured and filled with courses and extracurricular activities, making it difficult to add another activity to students' crowded schedules. Making a one-to-one peer support program part of the school district's service learning or career exploration curriculum offerings gives students a chance to become involved in mutually beneficial relationships with their peers who have disabilities. A supportive peer relationships program enables academically successful students, some of whom may be interested in learning about careers in human services, to receive credit for enrolling in a semester-long or year-long experience in providing social and academic support to their peers with disabilities (Hughes & Carter, 2006).

For example, a student aide program was started in a large junior high school with limited resources during a year when four students with fairly extensive disabilities were fully included in general education classes (Staub, Spaulding, Peck, Gallucci, & Schwartz, 1996). Many strategies had already been implemented at this school to address the wide range of learning abilities in the student body (e.g., cooperative grouping, multi-age grouping, thematic instruction, student-directed learning methods). Some student aides had minor special education needs, but, like the focus students, they received all their special education services in the general education classroom.

Following the implementation of the junior high student aide program, Staub and her colleagues observed many individually meaningful outcomes, including adaptations designed by the student aides that enabled their peers with disabilities to better participate in their classes and advocacy by student aides on behalf of their partners. For example, one aide found a way to modify a computer project so that his companion could operate the mouse. The low-cost student aide program meant that students filled many roles: aides acted as companions who provided opportunities for socialization, informal tutors who were creative in adapting tasks, and advocates. Although most comments about the program were positive, some students commented on the conflict that arose when their role required them to set limits like a teacher might do (Staub et al., 1996).

Peer Facilitators

Another peer partner model for inclusive high schools is the development of a peer facilitator program. In this model of peer support, a student without disabilities enrolls in a teacher's assistant course (an elective) and serves as a peer facilitator to a student or students within one class taught by a particular teacher. These peer facilitators (sometimes referred to as *peer tutors*) assist focus students with mobility, communication, note taking, role modeling, facilitation of natural supports among other students in the class, and development of other support strategies. In Kennedy High School in southern California, these peer facilitators are viewed as a support option that is less extensive than full-time support staff for the student but more extensive than part-time staff support (Rodifer et al., 1999).

Peer Buddy Program

The high schools in the Metropolitan Nashville School District promote inclusion for students with moderate and severe disabilities through their Peer Buddy Program. In this student aide model, the supporting peer enrolls in a service learning course and acts as an aide to a student with disabilities in one of his or her classes. The student with disabilities may have several peer buddies throughout the day. The supporting peer assists the student with disabilities with reading, note taking, studying, completing modified class assignments, communicating with teachers, and interacting with classmates. The buddies also have attended club meetings and sports events, gone shopping, and visited each other's homes outside of school.

The program began when teachers, administrators, and students at one high school, along with Hughes, Carter, and their colleagues (Hughes et al., 2001; Hughes et al., 1999) from a nearby university, became concerned about the lack of social and instructional integration being experienced by students with disabilities. The program spread to 11 other high schools in the district and has garnered praise from all constituencies involved (Copeland et al., 2002).

Because this is a credit-bearing course, the screening process for general education students who are interested is more structured than for an informal buddy system and includes several steps: 1) interested students are screened by school guidance counselors for attendance records and grades; 2) students complete an application and provide a reference from a teacher; and 3) applicants are interviewed by a special education teacher, who will monitor and evaluate their performance. Once accepted into the program, peer buddies receive an orientation and are matched with a student or students with disabilities, whom they then support on a daily basis. Grades for the course are based on attendance, positive attitudes, and active participation (Copeland et al., 2002).

Classroom teachers who have been involved with the program report that interactions between the peer buddies have not disrupted their classes and that the peer buddies have provided needed assistance to the partner with disabilities in unintrusive and nonstigmatizing ways (Copeland et al., 2002). Although initiated for the purpose of supporting students with disabilities in their classes, the peer buddies have often served as a bridge to the broader social network of their schools and neighborhoods. Peer buddies advocated for their partners, modeled acceptance for individuals with disabilities, and took the lead in creating social interaction opportunities. An additional advantage to peer buddy programs is that the peer buddies find that the support is reciprocal and "indicate that they derive as much benefit from providing support as their peers do" (Hughes et al., 1999, p. 21).

Organizing a Supportive Relationship Program

Getting a student aide or other supportive relationship program underway involves preparation and organization. The process includes recruitment and screening of applicants, orientation and training, and monitoring and evaluation. Student aides may complete journals about the focus student's academic or social progress and the course of the relationship and possibly develop some type of culminating report or creative project along with the focus student. The steps involved in getting a supportive relationship program started will vary somewhat according to students' ages, the size of the program, and whether the peer support experience involves academic credit or simply volunteering but typically will need to include recruitment, screening, orientation and training, and monitoring and evaluation.

Recruitment

Student aides can be recruited from service clubs, student government, or particular courses. Posters and flyers can be used to advertise the program, and guidance counselors can promote the program to potential enrollees. Especially if the program is new to the school, a special educator or panel of teachers and students with knowledge and experience of disabilities can conduct a brief presentation for student clubs or selected courses, such as all tenth-grade English or social sciences classes. Also, organizers can simply approach individual classroom teachers who they believe may be interested in spreading the word to potential participants.

Screening

Applicants should be screened with respect to their motivation for involvement in the program, their reliability, and their trustworthiness; guidance counselors should ensure that students have appropriate grades and motivation and are able to accommodate the student aide course within their program of study. Some programs require a recommendation from a teacher or counselor as part of the screening process (Hughes et al., 1999).

Orientation and Training

The teachers and other staff in charge of the program provide orientation and training for the student aides apart from the focus students. They talk openly about the purpose of the program, disability awareness, and the aides' responsibilities. Training also includes specific methods of assisting, praising and encouraging, helping with academic work, monitoring behavior, communicating, relating socially, and providing companionship for focus students. Suggestions for social integration activities and focus students' behavioral needs also are helpful

(Copeland et al., 2004). A manual providing this same information can be a valuable tool for clarifying expectations and further expanding the student aides' knowledge of disability characteristics and issues such as the use of person-first language or ways to handle bullying (Hughes et al., 1999). If the aide program is credit bearing, students also must be informed of any required assignments and grading criteria.

After receiving orientation and initial training (possibly at the end of the first week of school), focus students attend their classes accompanied by the student aide assigned for that class. Initially, the student aide strictly follows the teachers' plans for adapting course materials and activities; as the aide comes to know the student and the course, he or she often modifies or adapts the course curriculum and activities to enable the focus student to participate.

Monitoring and Evaluation

A special educator or other program facilitator should observe the students during the early stages of the partnership, looking at such things as the suitability of the level of support provided by the aide (e.g., signs of too much or too little assistance), the extent to which the aide is acting as a bridge between the focus student and classmates, and the quality of the class participation and schoolwork the focus student is producing. Student aides also could work with their peers to maintain assignment notebooks, chart progress data, and record the focus student's reflections on having a peer aide.

If student aides earn course credit, they are held accountable for their assistance to their peer and also for their own learning about the process of providing support. Grades can be based on attendance, teacher observation of the quality of support provided, and written assignments such as reflective journals or essays

(Hughes et al., 1999). Journal entries can be evaluated on elements such as the connections made between the initial training and the student's actual experiences (e.g., Have they witnessed evidence of prejudice or stereotyping at school? How did they respond? What was their peer's response?).

Outcomes of Supportive Relationship Programs

Researchers who have studied the outcomes of student aide, peer buddy, and peer facilitator programs have found a number of benefits for both partners. In addition to social and academic gains for the focus students, the aides themselves report meaningful outcomes that resulted from their participation in the experience. The partner's relationship often extends to include interactions outside the classroom (e.g., in the hallways or cafeteria), as well as after-school activities. These peer relationships, initially based on the support needs of one of the partners, can result in friendships between the partners and expansion of the focus student's peer network. Reported benefits include the following:

- *The focus students*—Increases in independence, social growth, and larger social networks (Copeland et al., 2004; Staub et al., 1996); increased active engagement and improved academic skills (Cushing & Kennedy, 1997; Dugan et al., 1995; Shukla, Kennedy, & Cushing, 1998, 1999); and decreased problem behavior (McDonnell, Mathot-Buckner, Thorson, & Fister, 2001) for students with varying disabilities
- *The student aides or support partners*—Increases in social networks; improved feelings of self-worth; improvements in their awareness and knowledge of, comfort with, and ap-

preciation of people with disabilities; greater patience toward their peers who learn differently and increased responsibility; increased expectations for the abilities of their peers with disabilities; friendships with peers with disabilities; and feelings of accomplishment (Copeland et al., 2004; Staub et al., 1996)

The research on student aide and peer support programs is now turning to questions about the differential effects of various types and levels of support for individual students. For example, high school students with severe disabilities in inclusive classes evidenced higher levels of social interaction and greater contact with the general education curriculum when they were supported by two peers rather than one (Carter et al., 2005). This finding has implications for the design of peer support programs and also for the use of paraprofessionals as classroom support agents. When peers provide direct support to students with disabilities, the role of paraprofessionals can shift to classwide monitoring and facilitation for a number of students; this shift has been shown to result in greater social and academic benefits (Shukla et al., 1998, 1999).

GOAL-SETTING AND PROBLEM-SOLVING APPROACHES

Peer goal-setting and problem-solving groups are ongoing peer support systems under the direction of a teacher or other adult. Specific variations of these more structured groups include the following:

- Peer planning
- Circles of Friends, MAPS (also called Making Action Plans) and PATH (Planning Alternative Tomorrows with Hope) (Falvey et al., 1997; Forest,

O'Brien, & Pearpoint, 1993; Vander-cook, York, & Forest, 1989)

- Personal Futures Planning (also called person-centered planning; Browder, Bambara, & Belifore, 1997; Kincaid, 1996; Mount, 2000; O'Brien & Lyle O'Brien, 1998)

- Collaborative problem solving (CPS) by peers (Salisbury, Palombaro, & Evans, 1993)

Positive social relationships and increased understanding of diversity among peers can result from each of these more structured peer support approaches (Carter et al., 2001; Fisher & Snell, 1999; Haring & Breen, 1992; Peck et al., 1990).

These approaches for lending peer support have several common elements:

1. An early phase that involves teachers (and, in some cases, family members or friends) providing information about a classmate with disabilities using sensitive and nonstigmatizing words suited to the typically developing peers' level of understanding

2. Ongoing, active group problem solving around issues related to the classmate with disabilities

3. Identification of informal goals for group actions that have been planned to resolve identified difficulties and to support the classmate

4. Regular, informal discussion of the progress and outcomes of peer support, with revision of group goals

The unique strategies used by peer problem-solving groups involve students' meeting together with an adult on a regular basis to learn more about the individual or classmate, to discuss issues around interaction, to problem-solve difficulties that arise and ways to lend support, and to assess the group's progress

on resolving difficulties and lending support. When the focus student is a part of the group, he or she is drawn into the discussion as much as possible and involved in any decision making. Whether the individual is part of the group depends on the student, the topics being discussed, and the peers who are involved.

Peer Planning

Peer planning is an ongoing peer support system that operates under the direction of a teacher or another school staff member; it uses same-age peers or the classmates of a child with disabilities to provide ongoing support and relationships for the child. Typically, the entire class, rather than a select group of peers, is involved in peer planning. Because peer planning involves whole-class problem-solving sessions, it can be incorporated into regularly scheduled class meetings (Developmental Studies Center, 1996; Vance & Weaver, 2002) in which students share and air classroom or school concerns that may not relate specifically to the class member with disabilities (Figure 3.6). Peer planning can be instrumental in creating a feeling of community within a classroom and can supplement more formalized peer support groups. The least intrusive (or least special) way to implement peer planning and some of the other peer support approaches described in this chapter is to use them for the class as a whole.

Peer planning is a highly successful strategy for students from second grade to middle school; simplified variations can be used with younger children. The amount and ways in which peers are involved, as well as the ways in which adults facilitate peer planning groups, will be heavily dependent on the focus child's age, disability, communicative abilities, behavior challenges, and personal preferences. One benefit of peer planning is

When Allen, a second-grade student with autism, became a member of Ms. Carey's class, the students quickly formed a peer planning group. After an informational session that taught the students more about Allen and autism, the class discussed Allen's tantrums, which the students had seen many times during the first few weeks of classes. Discussion questions included, Why does he do this? Does this mean he dislikes us? What should we do? How can we help? One thing the students had learned was that the word "no" had a negative effect on Allen and often led to tantrums, perhaps because he had heard the word so much during his life. So, the students, with their teachers' assistance, drew up a list of alternative ways to say *no* ("Please stop," "Do it this way," "un uh," "Come on, this is mine") and to redirect Allen when he was doing things he shouldn't do (get him interested in something else, use gestures). The class discussion led to a list of ideas about why it is important to ignore Allen when he has tantrums and how to do so:

- Listen to the teacher instead of Allen.
- Tantrums may become less important to Allen if no one pays attention.
- Do our work and be positive role models for Allen.
- Pay attention to the good.
- Teach Allen to communicate with us in positive ways.

Over the next few weeks, students practiced using these ideas while Allen's team of teachers tackled his communication system. Soon, Allen's tantrums diminished to almost none.

Figure 3.6.   Peer planning for Allen.

that, by involving all students in a classroom, there will be more consistency across classmates' interactions with the focus student and more success experienced as students relate to the student with disabilities in their classroom. Second, as class time can be taken to problem-solve and practice, no special meeting time is needed.

The support that comes from peer planning must be individualized and will change over time. Some students will need peer support only temporarily, but others will benefit from support throughout their school careers.

Sherica, a preschool student in a Head Start class who has limited communication and movement, may need an adult to facilitate "playing" with her fellow students and to explain to fellow students why her arms, legs, and mouth don't work like theirs do. Peer planning might involve having the peers think of ways to include Sherica while they engage in sandbox play, play at the table, or sit in a circle for weather and music.

Figure 3.7 illustrates a Problem-Solving Map that several of Melanie's fourth-grade classmates completed with the facilitation of the classroom teacher, who was having difficulty getting Melanie to come inside after recess. The peers participated in a small-group peer planning session for Melanie and were asked to apply the problem-solving steps that they had learned in a recent class meeting. They also had acquired, through other peer planning sessions and their daily social and supportive interactions with Melanie, a sense of the sorts of solutions that would suit Melanie's needs, abilities, and personality.

Circles of Friends, MAPS, and PATH

Circles of Friends (often simply called Circles), MAPS, and PATH are tools used to aid a person with disabilities to meet his or her goals and dreams, including those related to securing meaningful social rela-

Problem-Solving Map

Title of the map: *How to support Melanie*

Setting: *Outside on the playground*

Statement of the problem: *How to support Melanie to come in from outside with the class.*

---

1. **How have you responded to the problem in the past?**
    Said, "Melanie, come inside with me. We get to have library next!"
    Told her, "That's not the way a fourth grader acts."
    The teacher said Melanie could have a sticker if she came inside.

2. **Did these responses work?** *NO!*

3. **What are some other possible solutions to the problem?**
    Let Melanie be in charge of getting the class to line up. Give her a whistle.
    Melanie will pick a friend to count to 30 with her to get the class to line up.
    Melanie can carry in supplies with a friend.
    Have a race to get in line.

4. **Which is the best solution, and why?** *Pick a friend to count to 30. Because she likes to count and she likes to be first in line.*

5. **When will you try it?** *Tomorrow*

6. **Who will try it?** *Brianna, then Aimee, then Mason*

7. **How will you know if the solution works?** *Melanie will come inside with her friends and participate in classroom activities. But she might not want to count every day, so we will try the other ideas, too.*

Figure 3.7.   Problem-Solving Map written by Melanie's friends.

tionships and peer support. The first two tools are peer support group processes that have been used in integrating and including students with a wide range of disabilities since they were introduced by Forest and Lusthaus in 1989 (MAPS originally stood for the McGill Action Planning System but also stands for Making Action Plans). The Circles process was described in Chapter 2 as a process that can be used alone as a way to build awareness and understanding of the differences in social relationships that individuals with and without disabilities often experience; however, Circles may also be used as the first step in the MAPS process.

The MAPS process involves the focus student and a small group of peers who 1) get to know the focus student, 2) learn more about the focus student and his or her relationships and routines compared with the peers' own relationships and routines, 3) brainstorm with the focus student and with adult facilitators (teachers and family members) an "ideal day" or schedule for the classmate, 4) design an action plan to achieve the changes, and 5) work to realize and improve that plan. There are some general guidelines for using the MAPS process, but the authors encourage users to adapt those guidelines as needed (Falvey et al., 1997).

PATH (Planning Alternative Tomorrows with Hope) was developed in the early 1990s by Pearpoint, O'Brien, and Forest. It is a more far-reaching action planning process that can be used on an ongoing basis to record progress on the action plan and next steps. The PATH process first uses the MAPS process for aiding the support team to get to know the focus person; then, an *action plan* is developed to assist the focus person in reaching his or her long-term goals (Falvey et al., 1997).

MAPS Process

As with any peer support approach, the student's educational team must first determine why and how they are going to use the MAPS process before adding it to the IEP. The team explains the process to and seeks permission from the student's family; typically, one or more family members become involved, at least in the early meetings. In addition to a student's peers, group members often include one or more school staff members. Because special and general education teachers and paraprofessionals usually are familiar with the focus student and his or her peers, they are often included; one adult usually serves as the group facilitator.

Group membership is voluntary, and meetings are loosely arranged on a weekly basis, at a common time, and in a fixed location. The first few meetings can involve the Circles process. They also are devoted to discussion of the following topics and questions:

1. *What is the person's history or story?* Family members and friends relate the important milestones in the student's life.

2. *What is the dream?* Group members talk about their wishes for the focus student for the present and the future. The "vision" should be based not only on current realities but also on hopes for the person.

3. *What are your nightmares?* This question is difficult—some choose to omit it with younger groups—but it forces group members to think about what they must work hard to prevent from happening.

4. *Who is the person?* The group brainstorms for adjectives that describe the student; once a lengthy list has been generated, team members identify three words from the list that best describe the student.

5. *What are the person's strengths, gifts, and talents?* The group facilitator asks members to review the list of descriptors as a means of identifying the student's unique strengths and talents. The facilitator encourages team members to think about what the focus student can do, what he or she likes to do, and what he or she does well.

6. *What does the person need?* What do we need to do to meet those needs? Team members focus on the activities, events, things, people, and so forth that they think are necessities or requirements for this person presently and in the future. The group then arranges the list by priority.

7. *What is the plan of action to avoid the nightmares and to make the dream come true?* Team members begin this task by outlining a routine school day for peers without disabilities who are the same age as the focus student. Then, the team begins to add things to make that day a good one for the focus student; they begin to explore options to meet the needs identified in Question 6 in the context of a typical school day. Answering this question lays the groundwork for developing an action plan (Falvey et al., 1997).

For those questions requiring consensus, team members will need to brainstorm first and then work to reach a consensus. Thus, the facilitator will want to review brainstorming guidelines (e.g., "We want quantity, not quality," "No judgments yet," "Everyone participates") and consensus-reaching guidelines (e.g., "Let's find the best word," "Let's explain and compare our options, then locate our common ground"). As in other peer support group meetings, it is helpful to use large sheets of paper that can be displayed on the wall to keep track of the group members' answers to each of the seven areas of focus. These notes can be kept for future reference as the team moves on to its next task.

Once the questions have been answered, the adult facilitator assists the student's peers in defining a plan of action, which consists of activities and actions individual members can undertake to make the student's ideal day become more of a reality. To devise the plan of action, the facilitator might ask group members to review a timetable of the student's actual day (contrasted with an ideal day) and ask questions such as, "Does it make sense for the student to be doing this activity?" "Do any changes or modifications need to be made?"

Student Snapshot

The MAPS group for Donna, a high school student with multiple disabilities, identified several important components in her plan of action, including the following:

1. *Increase the circle of friends at high school.*

2. *Train friends and others to be able to assist Donna with her insulin.*

3. *Investigate the possibility of working as an assistant in the child care program offered at the high school.*

4. *Identify opportunities for Donna to present at conferences advocating for persons with disabilities (Falvey et al., 1997).*

The meetings that follow those initial meetings are focused on making the plan of action work: planning needed steps, taking action, evaluating that action, and generating ways to improve the plan. The sense of responsibility to the focus person by the group and individual members, coupled with regular celebration and problem solving, constitute the essential elements of a cohesive and effective MAPS process.

Creating a PATH

A more far-reaching person-centered planning process first uses the MAPS process for aiding the support team to get to know the focus person and then uses PATH to create an action plan (Falvey et al., 1997). The PATH process also occurs in a group meeting and typically includes family members (parents, siblings, and others), people from the community who are involved in the focus person's life, peers, teachers, and possibly community service providers. The focus person is involved in selecting the members of his or her team. The group process is led by two facilitators who are trained in the process: One person facilitates the discussion, and the other is a graphic recorder. The graphic recorder draws the PATH document on a large sheet of paper posted on a wall and large enough for everyone to see. The discussion addresses these questions (Falvey et al., 1997; Forest et al., 1993):

- What is the *North Star* or the dream the person has for his or her life?

- What *goals* are *"possible and probable"* 1 year from now? (Other timelines can be used, but 1 year is often helpful because it corresponds with an academic year and the duration of an IEP.)

- What is the situation *now?* (What does the present look like in comparison to the North Star?)

- Who should we *enroll* to make the journey with the person and provide support? At this point, those team members present who commit to being on the person's team and providing support sign the PATH document.

- What are the *strengths* and supports available?

- What *steps* will be taken, and by whom, within 1 month?

- What *steps* will be taken within 3 months?

- What are the *first steps*?

As is true with any person-centered planning and support approach, the group needs to stay in close touch with who the process is for; the focus person should be turned to often to be sure that the picture being created accurately reflects him or her. Also essential is for group members to confirm that the personal information being shared will be held in confidence.

The focus person's support circle then decides when to meet next in order to review progress, discuss any hurdles, and update the action plan. The PATH document can be digitally photographed and then printed to provide copies for the person and his or her support circle; large-format copying machines also can be used to reduce the document to a smaller size so that individual copies can be made.

Both the MAPS and PATH processes result in goals and action plans related to social relationships and social support; however, as they address all aspects of a person's life, and not only social needs, they also can provide useful input for other goal areas on a student's IEP.

Personal Futures Planning

Personal Futures Planning (Mount, 2000), also called *person-centered planning* (Brow-

der et al., 1997; Holburn & Vietze, 2002; Kincaid, 1996), is a group support process quite similar to MAPS and PATH. Typically, the focus person is high school age or older, and group members extend beyond peers and family to include community members (e.g., co-workers, people at local businesses frequented by the individual, support agency representatives). As with other peer problem-solving strategies, the group's focus is on identifying and achieving outcomes for the focus person.

During initial sessions of the support group, the emphasis is on the *personal profile* of the focus person:

1. People the focus person knows

2. Places he or she has lived

3. A history of critical life experiences

4. Current health

5. Choices made by the focus person and by others

6. Behaviors that resulted in gain or loss of respect by others

7. Strategies that have worked and failed with the focus person

8. Group members' hopes and fears for the person

9. Barriers and opportunities the person faces

10. Capacity themes (i.e., a summary of the person's gifts, preferences, and dreams) from the focus person's personal profile that group members discover

This personal profile, though more complex in its coverage, is comparable to the information obtained from the seven questions in the MAPS process. Large drawings accompanied by simple key words are constructed for each of the 10 areas of personal history so that the group, including the focus person, can retain these discussions. This information allows the group to generate a Personal Futures Plan, which lays out a vision that encompasses home, work, community, relationships, and making choices and exercising competencies, thus achieving the following five outcomes (O'Brien & Lyle, 2000):

1. *Community presence:* Increasing the person's visibility within and access to the community

2. *Community participation:* Expanding the person's friendships and other satisfying relationships

3. *Encouraging valued social roles:* Enhancing the person's reputation and increasing the ways the person can make a valued contribution

4. *Promoting choice:* Enabling the person to have more control and choices in his or her life

5. *Supporting contribution:* Assisting the person to grow and to develop more competencies

Similar to other structured peer support groups, the support group's task is to implement the plan through member action, group problem solving, updating and improving the plan, and celebrating accomplishments.

Collaborative Problem Solving by Peers

The CPS process (Salisbury, Palombaro, & Evans, 1993) has been successfully installed in elementary schools in which students with mild to profound disabilities are members of general education classrooms (Salisburty, Evans, & Palombaro, 1997). CPS can serve a number of purposes but has been tailored by Salisbury and other educational researchers (Giangreco, Cloninger, Dennis, & Edelman, 2002) for use with educational teams and peer networks to generate adaptations and other support strategies to enhance the inclusion of students with disabilities in activities with their peers.

Salisbury et al. (1997) studied the implementation of CPS by teachers who had students with severe disabilities in their classrooms. The kindergarten through fourth-grade teachers who volunteered to participate first attended a half-day in-service session focusing on basic information about inclusive education and the eight-step CPS process. These classroom teachers and the special educators involved with their students also drew up criteria to guide their implementation of inclusion. For example, inclusion criteria might be stated as follows: All students will participate actively in each class activity, using adaptations when needed; the focus student's perspective is kept in mind when considering choices or decisions; and the results are judged by the amount and quality of the focus student's participation and inclusion. Any threat to these inclusion criteria would alert teachers that problem solving was needed.

Once the inclusion criteria were established, teachers role-played the CPS process until they could use it consistently (Salisbury et al., 1993). To make it easier for children to use, the CPS process was streamlined from eight to five steps (Figure 3.8). Then, teachers began initiating the use of the process in the classroom whenever their inclusion criteria were not met (Salisbury & Palombaro, 1997).

Salisbury et al. (1997) documented that, over the course of the 2 years during which she and her colleagues collected data on the school's use of the CPS process, teaching teams as well as classroom peer groups used the CPS process both during preplanned sessions and spontaneously, as participation issues arose for students with severe disabilities. After approximately 4 months of implementation, students and teachers began to use the CPS process routinely. The CPS process was incorporated into ongoing classroom practices and used intuitively as a generalized approach to problem

---

The Five Steps of Collaborative Problem Solving

1. **What's happening here?**   This is where you decide what the problem is. Sometimes that's hard because you know something's not right, but you don't know exactly what it is. Talking about it with other people helped us figure things out.

2. **What can we do?**   This is the fun part. It's where you can brainstorm tons of ideas about possible solutions. They all get written down so that you can think about which one to try first.

3. **What would really work?**   In this step, you ask two questions for each possible solution. First, you ask, "Will the solution be good for all kids?" Second, you ask yourself if you or your group can really do this solution. "Do you have all the materials you need?" "Is there enough time to do it?"

4. **Take action!**   In this step, you first have to get everyone in your group to agree on which solution you want to go with. Remember, you pick the solution the group thinks is best and try it. You can always go back and try another way if you need to.

5. **How did we do? (Did we change things?)**   In this last step, you need to figure out if your solution worked the way you intended it to. Did everyone's needs get met or are there still things to be worked out? How did members of your group feel about the CPS process? Do you need to take further action?

Figure 3.8.   Collaborative problem solving for students. (From Salisbury, C.L., & Palombaro, M.M. [Eds.]. [1997]. *No problem: Working things out our way.* Pittsburgh: Allegheny Singer Research Institute, Child and Family Studies Program; reprinted by permission.)

solving. Teachers reported that the process was easy to use, promoted students' ownership of classroom activities, and enhanced students' problem-solving skills.

Inclusion challenges that were problem solved in the participating classes included

- How to modify Field Day activities so that all students could participate

- Ways to enable all students to participate in indoor games during classroom recess

- How to enable a student with significant physical disabilities to participate in a math-related dart game

- How a student in a wheelchair could sit with peers at lunch

In addition to the benefits for students with and without disabilities, and the ease of implementation for teachers, these CPS steps are "portable" and can be incorporated into any of the peer group methods. They also may be used by peers as a way of resolving problems that arise in any of the less-structured strategies of peer support that are described in this chapter.

IMPLEMENTING PEER SUPPORT GROUPS

How does a school or an educational team establish a peer support program to include students who have little or no membership in their school and classes? This section provides some general pointers for implementing peer support groups, which may be schoolwide, grade-level specific, or designed for a particular classroom. These guidelines are similar for each type of support group and for most age groups.

Preparation

Schools that seek to include all students are likely to have begun several practices that prepare the way for creating peer support groups. These practices might include staff in-services on disability, infusion of grade-level curriculum with content on disability (health, science, and literature), and disability-awareness activities suited to students' ages. The educational team of any student targeted to receive peer support, along with family members, must first sit down and discuss ways that they feel the student can be included and encouraged to interact with peers. The team should decide whether a peer support group is needed and what the peer support group would entail.

When students without disabilities and the focus student are not familiar with one another, they will need time simply to be together and to get used to one another. This stage should take place during the first few weeks of school or upon the arrival of a student with disabilities to a new school. During this initial phase, teacher modeling is one of the primary teaching strategies; although indirect in its approach, it is powerful—most students will be closely watching adults for direction on how to interact with the new student (Snell et al., 1995).

Seeking Permission from the Focus Student

Prior to involving a focus student in a peer support group, the peer planning process and the reasoning behind it need to be shared with the focus student (in a way that he or she can understand) and with his or her parents or guardians, thus allowing them time to consider whether they are comfortable with a peer support group approach. The focus student and his or her family members are given the option to refuse or to modify the way in which the student's disability, no matter how mild or severe, is discussed with classmates; however, it is essential that the typically developing peers who will become supportive partners to the focus student be provided with information that will aid their understanding of the focus student's social-communication, physical, and intellectual needs and abilities.

Recruiting Volunteer Peers

When the inclusion of students with extensive support needs and the concept of a peer support program is new to a school, particular grade levels or classes (e.g., all ninth-grade English classes) might be targeted to initiate the program. For example, with elementary and middle school students, it is often useful to use the Circles process to sensitize peers to the similarities and differences they have with the focus student(s). Once the similarities and differences have been identified, a videotape such as *Shakif's Map: Charting Your Journey* (Dobbin, n.d.), which illustrates the MAPS and PATH peer support purpose and process, can be played, followed by a group discussion.

When focus students have been in the school for some time, peers can be recruited following Haring and Breen's (1992) approach to recruiting for peer networks by using teachers' recommendations of typically developing peers who have had prior contact with the focus student (peers who shared a class or a school job, had a common interest or hobby, or who the focus student expressed an interest in getting to know). Once potential peers have been identified, the adults initiating the program should meet with the recommended students, explain the way the peer support network would work, and, if interest is expressed, ask these peers to enlist several close friends, thereby recruiting an established social network.

Once peers volunteer to participate in a support circle, it may be appropriate to seek permission for the students' participation from their parents (Fisher & Snell, 1999). Membership and participation in these groups must remain completely voluntary for all students involved, and students should have periodic opportunities to withdraw from the group (Haring & Breen, 1992).

Sharing Information About Disability

One of the first activities in a support group, after the initial organization, should be to share basic information with the typically developing students regarding their classmate with disabilities, especially if the peers have a lot of questions or concerns about the focus student. The basic information should include facts about the student, such as the school or classroom he or she used to attend; the number of siblings he or she has; the student's likes and dislikes (e.g., favorite foods, games, hobbies, television shows); and other personal information. The focus student is often part of this initial disclosure of information and can contribute to the discussion, even if he or she uses an alternative method of communicating. If peer support has been built into a student's IEP (Chapter 1 describes this approach), the process should be ready for implementation when the school year begins. The initial informational session should serve to dispel any myths or fears regarding the student's disability that are not factual.

When Daniel, a second-grade student with extensive physical disabilities and no formal communication system, was first included in his second-grade classroom, a few of the students were fearful of sitting next to him in case they might "catch" his illness. After a brief, child-oriented discussion about cerebral palsy, their fears were alleviated.

Scheduling

Peer planning or peer support groups need to meet consistently in order to plan for and support one or more students. Because smaller support groups will meet separately from the whole class, they will need to arrange in advance when and where they will meet (e.g., in a particular classroom, over lunch, every Thursday). Peer support programs that involve high school students enrolled in a credit-bearing course may reserve particular days to meet together or select a specifically arranged time—usually about 30 minutes weekly.

Peer Control of the Group

It is crucial that the adults be facilitators, not controllers, and that they allow students to voice their opinions openly. Promoting peer control of the group, however, does not mean that adult facilitators cannot identify issues for the group to discuss or problem-solve.

Following initial organizational sessions, many teachers find it helpful to make notes of the discussions on the blackboard or on large pieces of paper (using an adult or peer recorder, depending on writing ability). Wall-displayed notes are particularly useful when the group is brainstorming or when they are formulating a set of guidelines (e.g., other ways to say no to Charles) or a plan of action (e.g., involving Miranda at lunch, looking out for Carla in crowds). These notes can serve as an ongoing set of reminders to the class or group and can be helpful when reviewing progress or making revisions.

Problem-Solving Strategies

Problem solving is central to all peer group processes. These processes, as they are used by teachers and peers, are discussed in more detail in another book in this series, *Collaborative Teaming* (Snell & Janney, 2005); however, they also will be reviewed briefly in this section. A problem-solving process consists of a series of general steps and some procedural and interpersonal considerations (Beck, 1997). A typical sequence of problem-solving steps is

1. Identify the problem.
2. Gather information.
3. Generate possible solutions (e.g., through brainstorming).
4. Evaluate the possible solutions against predetermined criteria and choose the best one(s).

5. Make an action plan: Who will do what? When? What preparations need to be made?

Interpersonal considerations when engaged in problem solving include establishing a climate of trust, getting input from all parties, and reaching decisions through consensus. Procedural considerations include generating a number of potential solutions before making a decision and identifying the criteria by which solutions will be judged (Beck, 1997). Criteria for evaluating potential solutions to a peer support problem might be that 1) both the focus student and the peer partner will be comfortable implementing the solution, and 2) the solution will result in fuller participation in valued age-appropriate activities for the focus student.

Teachers will first need to explain and model the steps, then teach their students to apply them and to engage in cooperative interpersonal behaviors. It is useful to list the problem-solving steps and phrases to identify each step on a wall chart, and then teach students to apply the steps consistently until they become independent in using the process.

DISCUSSION

Some readers may feel that the approaches presented in this chapter ask children to take on too much responsibility for their classmates with disabilities; however, we have found that these experiences enable typically developing peers to learn valuable life lessons about respecting and being attentive to others' differences. Both children and teenagers learn skills and form attitudes and values from peer support activities that they will use throughout their lives. By contrast, many of us who did not grow up playing and studying alongside peers with disabilities may still experience some uneasiness and fear around people who are different from us.

Relationships among children and adults change from year to year. When students with disabilities move with the same peer group from grade level to grade level, the ensuing comfort level makes it easier for relationships to be maintained and to evolve. So, what happens to these relationships between students with and without disabilities when they move into middle school and high school? Some of them continue as they had been, and some gradually or even abruptly come to an end. Friendships do not necessarily have to be sustained in order to be meaningful; what one learns from friends is built on in other relationships. When students lose friends, however, it is also important that others take their place.

Peer support should continue to be an IEP accommodation throughout school for students with significant disabilities, poor social skills, or no supportive relationships. Because social relationships change and become more complex as students mature, creating opportunities for meaningful interaction between peers with and without disabilities should become more intentional over time and should not simply be left to chance. Facilitating the growth of networks of supportive peer relationships is essential, given that social behavior is reciprocal (Strain, 2001); all of the programs and intervention approaches described in this chapter seek to create a better fit between students with disabilities and their social environment. The next generation of research on social relationships and peer support for students with disabilities will help educators and parents to be more attuned to the specific supports and strategies that are best suited to individual students (Frea, Craig-Unkefer, Odom, & Johnson, 1999).

Chapter 4

Teaching Social Skills

When children and adolescents have inadequate social skills for their age, they are less able than their socially competent peers to develop positive relationships with fellow students, and their learning at school is often threatened. Researchers who study social skills in children agree on the following:

1. Children and adolescents who are at risk for not learning positive social behavior or who have identified disabilities often need some instruction and guidance in social interaction.

2. Social skills instruction can have positive outcomes on children's acceptance by peers.

3. To improve inadequate social skills, it is important to assess, target, and intentionally teach the necessary skills.

This chapter describes methods to assess and build social skills. The concept of social competence is explained and then used as a basis for detailing the social difficulties that many children must learn to overcome. Three students, Daniel, Melanie, and Sam, are used to illustrate skill difficulties and ways that teachers can address them.

Student Snapshot

Daniel is a 6-year-old second-grade student with multiple disabilities, including cerebral palsy, visual impairment, and a seizure disorder. He uses some augmentative devices to communicate and uses a wheelchair operated by others. Daniel's parents communicate with their fellow core team members daily via a written logbook in addition to attending regular meetings. Daniel's physical therapist, occupational therapist, speech-language therapist, and vision consultant are also active members of his team, though they are generally less available than the other team members; they provide updates at weekly meetings through written

notes. Daniel is learning to react to an object schedule, to initiate interactions with and respond to his peers and teachers, to make choices, and to reject things he does not want. Daniel's team has devised many adaptations to actively involve him in classroom activities.

Student Snapshot

Melanie, a fully included fourth-grade student with autism, shakes her head yes and no to communicate and also uses a picture communication book, some signing, and infrequent words. Melanie's parents are active participants on her team and attend core team meetings every month in addition to having frequent verbal exchanges between meetings. Melanie's general education and special education teachers meet weekly to plan and problem-solve, and her classroom teachers interact daily as they work together to implement her program within the fourth-grade class. Melanie is working on following school routines and actively participating in them (e.g., arrival, lunch, recess, class job). She has some reading and writing skills and enjoys using the computer. Socially, Melanie is a loner, and her interactions with peers are often unsuccessful unless she has adult support. Melanie is learning self-calming methods to use when she becomes angry or fearful.

Student Snapshot

Sam, a highly articulate 15-year-old, has pervasive developmental disorder, obsessive-compulsive disorder, and Tourette syndrome. He is enrolled in six general education ninth-grade classes and a one-to-one resource period; Sam receives 100% support and monitoring throughout the day and during class transitions, which are difficult for him. Sam's team is highly cohesive and provides strong support, and his parents contribute and are very pleased with Sam's progress.

Sam often interacts like a small child or an adult, rarely like a teenager. He needs situations that allow guided practice to develop his proper role. Sam is learning to reduce his inappropriate references to his and others' biological functions.

Teachers use redirection and other specific approaches to prevent Sam from getting into an agitated state; his disability is characterized by periodic and intense mood swings, which usually require him to remove himself from the situation and calm down. During these periods, Sam can become highly inappropriate and may be aggressive. Sam is learning to recognize and control his inappropriate behavior during classes and in the hallways and cafeteria. Reading the social stories prepared for him by his special education teacher assists him by cuing positive social behaviors and reassuring him that support will be available if he needs it.

CONCEPTS OF SOCIAL SKILLS AND SOCIAL COMPETENCE

Social skills are behaviors that allow people to initiate and maintain positive social relationships, contribute to peer acceptance and adjustment to school or work, and enable people to cope with and adapt effectively to a variety of social environments (Walker et al., 2004). They include five dimensions (Calderella & Merrell, 1997):

1. *Peer relations skills*—greeting others and sharing

2. *Self-management skills*—recognizing feelings and dealing with criticism

3. *Classroom survival skills*—listening and following directions

4. *Compliance skills*—accepting no for an answer

5. *Assertion skills*—negotiating

The purpose of improving students' social skills is to enhance students' overall social competence. *Social competence* includes both an individual's effectiveness in influencing the behavior of a peer and the appropriateness of the behavior

(given the environment, culture, and context) (Odom, McConnell, et al., 1992). Whereas social skills are specific actions that result in effective participation in social situations, social competence is an overall judgment that relevant others (parents, teachers, peers) make about an individual's behavior and interpersonal functioning (McFall, 1982). Effective, age-appropriate social skills are required for social competence, but so is the absence of problem behavior, the ability to accurately perceive social cues, and generally positive relations with others (Vaughn & Haager, 1990).

Gustafson and Haring (1992), in their work on the social competence of children, described a model for social competence. This model is a combination of several social competence ideologies but relies primarily on work by Dodge (1986) with input from Greenspan (1981). It has clear implications for assessing and teaching students with social competence problems. This model (Figure 4.1) views social behavior as a function of the interaction between a person and the environment. That is, a person entering a social situation brings predispositions to think, feel, and act in certain ways (e.g., aggressively, compassionately, selfishly, friendly). These predispositions are influenced by biology, past experience, modeling by others, and developmental characteristics; however, a person's behavior in any given situation is influenced by environmental factors, which include both the physical aspects of the setting (e.g., heat, light, noise, space) and the perceptions and expectations of other people (e.g., peers may expect the student to be shy and withdrawn or personable and outgoing).

According to this model, social competence has multiple components: cognitive, affective, and behavioral. The *cognitive component* comprises what one thinks before and during engagement in a social interaction. The *affective component* of social

---

Prior to interaction, the focus person enters the situation with beliefs, biological characteristics, and past experiences that influence goals and expectations regarding the situation; the environment holds physical and social variables that will influence subsequent behavior.

1. **Encoding**—covert process of perceiving and discriminating social cues; affected by past experience, predispositions, external "triggers," biologically determined response capabilities, ability to focus attention, general mood, and affective tendencies

2. **Interpreting**—covert process of understanding encoded information in a way that reflects one's personal perspective; goals for the situation are set or revised

3. **Response search**—covert process of generating possible alternative responses

4. **Response decision**—covert process of evaluating possible alternative responses and deciding which to do; affected by self-control, emotion, knowledge of possible responses, and past experience

5. **Enactment**—overt, observable actions and communications exhibited in a social interaction

---

Figure 4.1. Stages in a model of social competence. (*Sources:* Dodge, 1986; Gustafson & Haring, 1992.)

competence involves the emotions experienced during the social interaction process. And, of course, the outward, observable actions and communications exhibited in a social interaction manifest the *behavioral component.*

In order to understand how these components of thinking, feeling, and behaving come into play in a social interaction, it is helpful to analyze the stages in which a social interaction occurs. This model of social competence proposes five interrelated stages: encoding, interpreting, response search, response decision, and enactment. An individual may have problems with any of these five stages, resulting in social skill and social competence impairments.

Encoding and Interpreting

The initial input into a social interaction is the "self" that one brings to the encounter—the predispositions and social goals generated by experience, biology, temperament, character, ability to focus attention, and mood. The environment contains other input features: the number of other people and their receptivity, the activities going on, even the temperature. When entering a social situation, one has a goal, which may not be explicit or even visible but is an expectation of the outcome of the encounter. Goals may not be directly visible but might be expected, given the student's past behavior or reputation. A lack of social skills may mean that a child seeks a self-centered goal at the cost of another more relationship-enhancing goal (e.g., "I am going to win" versus "I want to have fun with everyone in this game").

Encoding encompasses perceiving the information or stimuli in the environment; *interpreting* entails understanding that information. (Synonyms for these terms and overlapping concepts include *social sensitivity, social insight, social cue discrimination,* and *social perception.*) The beliefs and expectations that an individual has about the situation (e.g., "I don't trust him," "People always pick on me," "I am going to have fun!") affect the discernment of social cues and play a role in generating emotions, which in turn affect the interpretation of those cues. For example, some students might misinterpret social cues: A peer's innocent smile might be thought to mean "She must want to be my girlfriend!" Or, a neutral look from a peer might be interpreted as "He doesn't like me."

When Sam picks up his lunch and looks for a place to sit in the cafeteria, he sits at the first table he sees that has vacant seats, whether he knows the other students sitting there or not. He does not scan the cafeteria for people he knows and does not "read" the expressions on the faces of the strangers he sits with. When the students do not strike up a conversation with Sam, he becomes upset and leaves the cafeteria without eating.

Though some children misinterpret social cues, others may fail to notice significant social cues from their peers or from adults because of sensory or intellectual disability and, consequently, might fail to adjust their goals for the interaction. For example, if an adolescent girl with a visual loss does not notice that the peer to whom she is talking is bored or is attending closely to a video or another peer, the girl may persist inappropriately in her goal of carrying on a conversation.

Interventions for the first two stages of social competence include 1) increasing the student's ability to notice and accurately interpret social cues and 2) helping the student to recognize cues that trigger habitual antisocial responses so that self-control strategies can then be employed. Ineffective or inappropriate social responses also can be improved by learning to better read others' emotions and recognizing one's own emotions. Certain cognitive interventions focus on teaching the student to recognize irrational beliefs and other maladaptive ways of thinking (e.g., one experience of being left out of a game generates the thought, "The other students *always* leave me out because nobody likes me"), and to replace them with more accurate perspectives (e.g., "We all get left out at times, but it's okay. I can find something else to do, and I can play with them next time.")

Response Search and Response Decision

The *encode–interpret* process is followed by a *response search–response decision* process. (Re-

lated terms include *social problem-solving, generating alternatives,* and *evaluating alternatives.*) This second pair of components also has a reciprocal relationship. Searching for and deciding on a response involve consideration of the range of possible ways one might react to a social situation, evaluating the possible outcome of these responses, and then choosing how to react. Generating and selecting an effective and/or socially approved response requires skills in problem solving; one must define the problem accurately, have knowledge of various responses, and have the intellectual ability to do hypothetical, if–then reasoning about the consequences of responding in various ways.

Students with poor social skills may have various difficulties with this process. Some may not have learned or even been exposed to appropriate responses; some may be challenged by the intellectual ability required for abstract thinking; and some may have difficulties with *anxiety, impulsivity, self-control,* or *emotion regulation.* Anxiety and other affective states have considerable bearing on social problem solving. Although the problem-solving process is cognitive, the internal statements that one has made about the situation (e.g., "He thinks I'm stupid" versus "I probably misunderstood what he said") can circumscribe the sorts of responses that will be examined (e.g., aggressive versus considerate). In similar fashion, impulsivity can induce a student to automatically choose the easiest, most well-practiced, or most quickly rewarded response available (e.g., punching the antagonist in the nose). If it is strong enough, anxiety can completely override one's problem-solving ability and skills in self-control.

Sam's anxiety in making the transition between classes means that he probably will not notice people he knows and will be less likely to smile or greet others. When students approach him to say, "Hi," he has difficulty controlling his anxiety and has even cursed at them or struck out.

Notice that the response search and decision steps are not directly observable, making them challenging to teach and to monitor; however, students can learn, with modeling and supported practice, how to problem-solve and choose responses that help them to achieve their social goals. Cognitive interventions teach new "scripts" for the problem-solving process; for example, instead of reacting impulsively in anger or frustration, Sam might be able to learn to stop and say to himself, "Okay, I can handle this. Let me think about what I can do next that won't get me into trouble." This strategy gives Sam time to calm himself and to think more clearly. Increasing his latency—the time between the stimulus (e.g., the crowded, bustling, noisy hallway) and his response—increases the likelihood that he will choose a thoughtful, appropriate response rather than an impulsive one.

Enactment

Enactment, the outward, observable actions and communications exhibited in a social encounter, comprise the behavior component. Carrying out an act as simple as approaching a peer group and joining in a play activity can be daunting for some children. A more complex interaction, such as resolving a conflict over a broken or missing electronic game, can require skills that are challenging even for socially sophisticated students. Successful enactment requires knowledge of behaviors that suit the situation. How well executed the response is can be another concern during this behavioral process. If a student selects a prosocial response (to join a peer group) but tries incompetently to do so, the outcome is often not successful. Alternatively, if the student's attempts to enter the peer group are inefficient (too slow, incomplete) the student also might be unsuccessful. Consider fourth-grade student Melanie, who

is learning ways to approach her peers and initiate interactions.

Melanie has learned to use a successful strategy to join an ongoing play group at recess; she stands close, watches and then suggests a novel way her peers might change the activity. Often, however, she tries once but is not persistent enough or her peers do not understand her ideas for play, and she is not included successfully.

When a social skill is weak or newly acquired, emotions such as anxiety can greatly interfere with one's ability to respond effectively, particularly in a new or unexpected context.

Sam has been practicing his self-calming strategies during his resource/study hall with Ms. Otis, the special education teacher. He has role-played these strategies with a peer and has been successful in using them during class changes in the hall. Today, he is on his way to geography class to take a test that will have a significant impact on his semester grade. When a friend approaches and holds up his hand to give Sam a high-five, Sam yells at him and then runs to the boys' bathroom to hide.

Interventions for the enactment stage of social competence entail learning new social skills through modeling, repeated practice, and generalization, as well as improving existing skills so that they are fluent or automatic. *Because enactment is the observable behavior, it is what adults and peers focus on most despite the complex process that precedes the behavior.* For example, prior to reacting to a social situation, a child may observe that situation (encode), have expectations about it (set goals), think about its meaning (interpret), modify his or her expectations, formulate how to behave or what to do (response search), decide what to do (response decision), again adjust his or her goals, and then finally behave (enact).

This last step, the actual behavior, is usually the primary stage in the social competence model toward which teach-ers and parents direct their instruction and their reactions; however, the other steps are also worthy of attention for many students. Many of the interventions that address the intellectual and affective com-ponents of social competence involve im-proving a student's self-control.

Difficulties with skills necessary for self-control, such as accurately perceiving so-cial cues, refraining from impulsivity, and considering alternatives, can become tar-gets for intervention when the steps or processes are made overt by teaching stu-dents to discriminate aspects of their own thoughts and feelings. For students who are less sophisticated conversationalists (e.g., Daniel, Melanie), much of social skills training may address the behavior component of social competence, specifi-cally enactment. But for other students (e.g., Sam), systematic instruction and practice in thinking about social interac-tions in a different way can yield positive results. Skills such as identifying steps to-ward a goal, considering alternatives, and using strategies to reduce anxiety or ten-sion are addressed in some of the social skills curricula listed later in the chapter.

Influence of Peers

Peers influence a focus student's social behavior in multiple ways, including the extent to which they initiate and respond to the student and the nature of those ex-changes (e.g., student is shunned or wel-comed, listened to or ignored). In addi-tion, following the enactment stage, the focus student's behavior is open to inter-pretation by peers. For example, whether the behavior is attributed to being under the focus student's control (e.g., "It was her fault") or to factors outside the stu-dent's control (e.g., "She couldn't help it") will factor in to determining peers' feelings and responses to the behavior (Frederickson & Turner, 2003).

Implementing activities and programs such as those described in Chapters 2 and 3, which influence peers' under-standings of their classmates with disabil-ities, can help to create an accepting environment in which a student's efforts to attempt new social skills will be per-ceived more favorably and rewarded more reliably. Classmates also can be given explicit training in how to initiate and sustain interactions with their peers with disabilities.

Student Snapshot

 Melanie has a history of either not trying or trying and giving up in joining an ongoing peer group. Her peers have come to view her as a withdrawn classmate, not an enjoyable play partner. Melanie's teachers consider a combination of approaches:

- Teach Melanie to be more proficient in her communication with peers.
- Teach Melanie's peers to better interpret her communication.
- Use adult facilitation to promote peer ac-ceptance and positive peer support for Melanie through classroom-based peer planning groups.

Interventions can be directed toward changing a focus student's thoughts, feel-ings, and actions; altering the antecedent events and the setting; and altering peers' skills and perceptions. The next section describes a way to classify or view social in-teraction difficulties that will be helpful to teachers as they assess and plan teach-ing methods to address social difficulties.

SOCIAL INTERACTION DIFFICULTIES

There are many ways to describe and clas-sify social skill problems. The approach used in this chapter sorts social interaction difficulties by the type of learning difficulty responsible for inadequate social skills: 1) the skills are not known; 2) the skills are known but are not performed, not performed well, or are not fluent; and 3) the skills may or may not be known but are overpowered by interfering or competing behavior problems (Gresham, 1997). A student often has more than one of these types of problems; a particular skill or skill set may be missing altogether, other skills may be weak, and problem behaviors may interfere with still other skills.

Individuals may not have necessary social skills because the skills have not been taught to them or the individuals have not learned them. Students with skill acquisition problems may not know how to greet others, how to start or carry on a conversation with peers, or how to join a group of socializing classmates.

Daniel has extensive limitations in his voluntary movements and is learning to use a communication system and make choices; he virtually never initiates an interaction with his peers. He is perhaps the most in need of learning to socialize.

The second group includes students who have the skills but do not use them or perform them poorly and need periodic coaching and feedback. Motivation and a lack of opportunity to use the skills often seem to be reasons why some students fall into the performance deficit or fluency problem category.

Melanie has practiced a strategy for joining a group with the special education teacher and a peer. She knows to approach, smile, and make a suggestion; however, on the playground, she is not persistent, and if her classmates do not understand her first attempt to interact, she gives up. Melanie partially knows what to do but is not fluent in using social skills or in generalizing them across situations and peers.

The third group includes students whose inappropriate behavior outweighs or overpowers their use of appropriate behavior and social skills. Problem behaviors (e.g., grabbing, pushing) may be easier to use and more effective for getting what a student wants (e.g., toys, a place in line) than the appropriate behavior (e.g., asking, waiting). Competing behaviors can be internalizing or overcontrolled behavior patterns such as anxiety and social withdrawal, or they may be externalizing or undercontrolled behavior patterns such as aggression and disruption (Gresham, 2000).

Sam sometimes receives assistance with getting out of a busy hallway or gets out of completing a class task if he explodes into an episode of hitting and refusing to work. Sam is less able than other students to say he needs help on an assignment or to indicate that it is hard for him to be in a crowded, noisy hallway.

Although not perfect, categorizing social skill difficulties into types of learning problems can help teachers as they design teaching programs. This method is used along with the model of social competence to structure the discussion of assessment and teaching strategies.

DESIGNING SOCIAL SKILLS INSTRUCTION

Figure 4.2 sets forth a five-step process for designing programs to teach social skills. As with any instructional process, this one involves assessment, targeting needed skills, designing a teaching program directed toward those skills, implementing the program, evaluating its effectiveness, and modifying the program as necessary. The process is described as it pertains to individual students who have rather significant social interaction and social relationship needs; however, the steps will be

Step 1. Identify social skill difficulties and the type of learning problem.

A. Assess the student on social skills expected for his or her gender, age, and cultural group, as well as other areas of concern (e.g., peer interactions, peer acceptance).

B. Identify the type of learning problem:

Acquisition problem—student doesn't have the skill or performance is weak.

Performance or fluency problem—student has the skill but does not know when to use it, is too slow in using it, cannot adjust the skill to suit the situation, or lacks proficiency in using it.

Interfering or competing behaviors—student has lots of competing, inappropriate behaviors; social skills may be known but are not efficient or effective enough to compete with the problem behaviors.

If a social skill problem is not identified, then explore other strategies that might be effective:

Improve peer/staff acceptance

Modify schoolwork and add supports

Arrange for opportunities to interact

Step 2. Set social skill goals for the student.

A. Pool and discuss existing information.

B. Write measurable goals and objectives or benchmarks.

Step 3. Select teaching options that match the student's specific social skill difficulty.

A. Review research-based social skill teaching methods.

B. Select methods that match the learning problem and context.

C. Consider the implications of peer networks.

D. Consider the use of commercial programs with a proven track record or potential effectiveness due to the presence of research-based components.

Step 4. Develop a teaching plan and consider the following:

A. Is staff training or additional staff/volunteer support needed?

B. Is parental involvement adequate; is a home component needed in the plan?

C. How will we schedule instruction and integrate it into student routines?

D. Will we group students, teach individual students, or both?

E. What materials and adult resources will we need?

F. How will we promote generalization?

G. What easy-to-use and meaningful ways will we use to monitor student progress before, during, and after training?

Step 5. Implement, evaluate, and improve the plan as needed.

Figure 4.2. A team process for designing social skills instructional programs. (*Sources:* Gresham, 1997; Walker et al., 2004; Walker, Schwarz, Nippold, Irvin, & Noell, 1994.)

the same whether applied to an individual student, a small group, or an entire class. Before detailing the social skills teaching process, it is necessary to address some preliminary issues: intervention strategies to build positive social relationships and the roles of team members in social skills instruction.

Intervention Strategies to Build Positive Social Relationships

Experience has taught many of us, and research has confirmed, the effectiveness of using multiple components in an intervention to build positive social relationships between students with adequate social skills and students who are at risk for or who demonstrate social skill difficulties (McConnell, 2002; Odom et al., 1999). The first three types of intervention strategies, discussed in Chapters 2 and 3, may prevent or even improve social skill problems and, therefore, are ongoing tactics that schools will want to implement before targeting and directly teaching social skills. These three types of strategies are "less special" and are likely to have a positive impact on multiple students:

1. Create opportunities for peers to interact, and support these interactions. These interventions include placement of students in inclusive settings, incidental teaching of social skills, arrangement of play and academic activities so that students "need" to interact, and use of cooperative learning and peer tutoring.

2. Improve the school atmosphere so that it is cooperative and accepting of diversity (see Chapter 2).

3. Build peer social support (through peer planning and problem solving, friendship activities, peer networks, and natural supports) for students who need it.

The fourth strategy is to provide social skills instruction based on assessment and a collaboratively developed plan; this strategy can either be applied in combination with the first three strategies or alone if the improvements made in the social environment are not enough to build needed social skills.

Social skill instruction can be focused on an individual student, a small group, or an entire class. When it is focused on an individual student, it should be part of the IEP process. When an entire class is targeted for social skill instruction, a universal or global approach is used. Teachers (often along with school psychologists or counselors) select a proven curriculum that is suited to the age group and

involves adequate amounts of teaching time (Walker et al., 2004). Often, a large group of age-appropriate skills (e.g., listening, greeting others, joining in, complimenting) are systematically addressed. Teachers may elect to use class meeting time, teacher advisory periods, or class guidance sessions to provide direct instruction in selected social skills, using the steps of defining the skill and its use, conducting modeling and role-playing performances, and giving feedback. This direct instruction would be complemented by generalization strategies such as reminding, prompting, and reinforcing use of the skill across the day.

Another global approach to social skills instruction is curriculum integration (Williams & Reisberg, 2003). Social skills are not relegated to the status of an add-on to the curriculum but instead are infused into everyday classroom social and instructional activities. For example, as part of planning for a history or literature unit, teachers can identify the social skills that are to be infused into unit activities and taught in conjunction with academic content, such as pairing conflict resolution with a unit about the Civil War.

Roles of Team Members in Social Skills Instruction

A student's core team members (general education teacher, special education teacher, and parent) are often the most knowledgeable and concerned about the student's social skill problems and will have the most central roles in social skills instruction; however, sometimes other extended team members will have information that is relevant and that should be included in team discussions.

Role of Special Educators

Special education teachers do the following activities:

1. Facilitate the assessment of the focus student's social skills, the team's selection of social-skill goals, and the design and implementation of teaching plans

2. Pull in related-services staff whose expertise may be critical for students with physical and communication disabilities

3. Design their schedules to provide routine opportunities for focus students to be with peers and have support for their interactions

4. Model interactions with focus students

5. Sensitively answer peers' questions about classmates with disabilities

6. Provide and teach others to provide positive behavior support to students with problem behavior and instruction to students learning social skills

7. Teach peers strategies to support their class members

Daniel's special education teacher works closely with Daniel's therapists to determine ways that Daniel can communicate yes and no and make clear choices. The special education teacher coordinates times to explore these social interaction ideas with classroom staff, to try them out with Daniel and his peers, and to work with the second-grade teacher to integrate them into Daniel's schedule.

Role of General Educators

Classroom teachers and paraprofessional classroom staff are present in the classroom more than the other team members; therefore, they are fundamental to the process of fostering social skills. They do the following:

1. Model acceptance of all students

2. Answer peers' questions

3. Plan activities to meaningfully include students

4. Provide direct support to students as they learn social skills

5. Monitor day-to-day progress of social skills

6. Identify times and places in the schedule when social skills instruction is best or create new opportunities

7. Encourage classmates to lend support to peers who need it.

Role of Peers

Peers participate in social skills teaching activities as models and "prompters" for students who are learning social skills, as "encouragers" to classmates for their mastery of skills, and as collaborators with each other and with adults to seek solutions to focus students' social difficulties. Peer involvement in planning social activities helps guarantee that the content of the activity and the language used are age appropriate, that the exercises are enjoyable for peers, and that participation in the activity is not stigmatizing.

Early in the school year, Melanie's and Daniel's classmates learned how each of the students communicated. Classmates practiced ways to offer Daniel choices and "read" his choice. Melanie's classmates learned a turn-taking approach for communicating with Melanie as she used her communication book to tell them about her activities out of school.

Role of Administrators

Building principals lend administrative and school system support. In their leadership capacity, they can do the following:

1. Arrange schedules so that opportunities exist for social integration among students

2. Work with teachers to integrate special services in terms of classroom assignments and availability of special education support

3. Distribute teacher duties so special and general education teachers regularly

interact with general education students and students with disabilities

4. Promote the teaching of social skills by providing in-service training

5. Facilitate collaborative teaming in the school

6. Appoint a group of teachers, parents, and students to work with guidance counselors in reviewing and selecting an effective published program or curriculum when classwide social skills instruction is desired

The assistant principal at Sam's high school contributed to the planning of Sam's crisis management plan because, when necessary, it required the immediate availability of a staff member to assist in removing Sam to a location where he could calm down. The principal also arranged for a special in-service session for staff.

TEAM PROCESS FOR DESIGNING SOCIAL SKILLS INSTRUCTION

This section reviews each step of the team process found in Figure 4.2.

Step 1

Identify Social Skill Difficulties and the Type of Learning Problem

Step 1 is initiated when experienced classroom or special education teachers notice social inadequacies or unusual peer-to-peer behavior in students. They share their concerns and may decide to further observe the student, to use one or more of the teacher assessment methods described in Figure 4.3, or to involve the school psychologist or counselor in the assessment. Informal interactions about the focus student by team members or be-

tween teachers and parents can be very helpful at this early stage.

In all likelihood, multiple assessment procedures will need to be conducted by more than one person, especially if a student has moderate to severe social difficulties. Many students have mild to moderate social competence problems that can be assessed using a social skills curriculum checklist (e.g., The Child Behavior Checklist [Achenbach 1991]), augmented by informal teacher observation during teaching sessions and in generalization contexts. The first and second sections of Figure 4.3 list early screening and identification assessments and social skill rating scales that are useful in gathering preliminary information regarding selection of target behaviors. These instruments identify general areas of concern that should then be further analyzed to target specific behaviors (Gresham, 2000).

In assessing students whose social skills and behavior problems are more extensive, it is sometimes useful for teachers to seek the assistance of the school psychologist or counselor, as the administration and interpretation of some of these assessments require training in using them. The measures involve indirect assessments conducted through interviews, rating scales, and questionnaires; they require prior observation and knowledge of the student. These assessments may or may not be helpful in clarifying a student's specific social difficulties. Assessment activities could include the following:

*   Counselors, psychologists, or teachers complete *norm-referenced assessments* or less formal *screening or behavior rating scales* that measure relevant aspects of social and emotional competence and screen for social skill or behavioral problems and indicators of risk.

*   Parents, peers, and/or teachers (and possibly the focus student) are interviewed.

Social skill and behavior rating scales for early screening and identification of risk behaviors and social problems

1. *The Child Behavior Checklist* (Achenbach, 1991)—This scale includes teacher and parent forms to nominate and then rate students suspected of having an antisocial profile. It has excellent psychometric characteristics and is used with children age 2–18.

2. *Assessment, Evaluation, and Programming System for Infants and Children (AEPS), Second Edition* (Bricker, 2002)—This scale provides a comprehensive assessment of children's development in all domains. Two subscales in the Social domain—Interaction with Others and Knowledge of Self and Others—are helpful indicators of social competence. Teachers and parents rate children on a hierarchy of functional goals and objectives, which provides useful input for individualized education program development.

3. *The Early Screening Project (ESP)* (Walker, Severson, & Feil, 1995)—This scale screens preschool and elementary school–age children on their behavior and social competence via a sequence of three "gates" or stages: 1) teacher nomination and rank ordering based on behavior problems; 2) the highest ranked are then rated to check against norms; and 3) those who exceed normative criteria are both rated by parents and observed by teachers in structured and unstructured situations on their responsiveness to teacher demands and peer relationships. This scale is reliable.

4. *Social Skills Rating System* (Gresham & Elliott, 1990)—This scale includes preschool, elementary, and secondary school versions with a self-report version for fifth-grade students and older. A parent rating scale is included. The scale has national norms and excellent psychometric properties.

5. *Systematic Screening for Behavior Disorders (SSBD)* (Walker & Severson, 1992)—This scale is similar to the ESP but is used with children in grades 1–6. It is reliable.

6. *The Walker-McConnell Scale of Social Competence and School Adjustment (SSCSA)* (Walker & McConnell, 1995)—Two versions (K–6 and 7–12) of this scale exist. Both versions include national norms and excellent psychometric properties.

Informal social skill assessment procedures involving interviews and observations

1. *Direct behavioral observations during recess or other nonstructured times*—When directly observing students, there are numerous ways to measure and record defined behaviors or social skill deficiencies. Observational data can be used to confirm information gleaned from developmental assessments and also can serve as a baseline measure for interventions. The important elements are 1) a clear definition of relevant behavior(s) in observable terms; 2) observation in an unobtrusive, nonstigmatizing manner, during specified time frames (e.g., centers, recess), over a long enough period to obtain a representative picture; 3) a procedure that is simple for teachers to use while still allowing an accurate observation; 4) a simple description of each observation context (e.g., time, date, location, people present, activities, unusual events); 5) involvement of the classroom teacher; and 6) cost-effectiveness.

    One such method of direct observation entails using a stopwatch and recording the cumulative duration of the problem behavior over a recess or social interaction period of a set length of time (e.g., the second 10 minutes of recess) (Walker et al., 2004). Often, two rather broad behaviors indicate that children are in need of social skill instruction ("negative social behavior" and "alone" behavior); both behaviors can be observed simultaneously using two stopwatches (one assigned to one behavior and the other assigned to the second behavior). In this approach, two totals result from every observation—one for each behavior. Observational data are graphed for easier understanding.

2. *Curriculum-Based Social Skills Assessments* (e.g., McGinnis & Goldstein, 1997a, 1997b; Walker et al., 2004)—Most published social skills curricula provide an assessment tool in the form of a table or matrix. Social skills taught by a curriculum (e.g., greeting others, joining in, complimenting, expressing anger) are listed on the left column of the table. Students' names are written across the top row of the table. The teacher completing the matrix uses

(continued)

Figure 4.3. Assessment methods relevant to the identification of antisocial behavior and to social skill training. (*Sources:* Brown, Odom, & Buysse, 2002; McGinniss & Goldstein, 1997a, 1997b; Odom, McConnell, et al., 1992; Walker et al., 2004; Wittmer, Doll, & Strain, 1996.)

Figure 4.3.   *(continued)*

observations and interviews with others who know the students well to judge each student on each skill; therefore, judgments are less subjective. A numerical rating of 1 to 5 could be used, with "1" meaning "student almost never uses the skill," "3" meaning "student sometimes uses the skill," and "5" meaning "student almost always uses the skill." Teachers will look for low student scores (across skills for a single student); students who receive a rating of 3 or less on 75% of the skills will benefit from training on all skills in the curriculum and may initially be taught using one-to-one or small-group formats. Low average scores across the class (skills on which 70% of the class earns a rating of "3" or less) indicate skills in which the whole class, using a classwide approach, will benefit from additional training (Walker et al., 2004). Matrix information also can help teachers to group students with similar skill needs for small-group instruction (McGinniss & Goldstein, 1997a, 1997b).

3. ***Social Contact Assessment Form*** (Kennedy, Shukla, et al., 1997)—This rating and recording scale notes location, activity, people involved, school period, and perceived quality rating about social interactions or "contacts" lasting 15 minutes or longer.

4. ***Social Interaction Checklist*** (Kennedy, Shukla, et al., 1997)—This paper-and-pencil event-recording system assesses two dimensions of social interactions: 1) interaction duration and 2) occurrence of social support behaviors (i.e., greeting, information, access to others, material aid, emotional support, companionship).

5. ***Interactive Partnership Scale (IPS)*** (Hunt et al., 1996)—During this observation procedure, each focus student is observed for 10 minutes (20 intervals of 15 seconds each with 15 seconds to record data after each interval). For each communicative initiation (from a focus student to another student or from another student to the focus student) that occurs during an interval, several things are recorded: who the interaction partner is (e.g., paraprofessional) and the structure (e.g., initiation), function (e.g., request), focus (social or task-related), and quality (e.g., mismatch) of the interaction. The resultant data can be analyzed and used in various ways.

Measures of relationships and friendships

1. ***Playmates and Friends Questionnaire for Teachers*** (Goldman, Buysse, & Carr, 1997)—A teacher lists frequent and occasional playmates, special friends, and a rating of the extent to which he or she uses a range of strategies to promote friendships between specific dyads. The procedure gives a picture of the extent to which a student is socially integrated into his or her classroom.

2. ***School-Based Social Network Form*** (Kennedy, Shukla, et al., 1997)—This instrument measures students' friendship networks at school. Information is collected on individual students via interviews with peers and school staff who are familiar with the student, the student's schedule, and his or her social interactions. Information gathered includes number of social contacts in a 2-week period, with whom, length of time for which the individuals have known the focus student, the way in which they regard the focus student (e.g., a friend, liked), and whether or not the individuals have provided social supports to the focus person or vice versa. This instrument has good reliability and validity.

3. ***Acceptance Scale for Kindergartners (ASK)*** (Favazza & Odom, 1996)—This scale is used to assess the attitudes of kindergartners toward peers with disabilities. The instrument appears to be reliable for use with children in this age group.

4. ***Sociometric assessment of social status***—This commonly used general approach measures social status among children and adolescents. Sociometric measures use peer nominations on positive dimensions (e.g., a friend, liked) and possibly on negative dimensions (e.g., not a friend, not liked). Peers also can be asked to rate the extent to which they like to play with a familiar child who is named or viewed in a picture. Sociometric measures are not good ways to assess social competence, as they give summary scores; peer nominations are better than peer ratings, but both are questioned as to their validity with preschoolers with disabilities. (For more information, refer to Gresham [1986] and Odom et al. [1992].) The use of sociometric measures for decision making about screening or programming for individual students also has questionable validity (Hamilton, Fuchs, Fuchs, & Roberts, 2000).

5. ***Student Friendship Perception Survey*** (Hendrickson, Shokoohi-Yekta, Hamre-Nietupski, & Gable, 1996)—This series of open-ended questions and forced-choice questions is suitable for middle and high school students and addresses ways to be a friend to a peer with severe disabilities, reasons why students could be friends, and reasons why it might be difficult to be friends.

6. ***Assessment of Loneliness*** (Williams & Asher, 1992)—Students are interviewed to assess their understanding of loneliness. This instrument has satisfactory internal reliability for both typically developing students age 8–13 and their peers with intellectual disabilities. Ten questions address feelings of loneliness (e.g., Is this school a lonely place for you?) and perceptions of inclusion or exclusion (e.g., Are the kids at school friendly to you? Are there kids at school who understand how you feel?) In a private interview format (15–20 minutes), students are told that their answers to the questions will help adults understand their experiences in school. Students are told to listen as questions are read one at a time and then to record one of three possible answers: "yes," "sometimes," or "no."

Functional behavior assessment instruments

1. ***Functional Assessment and Program Development for Problem Behavior: A Practical Handbook*** (O'Neill, Horner, Albin, Sprague, Storey, & Newton, 1997)—This three-part assessment and program development manual provides guidelines for 1) interviewing family members and school staff who are well acquainted with the focus student, 2) observing the student's problem behaviors (noting time, location, and antecedents and consequences of the behavior) and making an educated guess as to the behavior's function, and 3) designing behavior support plans. It is suitable for all ages.

2. ***Motivational Assessment Scale (MAS)*** (Durand, 1988; Durand & Crimmins, 1988)—This scale assists in the indirect assessment of one or more motivating function(s) that potentially maintain a student's problem behavior. The rating scale is completed by individuals who know the student well. Research in which the intervention has been based upon the MAS-identified function has established the validity of this instrument. The instrument is suitable for individuals of all ages.

3. ***Communication-Based Intervention: Describe, Categorize, Verify*** (Carr, Levin, McConnachie, Carlson, Kemp, & Smith, 1994)—This three-stage functional assessment procedure can be used with individuals of any age. It provides guidelines for use with individuals who have minimal communication and social skills. In the first stage, the antisocial problem behavior is identified through interviews with staff, peers, and family members. Next, incidences of these behaviors are observed and documented using a card system. One card is used per incident and documents the location, time, and people involved; the antecedents; the behavior; and the consequences. Interviews are continued whenever new behaviors or questions arise. A team of individuals then examines each card and categorizes each behavioral incident by its apparent function (e.g., attention; tangible; escape; or unknown, nonsocial motivation). Cards on which the team agrees are further analyzed for distinct patterns. Programs for each category are written by the team and implemented to verify the team's categorization.

Planned observations of the student's social interactions or the lack thereof can verify whether further teacher intervention is necessary. Initially, informal observation involves *discussing* the social interaction concern and defining it in observable terms and *planning when and how to observe* the student during the school day. Interviewing others (e.g., family members, paraprofessionals, therapists) who know the focus student's typi-cal ways of interacting and behaving also can be used to identify social interaction strengths and needs.

Most commercial programs to teach social skills will provide a tool in the form of a table or matrix for assessing the skills in that curriculum. These curriculum-based assessments can be completed for individual students, or a matrix method can be used to rate each student in an entire class on a set of age-appropriate social skills identified as potential targets (McGinnis & Goldstein, 1997a, 1997b; Walker et al., 2004).

If the overall goal of a social skill program is to improve the focus student's social relationships, then it is necessary to gather information about peer relationships and friendships. The third section of Figure 4.3 describes tools that can be used to assess students' existing social networks, social acceptance by students' peers, and students' understanding of friendship and loneliness.

Other disciplines can aid with assessment when there is a need to improve student difficulties in communication, movement ability, sensory ability, or physiological/medical or psychological health. Functional behavior assessment can help teams understand the conditions that predict when behavior problems will occur and the consequences that seem to motivate or maintain the behavior problems. A functional behavior assessment is essential when social skill problems involve excessive inappropriate behavior, such as highly disruptive classroom behavior and aggression toward self or others. The last section of Figure 4.3 lists several tools for functional behavior assessment.

The basic strategy in functional behavior assessment is to gather information about the antecedents, behaviors, and consequences (ABCs) of the situations where the behavior problems do and do not occur. This information is then analyzed to determine the functional relationships among those three types of data. A functional behavior assessment is helpful in differentiating among acquisition, performance, fluency, and competing behavior difficulties and in determining the function of competing behavior (Gresham, 2000). A simple ABC form (as shown in Figure 4.4) may be used to record this information; a blank form is located in Appendix A.

Antecedents are the conditions or stimuli that precede a behavior. When seeking this information, the team focuses on the antecedents that seem to predict that the problem behavior will occur. These trigger stimuli include specific people, locations, types of comments (e.g., requests to work, reprimands such as *no),* types of tasks, and types of assistance used to teach the task (e.g., physical prompts). After each instance of the problem behavior, the observer should identify the people who are present and interacting in addition to the time, context, and location of the problem behavior.

After several disruptive weeks in school, Sam's team decided to do a functional behavior assessment over a 3-day period, recording any instance of Sam's disruptive behavior (aggression, cursing, yelling). They noted seven instances in 3 days, and each instance involved a fair amount of disruption to the staff and/or students. When Sam's team looked at the functional behavior assessment information, they found several situations that preceded Sam's problem behavior: crowded, often noisy situations (e.g., in between classes, in the cafeteria) and new or unique situations (e.g., field trips, staff changes).

Setting events are factors or conditions that may be less obvious and more distant from the problem behavior and that seem to alter the likelihood that certain categories of antecedents will result in problem behavior. Influential setting events can be biological (e.g., constipation, sleep deprivation), social (e.g., crowding, sequence of activities), and physical (e.g., room temperature, comfort of clothing).

Sam knows that when his special education teacher, Ms. Otis, is absent, he will probably eat lunch right after earth science instead of attending a tutoring session with her; this means he must eat during the time that the cafeteria is noisiest and most crowded. Therefore, when Sam learns that Ms. Otis is absent (social setting event), his behavior is more difficult all morning. Also, if Sam misses his morning medication (physical setting event), he is more

ABC Recording Form

Student: *Sam* **Observer:** *Ms. Otis* **Dates:** *9/12/05–9/14/05*

Class/routine: *All-day schedule* **Location:** *Hometown High School*

Behavior(s): *Aggression, yelling, cursing* **Possible setting event:** *Sleepy, stayed up late?*

Antecedents	Behavior	Consequences
What happened before?	What is the problem behavior?	What happened afterward?
Monday 9/12/05		
9:30 Transition between classes. Sam was accidentally pushed; he was moving slowly.	Sam cursed at his teacher and peers; he hit a student.	The teacher took Sam to the resource room [escape].
11:45 Lunch room. There were no empty tables in the corner.	Sam yelled at students sitting at the corner table.	The students laughed, and Sam laughed. The teacher talked to Sam, who was moved to an area without students [attention, escape].
2:00 Physical education class in gym. Volleyball game. The teacher asked Sam to go to his court.	Sam yelled and tried to hit the teacher.	The special education aide took Sam to the corner of the gym; he did not play the game [escape].
Tuesday 9/13/05		
9:30 Transition between classes.	Sam refused to move in the crowded halls; he yelled.	The teacher helped Sam to his next class [escape].
1:45 Earth science. A lab group with guys he likes.	Sam made comments about a female classmate's body; peers laughed.	The teacher gave Sam a dirty look [attention].
2:30 The regular bus aide left early. A subaide met Sam at his locker.	Sam yelled at the subaide and refused to go to the bus with her.	Ms. Otis talked to Sam [attention]; he got on the bus.
Wednesday 9/14/05		
10:50 Field trip in English class.	Sam struck out at the teacher and peers as they helped him on the bus.	Sam was removed from the bus and stayed at school in the resource room; he shot baskets in the gym for part of the day [escape].

Figure 4.4. ABC assessment of Sam's problem behavior. (Contributed by Johnna Elliott.)

likely to become anxious; this often leads to disruptive behavior.

Obtaining data about the frequency and/or duration of the problem behavior is another important aspect of the functional behavior assessment. The time sampling methods described in the second section of Figure 4.3 can be used for this purpose, or the exact frequency or duration of the behavior can be counted.

Adults' roles in maintaining problem behavior may not be realized until the team studies the results of a functional behavior assessment. One or several common functions usually act to maintain most problem behaviors. The student learns that engaging in problem behavior results in one of several consequences:

- Escape from or avoidance of a situation that may be boring, too difficult or demanding, disliked, painful, or scary (e.g., social interaction)

- Obtaining attention, assistance, comfort, or nurturance from others

- Obtaining some desired tangible item (e.g., food)

- Sensory reinforcement by repetitive movements (e.g., rocking)

When observing a focus student, teachers should note on the recording form the consequences for each instance of problem behavior. This entails writing down what actually happened following the behavior (i.e., what adults or peers said and did to the focus student, even if this involved ignoring). Teachers also might guess as to which of the four common functions seem to be operating.

The instructional assistants and special education teacher recorded any instance of Sam's disruptive behavior (aggression, cursing, yelling). When Sam's team examined the functional behavior assessment data, they saw that the observed consequences reduced or stopped Sam's disruptive behavior. Sam's aggression, cursing, and yelling seemed to either

get him out of a situation he disliked (i.e., escape) or get him attention.

Information obtained from a functional behavior assessment allows the team to predict when the problem behavior will occur and to make educated hypotheses about what function it serves for the person and how it is being perpetuated (Horner & Carr, 1997). This information influences the design of the behavior support program in several ways:

- The social, communication, or other skills that are weak or missing and need to be taught

- Ways in which staff might change the school environment or schedule to prevent the problem behavior

- When skill teaching should take place (when the circumstances predict the problem behavior might occur)

- When instruction and social interaction will be less difficult

A companion book in this series, *Behavioral Support* (Janney & Snell, 2000), offers a detailed and systematic approach for assessing and addressing problem behavior.

When observations and other assessments indicate a student's social skill impairments occur often enough to warrant concern, the team then analyzes the social skill problems to identify which type or types of learning problems are involved (i.e., acquisition, performance, interfering).

Step 2

Set Social Skill Goals for the Student

 During Step 2, team members share their knowledge about the focus student and any relevant data that were gathered during Step 1. Based on the information gathered from the observations, rating scales, interviews, and functional behavior assessment, the team sets goals for the student's needed social skills. If a student has even moderate social interaction and behavioral difficulties, it is possible that numerous skill needs have been identified throughout the assessment process. When choosing which of the student's skills to address, the team should keep in mind the long-term outcomes that will lead to the student's achievement of the dreams and avoidance of the nightmares that were discussed at the outset of the person-centered planning processes described in Chapter 3. Almost universally, the dream includes having friends as well as peer acceptance and support of varying types and degrees of closeness. It is also wise to begin with social skill goals that have been empirically validated as normative and also predictive of quality-of-life improvements for students (Strain, 2001). Knowing and using the following skills appears to be vital for all students, as these skills are needed for making friends and are essential prerequisites to additional, more complex skills:

- *Entering a group* of peers
- *Suggesting an activity*
- *Sharing* toys, materials, and so forth
- *Taking turns* with others
- *Maintaining an interaction* for at least four exchanges
- Exhibiting *social reciprocity* in conversation and other interactions (balanced mutual exchange of information and ideas)
- *Managing conflicts*
- Supporting others (e.g., by *offering help* and showing suitable *affection)*

Another important type of goal relates to the replacement of problem behaviors that compete with appropriate social behavior. The functional behavior assessment will help determine which skills should be targeted to replace the problem behavior and to provide acceptable alternatives for achieving the same outcomes. Many of these replacement skills will be communicative or social in nature (e.g., requesting a break, asking for help or attention).

Sometimes peer input will contribute to the team's discussion of social-behavioral skill goals and criterion conditions (when, where, with whom, and how well the student will need to perform these skills). Observation of the student's peers, as well as solicitation of their ideas during peer planning sessions, can assist the team in selecting age-appropriate social skills and in setting realistic criteria to judge whether teaching has been successful. Sample questions for peers include the following:

- What do you think Jose could learn to do instead of hiding his face?
- What is difficult about talking to, playing with, or being around Freda?
- What could David learn to help him make more friends?
- Who could Mary learn to use this skill with, and when should Mary use this skill?

Like other IEP goals and instructional goals, *social skill goals must be measurable if they are to be taught systematically and if student progress is to be evaluated.* One of the hallmarks of a measurable goal is that it specifies an *observable behavior* (e.g., "To increase initiations with peers by approaching and suggesting an activity" is observable, whereas "To be more friendly" is not). In addition to being observable, a measurable goal must state the *conditions* (i.e., where, when, with whom, and given what supports or accommodations) under which the behavior will occur, and the *criteria* (i.e., the frequency, duration, or degree of proficiency) that must be met to accomplish the goal.

Often, making social skill goals observable requires a task analysis of the steps required to perform the skill. When stating social skill goals in an instructional plan or on an IEP, the *goal statement* should exhibit the complete social skill under the stated conditions and in keeping with the criteria given; *short-term objectives* can consist of 1) differing conditions for skill performance or 2) the steps of the skill as revealed by task analysis. If *benchmarks* are used, they reflect increasingly difficult criteria. Social-communication goals and objectives or benchmarks for Melanie might include:

- To initiate simple interactions (e.g., greetings, requests) with peers during consistently structured daily routines (e.g., arrival, snack, activity centers) at least three times per day for 5 consecutive days.

- Given an adult model paired with signs and objects of interest visible as cues, Melanie will make simple requests from peers during consistently structured daily routines at least three times per day for 5 consecutive days.

- Given only a peer model, Melanie will make simple requests from peers during consistently structured daily routines at least three times per day for 5 consecutive days.

- Given a peer model, Melanie will respond physically or verbally to a greeting from another peer.

- Melanie will respond with a gestural or verbal greeting to a greeting from a peer.

Step 3

Select Teaching Options that Match the Student's Specific Social Skill Difficulty

During Step 3, team members select teaching approaches and strategies that match the focus student's social skill shortcomings and type of learning problem (i.e., acquisition, performance, interfer-

ing behavior). First, they review research-based methods for social skill instruction. Then, they select methods that fit the focus student's current social abilities and developmental characteristics and that match the student's type of learning problem and context. Next, the team examines commercial social skills programs with proven efficacy. The team also may need to consider factors such as the focus student's peer networks and the student's special communication needs and/or behavior problems.

A social skills program is much easier to implement—and, therefore, more likely to realize improvements—when all team members participate in planning the program and reach a consensus on the final plan. When teams apply their own set of feasibility criteria to the options they are considering, it is often easier to reach a consensus objectively and to avoid staking out personal territory among the teaching options generated. Teams have many teaching strategies (behavioral, cognitive, affective, and self-management) from which to choose that have been proven successful in teaching social skills and in modifying socially inappropriate behavior. In most, if not all, cases, a combination of methods should be used.

Figure 4.5 analyzes the research base on social skills instruction. A number of supporting resources can be consulted for additional information about the topic of research-based social skill teaching methods (Gresham, 1986; Kamps, Potucek, Lopez, Kravits, & Kemmerer, 1997; Koegel, Koegel, & Parks, 1995; McConnell, 2002; Schneider, 1992; Sugai & Lewis, 1996; Walker et al., 2004.)

Behavioral Strategies

Behavioral methods and strategies—modeling, role playing, coaching, prompting, scripts for prompting interaction, and ma-

What the Research Says

Meta-analyses and reviews of research on social skills training for students with high-incidence disabilities or at-risk profiles have revealed mostly "small" effects (Beelman, Pfingsten, & Losel, 1994; Forness & Kavale, 1996; Kavale & Mostert, 2004; Mathur, Kavale, Quinn, Forness, & Rutherford, 1998) and limited generalization and maintenance of the skills trained—findings that are disheartening at first glance—however, several explanations have been offered that bring the validity of these findings into question (Gresham, Sugai, & Horner, 2001):

1. The intervention programs used in many of the studies that were analyzed did not use effective and potentially effective published training programs.

2. The average duration of the interventions was less than 30 hours, and many of them were conducted in contrived settings that did not match the participants' everyday social contexts.

3. Many of the studies did not tailor the intervention to the type of social skill problem (i.e., acquisition, performance or competing behavior) experienced by the participants.

4. The studies reviewed taught students specific social skills but then assessed broader outcomes such as social status, self-concept, and social competence, creating a mismatch between the interventions and the outcomes measures (Gresham, Sugai, & Horner, 2001; Kavale & Mostert, 2004).

In contrast with much of the research examined in these meta-analyses, social interaction skill programs that avoided these pitfalls have demonstrated much more success, including the following findings.

*   A review of 23 group-design studies of young children with disabilities who had received social skills interventions revealed that the most effective interventions used some combination of modeling, play-related activities (for young children), rehearsal or practice, and prompting (Vaughn et al., 2003).

*   Both child-specific intervention procedures (social skills training, prompting and reinforcing social interaction in naturalistic settings, social problem solving, self-monitoring) and peer-mediated interventions have significantly increased an array of social interaction behaviors (e.g., initiations, duration of interaction, use of augmentative communication devices) for students with autism (McConnell, 2002).

*   Significant reductions in inappropriate behavior (e.g., aggression, negative verbal statements, grabbing) maintained for 2 years after 31 Head Start, kindergarten, and first-grade students with behavior problems were involved in social skills instruction that utilized reinforcement, peer tutoring, and parent support (Kamps, Tankersley, & Ellis, 2000).

*   Researchers who have evaluated the effects of comprehensive and multiple-component social interaction intervention programs for 83 preschoolers with disabilities found significant, socially valid effects on the social skills and peer acceptance of students with disabilities. Programs that *combine* direct, child-specific social skills instruction by a teacher; structured opportunities for peers to participate together in shared activities; and peer-mediated strategies have produced the most dramatic improvements in children's social success (Odom et al., 1999).

Figure 4.5. Research-based practices for social skills instruction.

nipulation of consequences—are particularly effective when students first are acquiring social skills (Schneider, 1992). These strategies all focus on overt behavior: Behavioral methods place an emphasis on seeing, then doing, then getting feedback.

Modeling

Modeling (i.e., recorded or live demonstrations of targeted social skills) is often used with coaching or while giving the student opportunities to perform the target skill and providing feedback. It can be used opportunistically, during the course of a play or cooperative learning activity. For example, as two students are learning to *take turns* while playing a board game, the teacher says, "Watch me while I take *my* turn," and after moving the playing piece on the board, hands the dice to the next student and says, "Now it's *your* turn!" Modeling also is used during formal, structured learning sessions.

Modeling is most effective when (McGinnis & Goldstein, 1997b):

- It is conducted by individuals who are competent in using the skill

- It is explicit (i.e., tells the observing student what he or she is doing and why, and points out the critical features to look for in the modeling situation)

- The person modeling is perceived by the observer as having desirable skills, knowledge, and/or status

- The person modeling is a member of the observer's social environment

- The person modeling has similar demographic characteristics to the observer

In some cases, negative modeling might be provided in contrast to positive models, and the person modeling would discuss with the observing students what is wrong with the performance (i.e., the critical features that are missing); however, this strategy should be used with caution, as some students may enjoy imitating the incorrect behavior (Goldstein, 1988).

Role Playing

Modeling is strengthened when students then act out the targeted social skill or emotional response through role play. The main actor chooses or is given conditions for the performance, such as to respond to a specific social situation and may be asked to take his or her own or another student's perspective, to play the role of a specific person, or to portray a particular emotion. If the situation would involve more than one student in real life, it is preferable to have other students rather than adults play those roles, as this creates a more realistic scenario, and the adult can then coach the students through the role play if necessary. Role playing usually involves feedback (praise, corrections) to the student or actor regarding his or her performance.

In structured lesson contexts, both modeling and role playing should depict situations that are similar to those that students actually encounter and that cover variations in the way the skill might be used in different settings (Sugai & Lewis, 1996). Teachers may want to encourage students to use recent social incidents as subjects for modeling and role playing. Students can recall the sequence of events, script them using approved behaviors and language, and then reenact the scene with a different ending. Photos or slides taken of typical interaction scenes can be used as a way to recreate the situation for students. Role playing that uses realistic contexts promotes skill generalization; students learn the broader range of situations in which social skills are appropriate and can practice adapting the skills to fit the situations.

Coaching

Coaching involves direct verbal instructions regarding the targeted behavior or skill, along with prompting and, typically, discussion and feedback (e.g., praise, suggestions). Modeling and coaching often are used together, either in a naturally occurring situation or in a social skill lesson, and can be directed toward an individual or a group.

Prompting

Prompts are virtually any stimuli (e.g., physical touch, pictures) that help a student to perform a skill or task correctly. The value of prompting is that it ensures correct performance and, therefore, prevents the student from making errors that can have a number of detrimental effects on learning. Verbal reminders and subtle gestures, such as pointing to the playing piece on a game board or giving a student the "Let me think" look, can be highly effective when new skills are weak or need to be generalized. For students with minimal verbal skills, gestures and other visual prompts are often the most effective way to convey helpful information about what to do next, as verbal prompts can be confusing or distracting and also can be more difficult to fade than visual prompts.

Scripts for Prompting Interaction

Students with few interaction skills can be taught specific scripts to use during social or academic interactions with their peers. These scripts may be written sentences, word cards, or pictures that are used to prompt students; scripts also may simply be a series of verbal phrases and/or actions used with a game or some material (e.g., handheld videogame, package of crackers) that a student is taught to use during interaction with a peer. Scripts can be social (e.g., conversation topics, recess game suggestions) or task oriented (e.g., "Check my work," "Help me").

Manipulation of Consequences

Manipulation of consequences involves the presentation and removal of positive and negative events or things based on the student's behavior. Both adults and peers are involved in manipulating consequences, but self-management strategies teach the focus student to manipulate his or her own consequences contingent on certain performances. Consequence strategies may involve reinforcing students who follow class or individual behavior rules (e.g., by praising, giving a high-five). They also include

enforcing rules by using correction methods (e.g., student rehearses the broken rule and tells why it should have been followed), warnings, or unpleasant consequences (e.g., loss of time during recess). In the long run, positive consequences are most effective because they build the needed skills, whereas punishing consequences do not teach appropriate behavior and may weaken the punishing adult's rapport with the student. Consequence strategies are usually combined with strategies to prevent problem behavior from occurring and to teach or reinforce the use of alternative skills. They need to be matched to the student and circumstances to be effective; they should be generated as a result of the functional assessment that was conducted to determine the purpose of the problem behavior.

Cognitive and Affective Strategies

Cognitive strategies, also known as *interpersonal cognitive problem-solving, social cognitive processes, cognitive restructuring,* and *cognitive-behavioral strategies,* concentrate on the focus student's developing greater cognitive awareness of social situations and thoughtfully selecting adaptive strategies for responding to them. Teaching strategies that address one or more of the cognitive processes preceding social behavior require students to make their thinking, planning, and behavior selection processes conscious (Walker et al., 2004). These strategies can be helpful in increasing students' self-control and independence, as they do not rely on adults to provide external control or alter the situation (e.g., praising the student, giving him or her reminders).

Various cognitive strategies teach students to: 1) identify a cue or trigger that is likely to create a social difficulty for them (e.g., being told *no* by an authority figure, facing a crowd of strangers) and 2) generate a range of alternatives/

behaviors, consider the consequences of each, and then to decide which is the best response. Cognitive strategies are especially relevant for students whose impulsivity competes with their ability to use prosocial skills effectively; these techniques do not teach social interaction skills but enable the individual to refrain from impulsively responding to a social challenge.

Affective strategies are sometimes employed alone but most often are interwoven with behavioral and cognitive tactics. They alter the emotions that accompany a demanding social situation, thereby enabling the student to have greater self-control. Strategies such as *positive visualization, deep breathing*, and *physical relaxation techniques* are intended to calm the emotions so that clear perceptions, problem solving, and selection of effective social responses can occur. Students with mild disabilities whose anxiety or anger interfere with clear thinking when faced with certain types of social encounters may be good candidates for learning affective strategies.

Cognitive and affective strategies are complex and involve a combination of teaching methods, including modeling, role playing, prompting, coaching, and manipulation of consequences. The following teaching sequence is recommended in most social skills programs using cognitive strategies (Etscheidt, 1991; Goldstein, 1988; Harris & Pressley, 1991; McGinnis & Goldstein, 1997a, 1997b):

1. In a structured group or individual session, the teacher conducts a didactic lesson in which the strategy is defined and explained and the rationale for its use is provided.

2. Instructors model the strategy to "show" students how to think about the process; that is, the teacher thinks aloud, "Now I need to ask myself: 'What would happen if I did

that? Will that help me to reach my goal?'")

3. Students role-play the skill, first with coaching from the teacher, then with decreasing assistance.

4. Students are prompted, coached, and reinforced as they learn to use the process and the strategy in situations during which they interact with others.

Cognitive and affective strategies are both more difficult to teach and more difficult to research than behavioral strategies because the processes are covert. Students' knowledge of the process and their ability to enact a strategy can be evaluated within a structured training context, but use of the strategy in a naturalistic setting can only be inferred by an observer or reported later by the student. A growing research base is emerging, however, that provides evidence of the utility of these interventions, when applied prescriptively and in conjunction with other supportive interventions (Smith, 2002). Descriptions of some of the specific cognitive and affective strategies used in teaching social skills follow.

Cognitive-Behavioral Rehearsal

Cognitive-behavioral rehearsal involves role play or rehearsal and problem solving. The student practices the target skill under controlled conditions (e.g., just before attending a class during which the problem often arises) and verbalizes what he or she will do in the upcoming social situation or actually performs the target skill as a means of reminding him- or herself what to do, thereby preventing problem behavior. Adapted approaches to this category of strategies include *social stories* (Gray, 1998) and *cognitive picture and script rehearsal* strategies (Grodon & LeVassuer, 1994). These two techniques, designed for students with intellectual disabilities, Asperger syndrome, or autism, provide the focus student with a social script (often accompanied by drawings) that leads him or her through the process of rehearsing for a difficult situation.

When using the *social stories* approach (Gray, 1998; Gray & Garand, 1993), the teacher, with input from the student, writes a "story" with accurate information about a type of social situation known to cause difficulties for the student (e.g., lunch in the noisy, crowded cafeteria). The story is written in the first person, and objectively describes what will happen in the situation and how other people will act, think, and feel. The story also includes some directions that tell the student what to do and how to accurately understand the situation. The student and/or the teacher read the story several times during the day and immediately prior to entering the difficult situation. The story cognitively prepares the student for success by replacing inaccurate and/or anxiety-producing expectations with rational expectations and cues for the socially approved behavior that is expected. Stories are read repeatedly, with

or without an adult, until the student's new behavior is automatic.

Limited research has been conducted on the social story method, but evidence of its efficacy is mounting. One study found that students with autism showed significant decreases in disruptive behavior when well-constructed social stories were implemented within natural environments (Scattone, Wilczynski, Edwards, & Rabian, 2002), a second (using a reversal design) showed a decrease in interruptions and tantrums for a 5-year old boy with whom a social story intervention was used (Lorimer, Simpson, Myles, & Ganz, 2002), and a third showed that two students with autism increased their ability to make activity choices and then to play appropriately with their peers (Barry & Burlew, 2004).

A student's social stories may be written individually on cards or paper, or several stories may be collected into an individualized book for a student. Students often enjoy writing, typing, or printing their own stories and then illustrating them with drawings or clip art. Figure 4.6 provides

---

A Story About Having a Conversation at Lunch

A conversation is when two or more people take turns talking about something. Students like having conversations with each other because it feels good to have friends and to be part of a group.

Sometimes, it is okay to have a conversation, and sometimes it is not okay to have a conversation. It is okay for teenagers to talk in the cafeteria at lunch. As long as students use a medium voice and talk about appropriate things, teachers do not care if students have conversations during lunch.

There are some things that it is okay to talk about with acquaintances. Acquaintances are people whom students see at school but do not know very well. There are other things that students only talk about with very, very close friends or family members. When students are having a conversation with acquaintances in the cafeteria at lunch, they talk about movies, TV shows, music, what they did last night, and their plans for the weekend. Students do not talk about the bathroom or other very private things when they are with acquaintances in the cafeteria.

Students enjoy having conversations in the cafeteria, on the bus, and in the hallways. When students are having a conversation, there are ways to act that make other students comfortable and other ways to act that make students uncomfortable. Students feel comfortable when everyone takes turns talking during a conversation. Students make sure the other person gets a chance to talk. After making one statement or asking one question, a student can stop, look at the other person, and wait for the person to talk. Students feel comfortable when everyone has a chance to talk.

Figure 4.6. A social story to prepare Justin for conversations with peers.

a social story that was written for Justin, a high school student with Asperger syndrome whose peer relationships were challenged by his difficulty understanding the norms for when, where, and with whom conversing was appropriate.

Cognitive picture and script rehearsal (Grodon & LeVasseur, 1994) employs cards with drawings and social scripts that, like social stories, are reviewed with the student before entering a potentially troublesome situation. The cards illustrate and describe in print: 1) the antecedent to the problem situation; 2) the student's target response, along with the thought process that leads the student to that response; and 3) the positive consequences of the response. Cognitive and script rehearsals focus on a specific situation that is problematic for the student, such as the transition from computer time (a favorite activity) to reading group (a nonreferred activity), or coping with unexpected schedule changes.

Social Problem-Solving Strategies

These strategies teach students to resolve problems by generating alternatives to the conflict, evaluating the pros and cons of each one, and then acting out the best option. In addition to the steps in the problem-solving process, skills taught include listening, taking turns, negotiating, the ability to assume the perspective of another, and the ability to maintain a positive attitude.

Self-Instructional Strategies

Self-instruction is the use of covert speech or "self-talk" (i.e., thoughts) to direct one's personal behavior. *Self-instructional training* can be used to teach a number of cognitive and affective strategies (e.g., social problem-solving, anger control). It was originally based on Luria's (1961) theory about the role of inner speech in children's development of self-control.

Luria proposed a predictable developmental sequence through which children typically learn self-control: 1) behavior is controlled by physical intervention from adults, 2) behavior is controlled by verbal directions from adults, 3) children talk aloud to themselves to control their behavior, and 4) behavioral dos and don'ts are internalized as covert speech or *self-talk* (i.e., thoughts) (Luria, 1961).

Luria's theory found its initial validation in Meichenbaum and Goodman's (1971) research, which showed that children who learned to self-instruct or self-talk through modeling and verbal mediation evidenced decreases in impulsive behavior. Other researchers (see Robinson, Smith, Miller, & Brownell, 1994) have found improvements in aggression and anger management following self-instructional training. Adults with mild intellectual disabilities showed greater improvement in targeted social skills (i.e., managing conflict and responding to corrective feedback) when solving social problems with the use of self-instruction (O'Reilly et al., 2004).

Anger-Control Strategies

Anger-control strategies help individuals to identify when they are angry; recognize the conditions that trigger their anger and the negative outcomes related to aggressive expressions of anger; and identify ways to cope with negative feelings, express anger in appropriate ways, and reduce aggression (Goldstein, 1988). Included are strategies such as *self-instructional training, cognitive meditation (thinking aloud), relaxation training,* and *cognitive restructuring* (creating a new template for interpreting an anger-provoking situation). Students with serious conduct problems and/or emotional/behavioral disorders who received an intervention package including problem-solving training along with self-instructional training showed decreased impulsivity, disruptive behavior, and aggression and increased their prosocial behavior (Conduct Problems Prevention Research Group, 1999; Robinson, Smith, Miller, & Brownell, 1994).

Student Snapshot

 Sam is learning to predict the situations that trigger his anxiety and, consequently, anger. He also is learning to stop before acting, to think about at least three possible things he could do, and then to choose one of those options when an anxiety-provoking situation arises. He chooses among 1) reminding himself that he has teachers and friends who will help him when he needs it, 2) saying "I can handle this" instead of "I can't handle this" (cognitive strategies), 3) asking to go to one of several places to calm down (e.g., study hall, resource room, shop teacher's office), or 4) staying where he is and using a relaxation breathing routine (affective strategies). Soon, Ms. Otis will work with Sam to try out these methods during natural opportunities in his schedule.

Self-Management Strategies

Self-management methods involve teaching that is directed toward improving the student's independent use of a social or behavioral skill. These strategies teach students to become independent or less dependent on adults' constant vigilance of their behavior (Cole & Bambara, 1992). Self-management methods usually focus on outward behavior such as use of a social interaction or academic skill, but they could be used to aid a student in using cognitive skills as well, such as when a self-instruction strategy is employed. The steps for using these strategies include defining the target behavior, identifying practical reinforcers that the student can earn, designing a self-monitoring system (e.g., checklist of steps to follow), teaching the student to use the system, fading the student's use of the system while main-

taining self-management, and encouraging use of the system across other natural environments.

Various combinations of self-management strategies have been demonstrated to increase rates of on-task behavior and school-work participation and decrease disruptive behavior for students with autism, intellectual disabilities, emotional/behavioral disorders, severe disabilities, and learning disabilities (Barry & Messer, 2003; Brooks, Todd, Tofflemoyer, & Horner, 2003; Callahan & Rademacher, 1999; Koegel, Harrower, & Koegel, 1999; Smith & Sugai, 2000). Many of these studies were conducted with small numbers of students, but it is clear that self-management approaches yield meaningful benefits for students and are also quite efficient with respect to the amount of adult effort and involvement required to implement them.

Self-Cuing

Self-cuing strategies involve the use of tools such as class schedules, checklists, lists of the steps of a task, and watches that beep to help remind students or cue them to perform a target skill or check on their behavior. Students who are taught to self-manage initially will learn somewhat artificial ways to cue themselves; if these artificial signals are faded and students are taught to discriminate the natural stimuli that cue their behavior, the method used becomes a cognitive strategy; however, self-cuing does not always need to be faded. It is entirely normal to use a daily agenda for the rest of one's life.

Self-Monitoring

Another type of self-management strategy is self-monitoring, whereby a student learns to check his or her own behavior. The student might record each time he or she does a particular behavior (e.g., completing an assignment, offering assistance to a peer) or whenever a predetermined signal occurs—for example, the student checks to see if he or she is on task, is making verbal responses to adults' or peers' questions, and is not engaged in self-stimulatory behavior (e.g., rocking, humming). Self-monitoring is a well-researched method that has been highly effective in improving social interaction behaviors (e.g., Hughes, Copeland, et al., 2002; Koegel, Koegel, Hurley, & Frea, 1992; Strain, Kohler, Storey, & Danko, 1994) and academic behavior (e.g., Carr & Punzo, 1993). Effective, individualized self-monitoring strategies have been developed for students of all ages (including preschool) and with all types of disabilities. Self-monitoring strategies are known to have a *reactive effect,* whereby simply increasing awareness of the targeted behavior can bring about behavior change.

Self-Reinforcement

Self-reinforcement means that students also learn to apply rules to give themselves positive consequences for performing the target behavior (e.g., talking to peers who approach them, keeping hands to themselves). These skill-based methods all require direct instruction and may be used by adults (e.g., teachers or guidance counselors), by peers who have been taught to apply the methods with their classmates, or by adults in combination with peers.

Contexts and General Approaches for Teaching Social Skills

Several of the teaching methods and strategies described previously will be employed when implementing a social skills program for individuals or groups of students. Social skill interventions apply these strategies within three broad teaching contexts: 1) opportunistic teaching, 2) structured learning, and 3) peer-mediated intervention.

Opportunistic Teaching

Opportunistic (or incidental) teaching involves teaching social skills when students are in the presence of other students and are engaging in daily routines and activities. It is an incidental teaching approach to develop socially competent performance of skills during daily "teachable moments," such as when interactions take place in natural circumstances (e.g., recess, classroom). Opportunistic teaching can be used to prompt students when they miss an opportunity to perform a targeted social skill (e.g., could have joined in a group but looked and walked away), when they misuse a skill and need correction, and to "debrief" students who use inappropriate behaviors when an alternative target social skill would have worked. Teaching during natural opportunities is very useful when a social skill is partially acquired but needs to be made more fluent. For students with intellectual disabilities, it is virtually a requirement of effective social skills instruction.

Structured Learning

In their *Skillstreaming* series, McGinnis and Goldstein (1997a, 1997b) utilize a social skills teaching method called *structured learning,* which essentially is a direct instruction approach that also incorporates generalization training using opportunistic teaching. It is probably fair to say that virtually all of the published social skills curricula that employ cognitive-behavioral and social learning (i.e., learning from watching others) techniques utilize a similar training sequence. Some refer to the method as *structured learning,* some might use the terminology *model–lead–test* (Sugai & Lewis, 1996), and others might simply use the term *direct instruction.*

When using structured learning, teachers convene a social skills training group of students of similar ages who need to learn or improve some of the same social skills. The training uses a cognitive-behavioral approach, following the sequence of steps described previously: 1) introduction of the skill, including its definition and the rationale for learning it; 2) modeling of the prescribed skill steps by the teacher or other adult facilitator, with verbal rehearsal; 3) role playing by the students, first with coaching and then with increasing independence; and 4) performance feedback by peers and teachers after the role playing. Opportunistic teaching of practiced skills throughout the day also is used, and self-monitoring techniques are incorporated. The modeling and role-playing components follow the guidelines for their use previously described. Figure 4.7 provides a sample page from *Skillstreaming the Elementary School Child* (McGinnis & Gold-

stein, 1997b), illustrating the skill steps and suggested role-play situations for the skill using self-control.

Peer-Mediated Intervention

Sometimes, peers are taught or guided to assist in instruction; they might be taught to demonstrate (model), remind (cue), or praise (reinforce) specific social skills. This approach is called *peer-mediated interventions*. Other times, peers might simply provide spontaneous models to which the adult calls attention.

Research has repeatedly demonstrated the efficacy of peer-mediated approaches for enhancing the social and communicative interactions of students of various ages and with a range of disabilities; they have been particularly successful for students

Skill 36: Using Self-Control

Steps	Notes for discussion
1. Stop and count to 10.	Discuss the importance of allowing yourself time to cool off and think.
2. Think of how your body feels.	Discuss how bodily cues may signal losing control (e.g., your hands become sweaty, you feel hot or weak).
3. Think about your choices: a. Walk away for now.	Students should ask to leave the area for a few minutes, if necessary, until they regain control.
b. Do a relaxation exercise.	Teach students Relaxing (Skill 56)
c. Write about how you feel.	
d. Talk to someone about it.	Discuss choosing someone who would be likely to understand.
4. Act out your best choice.	If one choice doesn't work, the student should try another one.

Suggested situations

School: You are behind in your schoolwork and must stay after school to finish.
Home: Your parents won't let you go to a friend's house.
Peer group: A friend borrows something and breaks it.

Comments

Students should use this skill when they are too angry or upset to identify what they are feeling and need to gain control before dealing with the problem. Tell students that sometimes when people are very upset or angry, it is okay to delay dealing with the problem.

Figure 4.7. Skill steps and teaching suggestions for a Skillstreaming lesson. (From *Skillstreaming the elementary school child: New strategies and perspectives for teaching prosocial skills* [p. 126] by McGinnis. E., & Goldstein, A. [1997b], Champaign, IL: Research Press. Reprinted by permission.)

with autism (see McConnell, 2002). Peer-mediated interventions have been as effective as child-specific interventions (e.g., one-to-one social skills training by an adult) in improving a variety of social and communicative interaction skills (Odom et al., 1999). One of the most valuable results of peer-mediated interventions is their striking effects on generalization of behavior across additional peers, places, and situations (Odom, Chandler, Ostrosky, McConnell, & Reaney, 1992).

Student Snapshot

 In Melanie's fourth-grade class, four girls are learning ways in which they can help Melanie interact with them. They all have learned a turn-taking, "conversational" approach that involves using Melanie's picture conversation book (with pictures from home and school activities) while "reading" signs and limited words and speaking slowly. Several of the girls have brought pictures from home to make the conversations more interesting, and the class has started its own conversation book. Once Melanie and her four friends are skilled at interacting with one another using Melanie's conversation books, the girls demonstrate their method of interacting with Melanie to the rest of the class; Melanie then picks other students with whom she would like to interact before school, at break times after seatwork, during recess, and at lunch.

Although the selection of peers for a student-to-student intervention should consider demographic characteristics (e.g., high school students with disabilities might prefer to be matched with same-gender peers) and the individual support needs of the student with disabilities, there do not appear to be any universal screening criteria. In fact, after examining more than 200 research studies of peer-mediated social skill interventions conducted with young children, Strain concluded, "Based upon the universal success of diverse peer intervention agents, the systematic screening of chil-

dren for this intervention role was abandoned" (2001, p. 34).

Considerations for Students with More Extensive Support Needs

Most of the social skills teaching strategies and approaches described in this chapter can be effective with students who have extensive support needs if appropriate goals are targeted and additional adaptations are made. The specific teaching strategies selected need to complement the student's social competence abilities (to observe, interpret, search options, plan a response, and carry it out), his or her means of communication, and his or her specific social skills needs.

Intellectual Disabilities

Students with intellectual disabilities may benefit more from behavioral teaching methods that first directly shape their desired behavior in the social situation to which the behavior applies and then teach their classmates to model and to prompt their behavior in social situations. In addition, despite their complexity, cognitive and affective strategies have been successfully applied to younger children with disabilities, students with autism, and students with severe and/or multiple disabilities by reducing the difficulty of the language involved in the cognitive strategy and by adding objects or pictures. For students who are less able than their typically developing peers to examine their own thoughts or to communicate easily, the use of concrete (tangible or visual) reminders can reduce the abstractions involved.

Communication Limitations

When students do not have a reliable means of communicating, team members should focus and problem-solve in this area first. *Although speech is not essential to social participation with typically developing peers, students without speech must have reliable ways to communicate.* When many students with disabilities first learn to communicate, they use body language and later combine several symbolic communication systems, such as speaking a few words or short phrases; using some manual signs; pointing to a set of picture symbols; using a simple switch-operated system, such as Cheap Talk (Enabling Devices); or working a complex, computer-based, portable communication system with speech, such as Dynamo (DynaVox Technologies). Time needs to be set aside to teach peers to interact using this often highly personalized system of communication.

Conversation books have also been validated as an effective means of increasing social interaction with students whose communication is difficult to understand. Hunt and her co-workers (1991) used this approach with students ranging in age from elementary school (age 6–10) to high school (age 15–18). First, individualized conversation books were created; these books contained photos of activities, people, pets, sports, and other events that the students enjoyed during and after school and a menu of conversation topics. Photos were regularly added and removed to keep the books current and interesting. Next, the students were individually taught to use a turn-taking structure to interact with teachers, using the conversation book to augment their communication systems (e.g., words and phrases, signs, conventional gestures). The conversation topics were changed or clarified by pointing to photos.

Then, peers were taught to interact with these students; they learned to refer to the communication book to ask questions about a picture in the book or to make comments and to wait each time the focus students answered to give them time to ask another question or to make a comment. This training was given in

5-minute sessions during the school day and repeated with all of the involved peers across many settings where informal interactions could take place. The training resulted in meaningful increases in conversational exchanges between students with fairly significant intellectual disabilities and their peers without disabilities, some of whom also had limited motor skills or behavior problems.

Melanie points to photographs in a notebook for some conversations but uses signs, gestures, and some words to express herself as well. She can read a printed daily schedule of activities, recognize many printed words, and understand a lot of spoken language. Melanie's teachers will use modeling coupled with simple words and gestures to teach Melanie's peers to interact with her by using conversational turn taking and a communication photograph album; Melanie will use her photograph album to add meaning to her signing and limited speech.

Some students might simply use a personal set of body language to express themselves; however, these behaviors may be primarily nonsymbolic and may include sounds, facial expressions, gestures, and movements. Meaningful interactions can take place once peers learn the student's "personal communication dictionary," particularly within the context of familiar routines and preferred activities. Instruction is geared toward the interaction itself (each partner learning how to initiate and respond so that he or she is understood) and toward refining the communication responses so that they are more conventional and consistent while also expanded.

Daniel's peers have learned to give him choices for leisure activities by showing, telling, and letting him feel (one at a time) each of two choice items that represent activities he likes (e.g., audiotape for a talking book, switch to operate musical video games). "Should we listen to the book?" (Daniel feels the tape.) "Or do the video game?" (Daniel feels the switch.)

They know to repeat the choices and pause after each, waiting for him to lift his head, which is Daniel's signal for making a choice.

Behavior Problems

An additional consideration for students with serious behavior problems is manipulating the environment to decrease incidents of problem behavior while the student is learning new social, communication, and self-management skills. The choice of strategies should be based on data that were collected to analyze the antecedents that predict whether the social-behavioral problems will occur. Strategies include things such as providing a choice of activities, allowing more mobile activities or movement breaks, rearranging the desks or the entire classroom, providing prompts or reminders, stating and reviewing class rules, using relaxation activities, and providing more hands-on materials. Of course, these tactics should be part of a student's overall plan for positive behavior support.

Selecting Teaching Methods that Match Type of Learning Problem and Context

The methods and the context (location, time of day, activity, people present) chosen for teaching a student should correspond to the type of social skills learning problem the student has: acquisition, performance or fluency, and interfering or competing behaviors (Gresham, 1997). The three types of learning problems correspond with the different stages of learning that apply to many skills, not just to social skills. First, students acquire a skill (e.g., making change); then, they focus on perfecting it and using it fluently in many differing school and community contexts. Social skills are no different; once a social skill has been acquired, its performance often needs improvement. Therefore, it is not unusual for students

to have some skills in the acquisition stage of learning and others in the performance stage. Students with interfering behavior will first need to learn that there are alternate social skills that also achieve the desired outcome (peer attention, escape from unpleasant situation) and that the problem behavior no longer works, but these students may be unpracticed in their newly acquired social skills and may need to improve their performance over time. Figure 4.8 summarizes the intervention methods and teaching contexts that match each type of social skills learning problem.

Sam's team devised a comprehensive set of prevention, teaching, and management plans to address both Sam's disruptive behaviors (aggression, yelling, and confrontational behavior) that appear to be maintained mainly by escape and his socially immature behavior (talking about biological functions) that appears to be maintained by peer attention. Then, Sam's team identified 11 social skills that they believed Sam needed and brainstormed methods to teach these skills to him. All three types of learning are addressed in these 11 target skills: acquisition learning (knowing peers' names), improving performance (opening doors, helping classmates), and learning appropriate alternatives (asking for a break, managing rejection or stressful class work).

Considering the Influences of Peer Networks

Sometimes existing student networks can work against social skills training; prosocial skills are not always maintained by the peer network while problematic behavior may be encouraged. In such cases, intervention to improve social skills and peer relationships is more complicated. The educational team may have to address specific questions regarding a student's social networks and adjust the social skills teaching plans accordingly:

Social skill problem	Description	Intervention match	Proper context
Acquisition or skill problem	Student doesn't have the skill or is missing a necessary step in performing a social skill sequence.	Use direct, structured instruction (e.g., modeling, coaching) and manipulate antecedents and consequences.	Use structured small group initially, then informal and naturalistic teaching.
Performance or fluency problem	Student has the skill but may not know when to use it, may be too slow in using it, may be unable to adjust the skills to suit the situation, or may simply lack proficiency in using the skill.	Use antecedent-control strategies (e.g., peer social initiations and networks) and reinforcement-based procedures.	Use informal, naturalistic approach employing incidental teaching with performance feedback; also use peer-mediated approaches.
Interfering or competing behaviors	Student has many competing, inappropriate behaviors; social skills may be known but are not efficient or effective enough to be used instead of the problem behaviors.	Use a combination of procedures while also teaching and strengthening alternative behaviors (e.g., improve school/home environment to prevent problem behavior).	Use both formal and informal approaches, but an informal approach to training in naturally occurring contexts is essential to replace existing behavior problems with needed social skills.

Figure 4.8.   Matching social skill problems to effective interventions and training contexts.

- *Does the student's social network limit his or her social opportunities?* What factors influence the networks that exist in the classroom (gender, race, athletic ability, socioeconomic status, aggressiveness)? Can these factors be manipulated to expand the social and behavioral roles the student can occupy?

- *What social roles might assist the student in developing new skills or social characteristics?* What roles are connected with desirable behaviors or skills? Are there, for instance, leadership or helping roles that are available to students in the class? Is it possible to place the student in these roles to enable the student to be favorably viewed by his or her peers in a way that is not possible during routine class activities?

- *Does the student associate with classmates who encourage or maintain problem be-*

havior? If so, social skills training, even if successful, may never generalize to everyday peer exchanges because the student's network does not support the new skills. Could intervention be directed toward the whole group or social network? As an alternate solution, could the student be supported in associating with another group (one that supports his or her positive characteristics)?

- *Are there peers in the classroom who can "positively elicit and support the student's new skills or characteristics without a social cost to themselves"* (Farmer et al., 1996, p. 251)? The focus student could be placed in the proximity of supportive and helpful students who can promote appropriate social behaviors. Classwide cooperative group activities, along with social skills instruction, can further these behaviors.

Teachers must be careful neither to set the focus student up for engaging in the problem behaviors nor to let the helping students become socially vulnerable themselves.

Considering the Use of Commercial Social Skills Programs

Most commercially available social skills programs address a specific age group and range of social skills and use a combination of teaching strategies. Basic considerations in choosing a published program are:

- Does the program target the appropriate population of students?

- Does the purpose of the curriculum match the students' needs and goals?

- Does the program promote social competence rather than merely the acquisition of discrete skills?

- Are the amounts of structure and effort required to implement the program reasonably balanced against the likely outcomes?

In addition to these basic questions, it is important to determine whether the program has a validated track record of success or, at the very least, incorporates the elements that predict effectiveness. For example, some published programs fail to adequately promote generalization and transfer of skills across people, places, and situations (Gresham, 1997). In addition to shortcomings in the design of some programs, implementation errors such as a lack of training intensity can result in poor outcomes. Reviews of the research on social skills interventions (Forness & Kavale, 1996; Kavale & Mostert, 2004) revealed that the average duration of the intervention program was less than 30 hours over 10 weeks.

Several of the various social skill programs are listed and partially described in Figure 4.9. Though this list should not be regarded as complete, the programs that are listed have been identified as having one or more characteristics that distinguish them as potentially effective training packages (Forness & Kavale, 1996; Gresham, 1997; Kavale & Mostert, 2004; McIntosh, Vaughn, & Zaragoza, 1991; Walker et al., 2004; Zaragoza, Vaughn, & McIntosh, 1991). These characteristics include

1. *Support for the program's effectiveness:* The program has some published empirical support confirming that it improves the social skills it addresses; if not, the program incorporates the elements that predict effectiveness and has some published consumer satisfaction support.

2. *Socially valid methods used to select target social skills:* The program addresses skills rated as important by reliable sources. For example, the authors of ASSET (Hazel, Schumaker, Sherman, & Sheldon-Wildgen, 1981) identified their core skills by reviewing published social skills literature; obtaining ratings of importance on these core skills from parents, teachers, and students; and seeking critical judgments from experts in the field.

3. *Prescriptive nature:* The program enables teachers to determine the particular skill impairments that create problems for a student and to judge whether it is a skill acquisition or performance impairment (Walker et al., 2004). Teaching students to use skills they already perform acceptably reduces their motivation to improve.

4. *Assessment of outcomes:* The program provides a means for measuring students' achievement of long-term, valued outcomes, such as being socially accepted by peers, developing positive relationships, and attaining improved social adjustment and mental health.

Most of the programs listed in Figure 4.9 are meant to be used prescriptively

Program	Relevant ages	Skills addressed and methods used	Program effectiveness
The ACCEPTS Program: A Curriculum for Children's Effective Peer and Teacher Skills (Walker et al., 1983)	Kindergarten through sixth grade	Teaches 28 social skills organized into three areas: classroom skills (e.g., complying with teacher requests, working on assignments), relating to others (e.g., friendship-making, getting along with others), and coping skills (e.g., coping with teasing); one-to-one and small-group formats are used, but the program may be adapted to the whole class	b; supported by research with pre-school and elementary school children (McConnell, Sisson, Cort, & Strain, 1991; Walker et al., 1983)
The ACCESS Program: Adolescent Curriculum for Communication and Effective Social Skills (Walker, Todis, Holmes, & Horton, 1988)	Seventh grade through twelfth grade	Addresses friendships, getting along, compliance with teacher requests, appropriate ways of making assistance needs known, and self-control; taught through structured learning	b; socially validated core skills (Walker, Colvin, & Ramsey, 1995)
ASSET: A Social Skills Program for Adolescents (Hazel, Schumaker, Sherman, & Sheldon-Wildgen, 1981)	Adolescents	Teaches basic social skills (e.g., giving positive and negative feedback) and addresses serious behavior problems; methods include videotaped modeling (scenes in which adolescents model appropriate and inappropriate behavior with peers, parents, teachers, and others), group discussions, role plays, and homework assignments	b; excellent content validity on core social skills and situations in which skills could be applied
DO-WATCH-LISTEN-SAY: Social and Communication Intervention for Children with Autism (Quill, 2000)	Preschool and early grades	Addresses play skills (e.g., sharing), group skills (e.g., turn taking), and basic conversation skills; direct skill instruction and observational learning in natural contexts	a
First Step to Success (Walker et al., 1997)	Kindergartners at risk for antisocial behavior	Has three components that address school intervention, family support and parent training, and support and assistance from community social service agencies 1. CLASS (Contingencies for Learning Academic and Social Skills): school component 2. Homebase: parent training model 3. Matching family needs with available community support services if the family is eligible (e.g., services for poverty, abuse)	First component based on 5 years of research; second component based on 25 years of research; third component the least well developed; cited by Joseph and *(continued)*

Figure 4.9. Commercially available social skills teaching programs. (*Sources:* Brown & Odom, 1994; Forness & Kavale, 1996; Gresham, 1997; Joseph & Strain, 2003; Walker et al., 2004; Zaragoza et al., 1991.) (*Key:* a, cited by Brown and Odom (1994) as incorporating many of the strategies known to promote generalization and maintenance of social behavior; b, cited by Forness and Kavale (1996) as having "potential effectiveness"; c, no research has been conducted but uses a strategic approach to selecting and teaching skills and incorporates many of the strategies known to promote generalization and maintenance of positive social behavior.)

Figure 4.9. *(continued)*

Program	Relevant ages	Skills addressed and methods used	Program effectiveness
			Strain (2003) as having high level of evidence of success
Let's Be Social (Social Integration Project, 1989)	Preschool and early grades	Addresses interacting, sharing, cooperative play, and making friends, among others	a
Navigating the Social World: A Curriculum for Individuals with Asperger's Syndrome, High Functioning Autism and Related Disorders (McAffee, 2002)	School age (students must have some reading skills)	Teaches three groups of skills: recognizing and coping with one's own emotions, communication and social skills, and abstract thinking skills; most lessons involve introduction of the skill, demonstrations, role playing, and then prompting and reinforcing the use of skills in natural settings	c
Playtime/Social Time: Organizing Your Classroom to Build Social Interaction Skills (Odom & McConnell, 1997)	Preschool and early grades	Teaches interacting, sharing, cooperative play, making friends, and so forth	a
The Prepare Curriculum: Teaching Prosocial Competencies (Goldstein, 1988)	Middle and high school students who are aggressive, withdrawn, or weak in prosocial competencies	Teaches problem solving, interpersonal skills, situational perception, anger control, moral reasoning, stress management, empathy, recruiting supportive models, cooperation, and understanding and using groups; teaching methods include games, simulations, role plays, and group discussions	a
Promoting Social Success: A Curriculum for Children with Special Needs (Siperstein & Rickards, 2004)	Elementary school	Has units on emotional and behavioral regulation, noticing and interpreting cues, social problem solving, and skills for making and keeping friends; methods include use of concrete examples and consistent language, modeling, and repetition; use for an entire class, with selected students receiving more intensive instruction	c
RECESS: A Program For Reducing Negative-Aggressive Behavior (Walker, Hops, & Greenwood, 1993)	Kindergarten through third grade	Teaches prosocial forms of peer-related behavior and uses sanctions (point loss and time-out) for negative and aggressive behavior, breaking rules, teasing, and bullying; uses scripts, discussion, and role playing; group contingencies (rewards and privileges) used at school while individual contingencies applied at home; program gradually extends from recess to the classroom and includes maintenance strategies	Support for powerful effects on the social behavior of aggressive children in grades K–3 (Walker, Colvin, & Ramsey, 1995)

Program	Relevant ages	Skills addressed and methods used	Program effectiveness
Skillstreaming in Early Childhood: Teaching Prosocial Skills to the Preschool and Kindergarten Child (McGinnis & Goldstein, 1990)	Preschool through second grade	Teaches persisting despite difficulty, joining in, coping with teasing, knowing when to tell, waiting your turn, and so forth; uses structured learning: didactic instruction, modeling, role playing, feedback, and transfer	b
Skillstreaming the Adolescent: New Strategies and Perspectives for Teaching Prosocial Skills (McGinnis & Goldstein, 1997a)	Sixth grade through twelfth grade	Includes six skill areas such as beginning and advanced social skills (e.g., apologizing), skill alternatives to aggression (e.g., negotiation), skills for dealing with stress (e.g., responding to failure), and setting goals; uses structured learning: didactic instruction modeling, role playing, feedback, and transfer	b; Greenleaf (1992) found positive effects for adolescent boys with histories of disruptive behavior
Skillstreaming the Elementary School Child: New Strategies and Perspectives for Teaching Prosocial Skills (McGinnis & Goldstein, 1997b)	Third grade through fifth grade	Organized into five groups of skills: classroom survival (e.g., asking for help, saying thank you), friendship-making, dealing with feelings, alternatives to aggression, and dealing with stress (e.g., accepting consequences, dealing with peer pressure); uses structured learning: didactic instruction, modeling, role playing, feedback, and transfer	b; Sasso, Meloy, and Kavale (1990) reported successful generalized outcomes for some students with behavior disorders
Social Skills Intervention Guide (Elliott & Gresham, 1991)	Preschool through high school	Designed to be used in combination with the Social Skills Rating System (SSRS) (Gresham & Elliott, 1990)	b; SSRS has excellent psychometric properties
Social Skills Lessons and Activities for Grades 4–6 (Begun, 1996)	Grades 4–6 (other books in the series address skills for PreK–K and Grades 7–12)	Teaches classroom survival skills (e.g., following instructions, listening) and skills for interpersonal problem solving, dealing with anger, accepting differences and dealing with peer pressure; uses structured learning: modeling, role playing, feedback, and real-life application (Each book provides 50 or more lessons covering age-appropriate skills.)	c

with either a whole class (universal approach) or with small groups of students. Small groups should be carefully composed of students who have similar or complementary skill needs; however, homogeneous groups of students with disabilities and behavior problems are less likely to obtain positive outcomes than heterogeneous groups of students with and without behavior problems (Ang & Hughes, 2002). One-to-one instruction, particularly when it involves pulling the student out of class on a regular basis, also has some serious side effects. Many researchers suggest that this approach be avoided unless school staff build in certain features to reduce stigma and to improve skill generalization (e.g., use in combination with classwide program, build in peer support).

Melanie's fourth-grade teacher has designated a half hour each day to social skills training. In combination with the guidance counselor and the special education teacher, Melanie's teacher offers 30-minute activities using the ACCEPTS program (Walker et al., 1983). Often, teachers are able to integrate academic skills such as reading, speaking, and writing into the social skills teaching. The ACCEPTS program teaches skills in three core areas: classroom social skills, relating to others, and coping.

Step 4

Develop a Teaching Plan

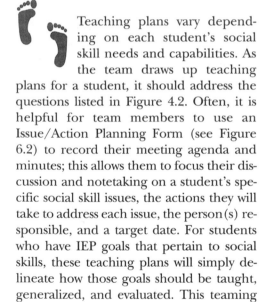

Teaching plans vary depending on each student's social skill needs and capabilities. As the team draws up teaching plans for a student, it should address the questions listed in Figure 4.2. Often, it is helpful for team members to use an Issue/Action Planning Form (see Figure 6.2) to record their meeting agenda and minutes; this allows them to focus their discussion and notetaking on a student's specific social skill issues, the actions they will take to address each issue, the person(s) responsible, and a target date. For students who have IEP goals that pertain to social skills, these teaching plans will simply delineate how those goals should be taught, generalized, and evaluated. This teaming strategy is discussed in detail in Chapter 6.

Step 5

Implement, Evaluate, and Improve the Plan as Needed

In Step 5, team members implement and monitor the results of teaching plans they have designed. For example, they will consider the difficulties the focus student may have with generalizing new social skills and plan ways to promote skill transfer. Teams will identify meaningful outcomes measures to assess the success of the program. Finally, teams will generate ways to strengthen programs that are not producing the skill improvements for which they have aimed.

Generalization Problems with Social Skills

In a structured lesson, students are taught to discriminate examples and non-examples of a skill and situations in which the skill should or should not be used, but, later, students need to learn to generalize that skill to a variety of contexts, which requires that they be more liberal about when to use the skill and which particular form of the skill to use (Gresham, 1997). For most students, teachers will follow or accompany structured, formal instruction that takes place in artificial contexts with conscientious teaching across many natural contexts (generalization training). Formal, direct interventions are recommended for students who have social skill acquisition problems. By contrast, students who have social skill performance problems will benefit more from opportunistic or naturalistic teaching in real circumstances that are part of the daily activities.

Using natural contexts with students who have performance problems shifts their learning to the more complex and less predictable set of stimuli that exist in ongoing school activities and social exchanges. At this point in social skills training, peer support and peer-mediated training can be a less obtrusive, more appropriate means for promoting generalization than having adults provide focus students with prompts, cues, coaching, rehearsal, and feedback.

- Structured and formal instruction, for skill acquisition: *Melanie and two girls are sitting with the teacher at a small table in the back of the classroom with Melanie's conversation book; they are practicing a turn-taking approach to conversing using words, gestures, and photographs.*

- Less structured, informal, and naturalistic, for generalization: *When Melanie's peers yell to her to join them at recess, the classroom assistant reminds Melanie to respond and act ("If you want to play, wave to them, and go after them").*

The opportunistic teaching approach used for generalization can involve prompting a student to use a social skill, modeling it or providing other prompts (e.g., gestures, picture prompts), giving helpful feedback, and reinforcing skill use. It is repeated over and over in different locations at varying times whenever the skill is needed. For students who have learned cognitive strategies, generalization training may involve reminders to recognize when to use a particular strategy ("Think about the five steps for solving a problem. What's the first one?").

Another strategy for supporting the transfer of skills from social skills lessons to the authentic social world is to assign "homework." McGinnis and Goldstein (1997a, 1997b) described several increasingly challenging types of homework assignments that are designed to promote generalization of targeted skills to the real world. First, the teacher assists the student to identify a time and place when the skill is certain to be needed; after using the skill, the student self-evaluates how well he or she followed the skill steps (not how successful the outcome was). As students become more proficient, homework becomes self-monitoring of skill use across the day or week.

Another approach that promotes generalization of social skills is to involve peers in the modeling and prompting process (peer-mediated training). Kamps et al. (1997) discovered that they could greatly increase incidental opportunities for peers to interact with classmates who had autism by forming special peer networks associated with many routine activities (e.g., lunch bunch, recess buddies, classwide peer tutoring). During these peer network activities, peers used simple modeling and script prompting methods to initiate interactions while teachers monitored the sessions and gave out praise and points.

To summarize, Elliott and Gresham (1991) urged including as many of the following elements as possible in social skills training programs:

- Teach behaviors that are valued in everyday settings and, therefore, will be naturally reinforced when they occur.
- Train across people, places, and situations that the student encounters daily.
- Fade training arrangements, such as special reinforcement, until they are very like those in natural situations.
- Prompt and reinforce the use of skills in relevant new situations.
- Include peers in training.

Students for whom the curriculum is significantly adapted require a systematic approach to planning for generalization across many social contexts. A useful approach is to construct a matrix listing the daily schedule across the top row and the student's social and communication goals down the left-hand column. The cells that correspond with scheduled, formal instruction in each skill can be marked with one code, and the cells that correspond with natural opportunities for using the skills with the support of opportunistic teaching can be marked with another code.

On Melanie's Program Planning Matrix, her team indicated the most appropriate times for direct social skills instruction and then indicated other times during the day when Melanie would need to use her new skills in order to increase her social interactions and peer support. The special education teacher then wrote up brief descriptions of the opportunistic teaching approaches that would be used for generalization and shared them with the team.

Many generalization errors seem to result when the acquired social skills are not as strong or efficient as the former behaviors used by the student in a particular social situation. Researchers have described these former responses as *competing behaviors*. The teacher's goal should be to teach the student social skills that are "functionally equivalent" to or just as effective as the problem or competing behavior in obtaining a desired outcome (Horner, O'Neil, & Flannery, 1993).

Student Snapshot

Since elementary school, Sam has demonstrated his dislike for active, noisy games in physical education by covering his ears, growing anxious, making noises, and refusing to participate. Beginning in middle school, Sam perfected a set of highly effective ways to get out of physical education; these methods include yelling, refusing to participate, asking to go to the restroom, and behaving aggressively toward others. By mid-October, Sam's team (including his physical education teacher) designed a program based on his functional behavior assessment. The team taught Sam several alternative ways for him to "escape" loud group games: Instead of participating in the group activities, he could ask for a short break, run on the track, perform exercises using headphones, or use a self-monitoring plan to keep track of actual participation in order to earn preferred activities. Because the competing behaviors were so ingrained and still occasionally worked with some teachers, the replacement behaviors were not automatic for Sam.

In cases of poor skill generalization, team members might ask several ques-

tions and then strengthen the student's program based on the answers (Gresham, 1997):

1. Does the student engage in undesirable behavior that achieves the same results as the socially skilled target behavior (e.g., ends disliked activity, gets attention)? Are the undesirable behaviors equally (or more) effective in obtaining reinforcement? (If the answers are positive, ask the second set of questions.)

2. If the undesirable behaviors are equally or more effective in obtaining reinforcement, are they easier for the student? Are they more likely to achieve the same function faster and more consistently than the socially skilled alternative behavior?

If the answers to the second set of questions are also affirmative, the solution lies in the following rule: *Decrease the efficiency and reliability of competing, inappropriate behaviors.* This is accomplished by not allowing problem behaviors to "work" for the student and ensuring that the social skills and appropriate behavior (even if imperfect) result in the function that the student seeks (e.g., attention, escape, tangibles).

Finally, the team should learn about trigger stimuli that might play a role in preventing the generalization of learning. To do this, they should ask this third question: "Are competing problem behaviors related to the presence of a specific stimulus (e.g., person, place, or thing) or are they associated with many stimuli and situations?" (Gresham, 1997, pp. 246–247) When the team members determine that singular people, places, or things act as triggers for problem behavior, they might try to change these stimuli to prevent the problem; however, if many circumstances provoke the problem behavior, then the best plan is to increase the efficiency and reliability of alternative behaviors.

Student Snapshot

Because they could not discontinue loud group activities during physical education, Sam's team decided to increase the efficiency and reliability of Sam's alternative behaviors. They determined ways to address his problem behavior when it did occur. Then, the physical education teacher and class assistant taught Sam several appropriate ways he could request "escape" from loud group games. Next, they planned and gave Sam's peers some instruction on ways in which they might support Sam by ignoring his problem behaviors; several peers agreed to run or exercise with him if he requested these alternatives. In addition, Sam was not allowed to leave physical education and sit in the principal's office when he engaged in his old problem behavior. Instead, he was taken by a teaching assistant to the far end of the gym (or to another gym) and was expected to complete an exercise activity.

Use of Meaningful Outcome Measures

When social skill teaching plans work, the student will make progress toward his or her social skill goals at a reasonable rate, and these improvements in student behavior will be noticed and appreciated by others who are important in the student's life. This meaningful outcome is sometimes called *social validation*; society (e.g., teachers, parents, peers, principals)

deems that the change is important. Another desired outcome is a positive change in the person's social relationships, which has been called *habilitative validity* (Hawkins, 1991). Answering the following types of questions will help educators evaluate their social skill teaching efforts by examining social relationship outcomes:

- Did the social skills or behavior change make a difference in the individual's social functioning, particularly in his or her participation and interaction in peer networks?

- Did social skill training produce changes in the person's status within his or her peer group?

Daniel's team keeps track of how often he responds to peers' comments and initiates social interaction; they also get a monthly count from Daniel's home of invitations to play that Daniel receives from classmates and those that classmates accept from him.

To be meaningful, a behavior change or social skill must be noticed by others and reach what is called the *just noticeable difference* level of performance; however, a just noticeable difference is often rather large and is regarded as significant only when it occurs across most or all environments that the student routinely uses.

Chapter 5

Models of Peer Support in Instruction

The term *peer-mediated instruction* applies when teachers involve students in lending instructional support to other students. Several of the methods to building peer relationships and support that have already been described in this book can be classified as *peer-mediated interventions:*

- Peer modeling (see Chapter 4)
- Peer buddy systems (peer monitoring; see Chapter 3)
- Peer networking (see Chapter 3)

This chapter focuses primarily on more structured approaches to peer-mediated instruction: cooperative learning and peer tutoring. In addition, some of the more instructionally focused peer-networking systems are briefly examined.

These peer-mediated instructional approaches are well suited to the philosophy and practice of inclusive education: They accommodate learner diversity, are well substantiated as effective methods for enhancing academic achievement and social development, and also foster opportunities for social relationships among peers. Academic benefits accrue as students experience the motivating influence of an instructional environment that provides better pupil–teacher ratios, more time on task and active responding, more opportunities for feedback, and more frequent opportunities for individualized assistance (Greenwood, Carta, & Kamps, 1990). Social benefits, which include improved collaborative skills and increased supportive behaviors toward others (see Figure 5.1), can be credited to the increase in opportunities for supported practice in working together toward common goals and learning to give and receive helpful feedback. Cooperative learning and classwide approaches to peer tutoring are nonintrusive ways to provide adaptations for students with disabilities, as no student is singled out for specialized intervention, yet each student's work can be individualized.

Although peer-mediated instruction is a valuable way of increasing joint instructional interactions among students with and without disabilities, it should not be employed as the *sole* tactic for nurturing positive social relationships among students with and without disabilities. Nor

---

Increased academic achievement

Improved intergroup relations

Improved self-esteem

High-level reasoning strategies and increased critical reasoning competencies

Greater ability to view situations from others' perspectives

Greater intrinsic motivation

More positive attitudes toward subject areas, learning, and school

More positive attitudes toward teachers, principals, and school personnel

Less disruptive and more on-task behavior

Greater collaborative skills and better attitudes, necessary for working with others

Greater feeling of individual control over one's success in school

Increased altruism and supportive behaviors toward others

Increased prosocial behavior

Improved skills at resolving conficts

Increased attendance

Figure 5.1. Outcomes often associated with cooperative learning. (*Sources:* Johnson, Johnson, & Holubec, 1994; Maheady, Harper, & Mallette, 2001; Slavin, 1991.)

We recognize and appreciate Monica Delano's work on a previous version of this chapter.

should it be used with the expectation that it will necessarily lead to friendships between students with and without disabilities. The nature of the interactions that occur and the relationships that develop between peers will depend to some extent on the tasks that are assigned to them. Tutoring, helping, and other peer-mediated instructional roles should not be assumed to be the key to developing close personal ties such as friendships; however, cooperative learning is associated with greater peer acceptance of students with disabilities than competitive or individualistic learning—even when contributions to the group task were imbalanced (Johnson & Johnson, 1984, 1989).

Cooperative learning, peer tutoring, peer networking, and several other peer-mediated instructional approaches are based on solid research foundations and offer innovative strategies for meeting the diverse needs of today's classrooms. Peer-mediated instruction provides opportunities for students with and without disabilities to learn together—which is not only a requirement for authentic class membership but also generates additional opportunities for students to learn from their interaction with one another. A further justification for the use of peer-mediated approaches lies in data revealing high levels of acceptability, feasibility, and consumer satisfaction from both teachers and student.

For example, a review of 14 studies of peer-mediated interventions for students with emotional and behavioral disorders found satisfaction ratings of 89%–100% among students and 100% among teachers (Ryan, Reid, & Epstein, 2004). Similarly, the middle school teachers who participated in Mitchem, Young, West, and Benyo's (2001) evaluation of a classwide peer-assisted self-management system gave the program satisfaction ratings of 100%; these teachers also rated the acceptability of the program's goals and procedures at approximately 95%.

Cooperative learning is one of the instructional strategies most frequently recommended for use by teachers in inclusive classrooms (Johnson & Johnson, 1999; Nevin et al., 2002; Putnam, 1998). When a group of in-service teachers evaluated their comfort level in implementing a selection of instructional practices that have been validated as effective for heterogeneous classrooms, they gave cooperative learning and direct instruction their highest scores (King-Sears & Cummings, 1996). These data about teachers' satisfaction, comfort level, and perceptions of acceptability bode well for the continued adoption and institutionalization of peer-mediated instructional practices.

Some practical guidelines for implementation of cooperative learning, peer tutoring, and peer networking, along with several case examples, are provided following a brief summary of the empirical support for these approaches.

COOPERATIVE LEARNING

Cooperative learning is an instructional method in which students work in small, mixed-ability groups and are responsible for their groupmates' learning as well as their own learning (Campbell & Campbell, 1995). Resources to assist in the implementation of cooperative learning are included in Appendix B.

Outcomes

Cooperative learning is perhaps one of the most extensively studied instructional methods. Hundreds of research studies on cooperative learning, in addition to numerous books and various reviews of the literature, have been published since the 1980s. Though continued systematic research is still needed, especially in the area of including students who require an adapted curriculum and multiple supports, results are quite encouraging. An extensive review of the literature is beyond the scope of this chapter (refer to Johnson & Johnson, 1989; Slavin, 1990, 1991, 1995); however, some of the promising benefits are highlighted in Figure 5.2. Continued research in this area will increase our understanding of the impact that cooperative learning has on specific student outcomes.

Components

Cooperative learning classrooms are places where heterogeneous groups of students learn to work together, accept one another, and achieve positive academic and social outcomes. Competition is replaced by cooperation, mutual support, and shared accomplishments. Though this may sound idealistic, there are several structured models of cooperative learning that support these outcomes (see Sharan, 1994, for detailed descriptions). All models for cooperative learning share what Johnson and Johnson (1989) identified as the five essential components of cooperative learning, which distinguish cooperative learning from generic groupwork:

1. *Positive interdependence:* All group members work together toward a shared goal. Each student plays a key

---

When cooperative learning is appropriately implemented, students achieve better outcomes than in individual or competitive situations.

- Slavin (1990) analyzed 68 studies of cooperative learning and found that in 72% of the studies, cooperative-learning groups outperformed control groups.
- Johnson and Johnson's (1989) meta-analysis of research found that achievement was higher when students worked cooperatively than when they worked individually.
- The key components of cooperative learning that are credited for these learning outcomes are positive interdependence, individual accountability, equal opportunity for success, cooperative skill instruction, and learning strategy instruction (Johnson & Johnson, 1989; Slavin, 1990).

There is strong support for cooperative learning as an approach to achieve academic gains in diverse classrooms, but how diverse should the classroom be?

More study will help address the following questions:

- Can cooperative learning facilitate the development of higher-order thinking skills (Davidson, 1985)?
- To what extent is academic achievement in students with disabilities meaningfully supported by cooperative learning? What accommodations will enable students with difficulty in attending to others, socially interacting, or communicating in general to achieve within the context of cooperative learning groups (Cosden & Haring, 1992; McMaster & Fuchs, 2002)?

Research suggests that cooperative learning is associated with gaining interpersonal skills and acceptance of differences.

- Acceptance of students with disabilities
- Positive relationships among members of different ethnic groups
- Improvements in interactions between students with disabilities and those without
- Increased academic engagement during group sessions
- Increased learning by all group members, including elementary students with autism and multiple disabilities (Dugan et al., 1995; Hunt et al., 1994; Slavin, 1995)

Figure 5.2.   Research findings and issues surrounding cooperative learning.

role in the group's success and takes responsibility for supporting the other group members. The group is successful only when each member achieves the goal.

2. *Individual accountability:* Each group member is required to learn the material or meet his or her individual goal. Group members may quiz one another to check for understanding. As the classroom environment becomes a cooperative community, students begin to develop a sense of caring for others and encourage each other to do their best.

3. *Cooperative skills:* Cooperative skills are the subset of social skills that involve synergistic interactions between group members participating together in group activities (e.g., taking turns, active listening, resolving conflicts). Teachers may instruct students in the use of cooperative skills through modeling, guided practice, and feedback.

4. *Face-to-face interaction:* Cooperative learning tasks require students to physically group together and interact with one another during activities. Depending on the specific activities, desks or chairs can be rearranged in small circles with a shared working surface; younger students often cluster together on the floor.

5. *Group processing:* During a cooperative learning activity, students are asked to reflect on how well they are functioning as a team. Group strengths and weaknesses are identified. Based on the identified group needs, students set improvement goals for the group.

To initiate cooperative learning groups in a classroom, teachers will need to take several steps. Of course, becoming conversant (through reading, observing colleagues, and attending in-service training) with the essential components and strategies comes first. Next, teachers may want to begin by teaching students some basic cooperative skills (e.g., listening, giving helpful feedback, reaching consensus) and integrating a selection of simple cooperative learning structures into their teacher-led instruction. For example, structures such as Think–Pair–Share and Numbered Heads Together (see Figure 5.3) are effective tactics to use during the review-and-connect or guided-practice portions of a direct-instruction lesson.

Once some of the basic cooperative learning components and strategies are understood, formal cooperative learning groups organized using the eight steps detailed in the next section can be implemented. These formal cooperative groups can be used for students to

- Complete independent practice activities (e.g., a science experiment, a set of mathematical problems)

- Teach themselves certain new information or skills (e.g., gather and read text and electronic resources about a social science or literature topic)

- Complete unit projects (e.g., produce a play, prepare a multi-media presentation about an animal species or historical event)

- Engage in discovery learning and inductive lessons (although additional adaptations typically would be needed to make such lessons suitable for learners with more challenging disabilities)

As even more experience and comfort with cooperative learning are gained, teachers are encouraged to explore more specific cooperative learning models (see Sharan, 1994), such as those that are briefly summarized in Figure 5.3. These models of cooperative learning correspond to particular subject areas, specific learning tasks, and age groups more

Cooperative learning structures that can be used with a variety of curriculum content

Think–Pair–Share

- The teacher gives the students a method for finding a partner (e.g., the person directly across the table).
- The teacher poses a question: "How many planets are in our solar system?"
- The teacher calls for time to "Think," and each individual student thinks or writes the answer.
- The teacher calls for time to "Pair," and the partners compare answers; if they disagree, they work together to find the correct answer.
- The teacher calls for time to "Share" and can then call on any student because everyone has had a chance to find the correct answer.
- The Think–Pair–Share structure is appropriate for warm up/review periods, checks for understanding, guided practice, and skill drills (Kagan, 1990).

Numbered Heads Together

- Students get into their cooperative groups and number off sequentially.
- A question or problem is presented to the students.
- The students in each group put their heads together, discuss the answer, and make sure everyone knows the answer and can explain it.
- The teacher calls a number (a spinner or die can be used), and everyone with that number stands or raises a hand and can be called on by the teacher.
- This structure is suited to checks for understanding (e.g., of material that the group has learned through reading), guided practice, and lesson summary and closure (Kagan, 1990).

Jigsaw

- The material to be learned or studied is divided among the members of each cooperative group.
- All group members who have been assigned the same material read and study together in "expert" groups.
- Group members go back to their original cooperative groups and teach their part of the material to their team.
- The Jigsaw structure is appropriate for the input portion of the lesson (i.e., instead of the material to be learned coming from a lecture or by each individual reading all of the material), project-based learning, and reviews (Johnson & Johnson, 1999).

Cooperative learning models that are designed for specific curriculum areas

Team-Assisted Individualization (TAI)

- Students work in heterogeneous groups of four or five, but each student has individualized materials and goals.
- Team members are responsible for helping one another, checking each other's work, and keeping track of the team's score.
- The teacher monitors all groups and may teach small groups of students while the others are involved in their teamwork.
- TAI is designed specifically for mathematics. Research has shown its superiority to traditional math instruction for mixed groups of students with and without mild disabilities (Slavin, Madden, & Leavey, 1984).

Cooperative Integrated Reading and Composition (CIRC)

- Students work on heterogeneous cooperative teams that are rewarded for team success and are responsible for ensuring the accountability of each team member.
- The program combines teacher-directed small-group instruction with team practice in oral reading, spelling, decoding, vocabulary, and composition.
- CIRC is designed for reading, writing, and language arts instruction in the upper elementary grades (Jenkins et al., 1991; Slavin, Stevens, & Madden, 1988; Stevens & Slavin, 1995).

Figure 5.3. Cooperative learning structures and models. (*Sources:* Jenkins, Jewell, Leicester, Jenkins, & Troutner, 1991; Johnson & Johnson, 1999; Kagan, 1990; Slavin, 1990; Slavin, Madden, & Leavey, 1984; Slavin, Stevens, & Madden, 1988; Stevens & Slavin, 1995.)

closely and, thus, will be more useful than other models.

Organizing a Cooperative Learning Lesson

Organizing class activities so that students learn cooperatively is not a trivial process. Teachers cannot simply place students into groups and tell them to work together on a task. The lesson needs to be planned. In order to meet the individualized learning needs of each student, teachers will need methods to modify schoolwork so that students can participate actively alongside peers in ways that are meaningful while also acquiring useful knowledge and skills. (*Modifying Schoolwork* [Janney & Snell, 2004], a companion book in this series, provides detailed information regarding methods of modifying schoolwork so that all students can actively participate in a classroom.)

Cooperative learning groups function best when teachers establish familiar routines and teach them to students. For example, methods for assigning roles, moving into groups, distributing materials, self-evaluating, and reporting back to the large group should all be accomplished through established routines. It is almost always useful to provide students with visuals to cue them in completing the steps of the task assigned to the group. Other helpful elements to include on a poster or checklist include a list of the roles to be filled by group members and the amounts of time allotted to various task steps. These visuals might be absolutely necessary to enable some students with disabilities to participate in the activity; however, they also are helpful for all learners.

The organization of cooperative learning groups usually includes eight steps.

Step 1
Determine Group Lesson Goals

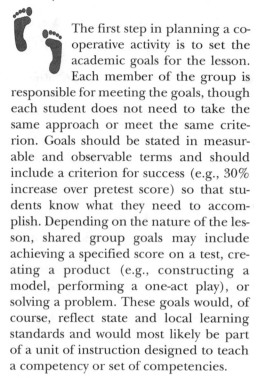 The first step in planning a cooperative activity is to set the academic goals for the lesson. Each member of the group is responsible for meeting the goals, though each student does not need to take the same approach or meet the same criterion. Goals should be stated in measurable and observable terms and should include a criterion for success (e.g., 30% increase over pretest score) so that students know what they need to accomplish. Depending on the nature of the lesson, shared group goals may include achieving a specified score on a test, creating a product (e.g., constructing a model, performing a one-act play), or solving a problem. These goals would, of course, reflect state and local learning standards and would most likely be part of a unit of instruction designed to teach a competency or set of competencies.

Step 2
Determine Individual Objectives

 To ensure individual accountability and to monitor progress, teachers should set individualized modifications and accommodations, including any individualized objectives for students who need them. Usually, group members with IEPs who have individualized objectives will have *simplified* or *reduced* versions of teammates' goals. A few students may have social-communication or motor objectives related to task participation, with less emphasis on academic content. Other students may have other accommodations in materials, assistive devices, or personal support.

Step 3

Assign Students to Groups and Arrange Seating

Cooperative groups are usually heterogeneous with respect to ethnicity, gender, ability, and socioeconomic status. At the beginning of the school year, when the teacher is unfamiliar with the individual students in the class, students may be randomly assigned to groups; however, once the teacher is familiar with students' academic levels and social skills, heterogeneous groups can be systematically created to form base groups. Occasionally, teachers may appoint temporary or "ad-hoc" groups for short-term projects while still relying on the base groups. Teachers also might allow students to create their own groups (self-selected groups) for some projects; however, this often leads to homogeneous groups (e.g., a peer network of high achievers in one group). Typical groups range in size from two to six students. Base groups should be rotated routinely to ensure that every student has an opportunity to work cooperatively with each one of his or her classmates.

In order to ensure face-to-face interaction, teachers also will need to consider the seating arrangement. If students are not already seated in clusters, planning should determine the method for directing students to help rearrange the furniture and/or to move to other locations.

Step 4

Assign Roles

Assigning group roles allows students to take responsibility for specific tasks during the group activity and fosters positive interdependence. Roles can be task re-

lated or process related. Teachers may assign roles that are well suited to the students' skills, or students may be asked to select roles that match their particular interests and skills. Figure 5.4 lists several cooperative group roles typical to cooperative groups (Johnson et al., 1994; Putnam, 1997). The roles of facilitator, recorder, reporter, and timekeeper are essential; others may be used as needed, depending on the task, students' ages, and so forth. Teachers can create a poster or other visual that lists the roles and their definitions and then rehearse the requirements for assigned roles prior to students' moving into groups.

Step 5

Determine Materials Needed

Getting, distributing, and returning materials is often a group role assigned to students; however, teachers will want to list and make accessible the materials students will need to meet both their group and individual goals. Giving each group only one set of materials is one way to promote positive interdependence among teammates.

Step 6

Target Cooperative Skills

Cooperative skills are those social and teamwork skills that are necessary for effective group participation. Younger students, typically, will need to learn skills such as staying with the group, sharing materials, taking turns, contributing ideas, and encouraging others. Secondary students may need skill development in active listening, giving and receiving constructive criticism, paraphrasing, time management, and conflict resolution.

Checker	Makes sure that each group member understands and agrees with the answer
Encourager	Encourages all group members to participate, and reinforces them for doing so
Facilitator, leader, or guide*	Runs the agenda, ensures that the group process is followed and keeps the group on task
Materials manager	Brings materials to the group and returns them to their place afterward
Noise controller	Monitors the noise level in the group and reminds others when they are too loud
Reader	Reads the problems, directions, or other written material aloud for the group
Recorder*	Documents the work of the group, takes notes, and writes answers
Reporter*	Reports the group's response to the large group if there is a "report out" session at the end of the cooperative group activity
Runner, courier, or scout	Goes to teachers for answers to questions, carries messages to other groups, and takes the group product to its destination
Summarizer	Summarizes the discussion or decision reached by the group
Timekeeper*	Periodically alerts the group to how much time remains

Figure 5.4. Cooperative group roles. (*Sources:* Johnson et al., 1994; Putnam, 1997.) (*Essential roles.)

Some students with disabilities may need help with cooperative skills related to their specific disabilities or skill repertoires; others will simply need to improve the cooperative skills in which they are weak (Cosden & Haring, 1992). For example, students with more severe disabilities may benefit from learning skills including recognizing and greeting group members and developing motor and attending skills to partially participate in group activities. Students with mild disabilities may need skills such as asking appropriate questions, asserting ideas in respectful ways, and listening to others in the group.

In order for students without disabilities to benefit from interactions in cooperative learning groups with members who have disabilities, a small repertoire of individualized skills may be needed:

• Communication skills that let group members interact effectively (e.g.,

being familiar with another student's yes/no or picture system or with his or her augmentative device; knowing how to prompt another student to participate without being obtrusive)

• Collateral peer support behaviors that let group members motivate each other to persist in cooperative group tasks (Cosden & Haring, 1992)

Learning cooperative skills requires instruction. Teachers should target and teach a few skills at a time by naming the targeted skill, giving the reason and circumstances for using it, telling and showing what it looks like, having students rehearse the skill, and giving students helpful feedback on their practice of the skill. Students also should learn to self-evaluate their use of cooperative skills individually and as a team. When giving directions for a cooperative group activity, teachers can ask students to rehearse the cooperative skills that have been targeted (e.g., "What should you do if you disagree with what someone says?" "What are some ways to encourage your teammates?") Teaching cooperative skills can be more difficult for younger students. Some teachers have found that discussions along with T-charts can help students define the social skills in terms that they understand (see first section of Figure 5.5 for example of a T-chart).

For students in several fourth-grade classrooms in which one classmate had autism, Dugan and her colleagues (1995) used the acronym SCORE to aide students in remembering the five social skills that had been targeted:

- Share your ideas with others.
- Correct each other's work.
- Offer praise to each other.
- React to others, but do so calmly.
- Encourage and help other group members.

Teachers first used classroom games to teach the social skills and then refined the skills in the context of cooperative learning social studies groups (Dugan et al., 1995).

Student Snapshot

Susan is a 10-year-old with cerebral palsy and an emotional disturbance. She walks independently but needs some assistance with fine motor tasks. Handwriting is especially challenging; therefore, Susan is learning keyboarding. Susan's social skills are delayed in comparison with those of her peers, and she sometimes has difficulty reading social cues and working cooperatively with others. Susan's accommodations include the use of oral and typed responses in place of written responses, a calculator, alternate-level reading materials, a peer buddy, shortened assignments, and self-monitoring behavior checklists. A teaching assistant works unobtrusively with Susan in the fifth-grade classroom as needed and lends support to the group as a

whole. Susan also attends a daily language arts tutorial with a special education teacher and participates in small-group counseling sessions twice per week.

Because Susan is accustomed to using checklists (for behavioral performance and to complete school tasks), she may benefit from having a checklist of her role responsibilities (e.g., being voice control technician means that you will . . .) and the cooperative skills on which she is working (e.g., ask others questions and listen to their answers; take your turn and let others have their turn).

Step 7

Plan How to Monitor Group Functioning

Cooperative group skills and task accomplishment often are monitored best through observations; teachers rotate among groups and note the cooperative skills they observe students exhibiting as they work in their groups. A grid with the alphabetized class list on the left side and the target cooperative skills written across the top can provide a simple way to code what teachers observe. Correctly used skills can be marked with a +, those prompted by peers or adults marked with a *P*, and those missing or deficient marked with a –. Analyses of these grids will help teachers determine when group or individual instruction may be needed. Some of this teaching can occur naturalistically, as teachers intervene when necessary to prompt, model, and reward the use of cooperative skills.

Step 8

Evaluate and Give Feedback

At the close of a cooperative group lesson, group members can be asked to provide their teacher with self-evaluations of their group's functioning. Evaluation questions can be task-related (e.g., Did

1. **Use a T-chart to define social objectives with children:**

Ask students to focus on one specific behavior on which they are working and brainstorm how it looks and sounds. Use a T-chart (as shown below) to record the students' definitions.

Using Quiet Voices

Looks Like	Sounds Like
Faces together—one foot apart	Whispering
Sitting close together	"One foot voice"
Knees touching	Soft voices
Looking at each other	Very quiet

2. **Process cooperative group lessons:**

Have groups process at the end of the group session for a few minutes.

- Initially, ask groups to use a smiley-face chart to evaluate themselves (chart below on left).
- Later, ask groups to answer two open-ended questions (chart below on right).

Have the entire class process afterward by discussing what happened.

- While students remain in their groups, facilitate discussion of the instructional and social objectives of the lesson.
- Have students refer to their group data to talk about how well their group did and what they will work on for the next lesson.
- Use your data to provide feedback to groups and point out positive examples of how students worked together.

Initial Group Processing Chart	**Later Group Processing Chart**
How did we do?	**Our social skills:**
We used quiet voices: ☺ 😐 ☹	How did we do?
We did our roles: ☺ 😐 ☹	What will we work on next?
Sign here: _____	Sign here: _____

3. **Monitor the use of social skills:**

- Discuss the skills before groups start.
- Inform students that the class will talk together about how well they did after the groups meet.
- Tell students that you will observe how they work throughout the group lesson.
- Move about from group to group and provide reminders and assistance on instructional and social objectives if needed.
- Collect data during the lesson on students' social objectives by jotting codes by students'/groups' names (see chart that follows).

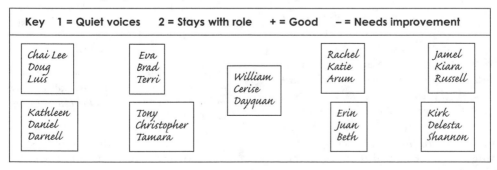

Figure 5.5. Methods teachers used with first graders to define, monitor, and process cooperative group skills. (From Ayres, B., O'Brien, L., & Rogers, T. [1992]. *Working together, sharing and helping each other: Cooperative learning in a first grade classroom that includes students with disabilities.* Syracuse, NY: Syracuse University, The Inclusive Education Project; reprinted by permission.)

we complete the task?) as well as process-related (e.g., Did we all fill our roles? Did everyone participate?). The teacher can then share feedback with the groups. Simple group-processing charts can help groups self-evaluate their progress in using particular social skills. (The second section of Figure 5.5 provides some examples applied to younger elementary students that are applicable, with modification, to older students.)

Figure 5.6 provides a cooperative learning lesson plan and a cooperative learning group agenda that illustrate the use of these eight steps. The lesson plan and agenda are for a fifth-grade science lesson and include adaptations for Susan, discussed previously.

Considerations for Individuals with More Extensive Disabilities

Some readers might wonder if it really is possible for all group members to achieve the group learning goals when one member has more extensive physical and/or intellectual disabilities. Others might question whether group members who have difficulty attending to and completing tasks due to short attention spans and distractibility will learn or will let others learn. Finally, some teachers and parents may ask, "What about those students who are disruptive? Will they learn or will they just disrupt the learning of others?" These are legitimate concerns. Two studies lend clear support to the likelihood that all students, including students with autism and multiple disabilities, can learn in a cooperative group context when the teacher preparation and support are adequate (Dugan et al., 1995; Hunt et al., 1994); however, the success of cooperative learning strategies often depends on the teacher's *preparation* for a cooperative learning group lesson and the teacher's supports given *during* the ongoing cooperative group activity.

Preparation

Teachers should work and plan in the following ways to prepare for cooperative learning groups that have members needing more support:

- Work collaboratively with other teachers and support staff.

- Set reasonable learning objectives, individualized for as many students as necessary.

- Make the necessary adaptations in materials, the way the task is designed, and the physical environment.

- Consider the abilities, behavior, and social networks of students with more extensive needs when determining group composition (e.g., put a nonreader with peers who read well, separate students who have serious behavior problems).

- Make adjustments to suit students who are not fluent in English or students who use alternative communication systems.

- Allow for any IEP accommodations required by students.

- If a student requires direct instruction on social interaction (e.g., staying on task, listening to others), find ways to teach the necessary skills within cooperative groups and at other times. Design behavior support plans with self-management features to be used unobtrusively by students who need them. (*Susan uses her self-management checklist system or is reminded to do so by her buddy; afterward, she reviews her performance by counting up the pluses on her checklist.*)

- Teach the social interaction skills needed by various class members for effective participation in cooperative groups (Cosden & Haring, 1992).

Cooperative Learning Lesson Plan

Content area: *Science* **Date:** *November 1*
Grade: *Fifth* **Teacher:** *Roberta Jones*

Lesson objectives:

1. Group lesson objective(s): *Using a list of 20 names of human bones and a diagram of a skeleton, students will label the bones and achieve a 50% increase over their pretest score.*

2. Cooperative skill objective(s): *Students will take turns, give positive encouragement to all, fill group roles, and give Susan encouragement and prompts only as needed.*

Adaptations/accommodations for individual learning needs:

Student	Adaptations/accommodation(s)	
Susan	*Shortened word list (10 bones)*	*Peer reader (Sandy)*
	Self-monitoring behavioral checklist	*Oral responses*

Materials:

For lesson introduction/review, directions, and closure: *Life-size skeleton model, poster with task steps, cooperative skill data sheet*

For each group: *Skeleton diagram, pictures of bones to cut out, science textbooks, scissors, pencils, crayons or markers, task checklist (illustrated on next page), self-evaluation sheet*

Lesson steps:

In large group: review bone names and functions from yesterday.

1. *Show overhead transparency of skeleton diagram. Demonstrate how to label two bones and find their functions in textbook.*

2. *Give directions for cooperative task (refer to poster); check for understanding. Give definitions of group roles (students respond using thumbs up or thumbs down) and rehearse social skills chorally (refer to wall chart).*

3. *Before dismissing students to move into their base groups, remind the Facilitator from the last cooperative lesson to use the Role Rotation guide to assign roles for today.*

Summary/closure: *Each group posts its chart on the bulletin board. Discuss group self-evaluations. Award links for group Challenge Chains to groups that completed the task and the evaluation sheet. Remind students of the individual quiz tomorrow.*

Group members with individual goals:

Susan	*Correctly label 8/10 bones*	*Max*	*Correctly label 19/20 bones*
Alan	*Correctly label 17/20 bones*	*Sandy*	*Correctly label 18/20 bones*

Comments:

Pair Sandy with Susan for the tutoring activity.
Remind Susan to complete her self-monitoring checklist when the lesson ends.

(continued)

Figure 5.6. Cooperative learning lesson plan and cooperative learning group agenda for a fifth-grade science unit on the human skeletal system.

Figure 5.6.   *(continued)*

Cooperative Learning Group Agenda

Activity: *Human skeletal system*

Date: *November 1*   **Time:**   *45 minutes*

Task: *Complete the human skeleton diagram by labeling the bones and writing one function of each.*

Members and jobs:

Facilitator: *Sunny*   Reporter: *Danielle*   Scout: *No one*

Timekeeper: *Mike*   Recorder: *Ross*   Materials: *Amber*

Check off each step as you complete it.

☐   1.   Cut out bones.

☐   2.   Give each group member an equal number of bones.

☐   3.   Find information on the function of the bones you have; write it on the bone cutouts.

☐   4.   Think of a way to classify the bones. Make sure everyone agrees.

☐   5.   Color the bones in each category the same color; make a color coding key.

☐   6.   Paste bones on the skeleton diagram. Make sure everyone agrees.

☐   7.   Give your skeleton a name and age; discuss the bone benefits and problems for a person that age.

☐   8.   Work in tutoring pairs to review the names of the bones (2 minutes per student in each role, set timer).

☐   9.   Complete the cooperative group evaluation sheet.

☐   10.   Clean up your area.

☐   11.   Report to the class: How did you classify the bones, and why?

Supports Given During the Lesson

To lend support to students before, during, and immediately after an ongoing cooperative group activity, teachers should take several actions:

- After some initial practice, remind group members of the specific ways they might support some of their fellow group members to enable their participation.

- Circulate among all of the groups, taking care to provide equal attention to each group.

- Use *planned attention,* which 1) is given only as needed, 2) reminds students to do the things they already know regarding working cooperatively and supporting one another, 3) motivates

group members to be less dependent on adults and more dependent on one another, and 4) is systematically diminished from more to less to none.

- Provide ways to generalize peer support of group members with additional learning needs across other classmates and different cooperative activities.

- Take notes on issues that need problem solving and on progress made by groups, use these notes during later discussions with groups and/or among teachers.

Effectively including a student with multiple disabilities or other complex needs within cooperative learning groups does indeed require thoughtful preparation and planning. Figure 5.7 provides an

Individual Adaptations Plan for Cooperative Learning Activities

Student: *Daniel* **School year/semester:** *2005–2006*
Teacher(s): *Lauren James* **Grade:** *Second*

Individualized education program goals:

Daniel will have at least one classroom participation or functional skill objective and one academic objective for each cooperative lesson. Additional incidental learning objectives that relate to the unit may also be targeted. Specific objectives will be determined at the second-grade team planning meeting for each thematic unit.

A. *Classroom participation and functional skill goals*

   Partial participation in cooperative group lessons, with objectives related to motor skills (cut/color/paste, touch-move to count objects, hand items to others), communication, alertness and attention

   Initiate, respond, make choices, reject using recognizable communication cues (yes = head move up; no = head dropped to side) and simple switches

   Use picture schedule and task lists to anticipate and terminate events

B. *Academic goals*

   Cut/color/paste pictures and words

   Identify pictures of 2–3 vocabulary words for each content area unit

   Identify numerals and count objects 1–10

Objectives for participation:

Aim for four opportunities for Daniel to engage in role-related interactions and six opportunities for academic responding (counting objects/recognizing numerals or cut/color paste) during each session. See Daniel's Classroom Participation Plan for directions on performing "Recognize numerals 1–10," "Count items 1–10," and "Cut/color/paste"

Cooperative learning group assignment:

At the beginning of the year, place Daniel in a base group with students from his second-grade class. As Daniel and other students get to know one another, he should rotate groups as other students do; ensure that at least two group members are practiced in understanding his communication and supporting his participation.

Role assignment:

Assign peer partner to share the role of checker, timekeeper, or materials manager with Daniel. Be sure selected peers have been trained in how to ask questions, assist with writing, and hand things to and take things from Daniel. (See peer support training directions, below.)

· *Checker — Daniel and a peer are in charge of checking off a list of task steps as they are completed. The peer shows Daniel the list and asks, "Are we on step 1?" "Did we finish step 1?" and so forth.*

(continued)

Figure 5.7. Daniel's Individual Adaptations Plan for Cooperative Learning Activities.

Figure 5.7. *(continued)*

- *Timekeeper—A peer sets the timer (which shows time available in red) and places it near Daniel. Three times during the activity, the peer asks Daniel, "Is it time to stop?"*
- *Materials manager—If Daniel is in his wheelchair, a peer pushes him to the materials table and places the materials on Daniel's tray. Daniel and the peer then take the materials back to the group. Depending on the materials needed for the lesson, Daniel may be able to hand out materials to each person in the group. If the activity uses individual materials, Daniel passes them out to group members with partial physical support from an adult.*

Positioning and environmental considerations:

If the group meets at a table, position Daniel in his wheelchair; if the group meets on the floor, position Daniel in his adapted chair.

Peer support during cooperative activities:

The peer who is sharing a role with Daniel will sit next to Daniel and support him in filling the role. A second peer will assist with the targeted functional or academic skill. Other peers have learned through peer support sessions how to communicate with Daniel and will be reminded of guidelines (e.g., only one person at a time should help/prompt Daniel).

Training/supervision needed by classmates:

Understand Daniel's ways of communicating (e.g., uses a variety of facial expressions, movements, and vocalizations to indicate likes and dislikes and to interact socially with others)

Ask questions related to participation goals (stand close, make eye contact with Daniel, hold two objects in front of Daniel, and ask, "Daniel, which marker do you want to use?")

Prompt (if Daniel does not respond within 3 seconds)

Understand consequences (do not "second guess"—that is, do not ask the question again after Daniel has given a response)

Provide physical support for motor skills (e.g., pointing, picking up object, coloring/writing, pasting. Daniel's friends from first grade, especially Stacie, Morgan, and Jamel, are very good at this.)

Adult supports during cooperative learning activities:

At the beginning of the year, the special education teacher will support Daniel during cooperative group activities and then will fade support as peers get to know Daniel better. Assistance will be provided when Daniel is filling his role or taking his turn; the teacher will step back to monitor (and assist other groups) in between Daniel's responses.

As adults fade support, they will circulate among all groups; they will not hover over Daniel, but keep an eye on his participation and move in to give more support if a peer interaction is floundering (peers are either doing things for Daniel or forgetting to include him).

example of a format that can be used once a semester to record and share with team members the general plans for adapting cooperative learning groups for a student with extensive support needs. The plan illustrated in Figure 5.7, which was developed for Daniel, a student with multiple disabilities, includes the modified instructional goals that should be addressed during cooperative activities, as well as suggestions for group and role assignments, positioning, and peer supports. Other sources that provide numerous examples of cooperative learning across different age groups and content areas may be consulted for additional possibilities (Ayres et al., 1992; Johnson & Johnson, 1999; Johnson, Johnson, & Holubec, 1993; Nevin et al., 2002; Putnam, 1997; Putnam, 1998; Villa & Thousand, 2002).

PEER TUTORING

Peer tutoring is one-to-one instruction on a particular topic, assignment, or skill by a classmate, a peer, or an older student; it is a well-established general method to promote learning in students. This instructional arrangement is particularly effective in *incremental learning,* in which there is a single correct answer or behavior response that the tutor is able to guide the tutee toward. There is *no single, correct way* to structure peer tutoring programs, but effective programs do have several features in common: careful planning of student pairings and content selection, instruction for tutors in how to tutor, and monitoring by teachers. This section introduces strategies for selecting and training tutors, describes a few examples of program designs that have varying amounts of supportive research, and presents a case application in which cross-age peer tutoring was implemented in a fifth-grade classroom.

Overview

Peer tutoring, which is encompassed by the term *peer-mediated instruction,* has been recommended by many researchers as an alternative or supplemental method to traditional instructional approaches such as lectures and student discussions. Advocates of peer tutoring assert that it provides the following benefits: increased student opportunity to respond, lengthened practice time for skills, and improved cooperation among peers (Arreaga-Mayer, 1998; Greenwood, Terry, Delquadri, Elliott, & Arreaga-Mayer, 1995).

Evidence of the instructional, social, and cost effectiveness of student-to-student tutoring has been mounting since the 1980s. Cohen, Kulik, and Kulik's (1982) meta-analysis found that structured programs that used tutors who knew the content well had better results; in 45 of the 52 studies examined, students who were tutored by older students made more gains than did those tutored by same-age peer tutors. (See Figure 5.8 for more evidence.) Narrative reviews by Maheady, Harper, and Malette (2001) and Utley, Mortweet, and Greenwood (1997) confirmed the overall favorability of peer-mediated instruction and interventions.

Although some might expect that students with behavior problems or intellectual disabilities would not be good candidates for tutoring or being tutored by their peers, evidence suggests otherwise. In their review of 14 studies of peer-mediated interventions for students classified as having emotional or behavioral disorders, Ryan et al. (2004) found positive outcomes across all types of peer-mediated interventions; both same-age and cross-age tutoring were beneficial for students of all ages across all subject areas, with tutors having even more positive outcomes than tutees. In a study examining peer tutors' effectiveness in implementing prompting procedures to tutees with intellectual disabilities, researchers discovered that not only did tutors reliably follow through on assisting their tutees, but the tutees also learned at the same rate with their peers as they did with their special education teacher (Miracle, Collins, Schuster, & Grisham-Brown,

---

Classwide peer tutoring has been effective in

- Improving spelling performances of elementary school students (Kohler & Greenwood, 1990) and students with mild disabilities (Harper, Mallette, & Moore, 1991); improving the spelling accuracy and level of engagement for students with mild intellectual disabilities and their typically developing peers

- Improving literacy skills in elementary-age English language learners and culturally and linguistically diverse elementary students (Greenwood et al., 2001)

- Yielding gains in spelling accuracy and lengthened positive social interactions between peers and classmates with learning and intellectual disabilities requiring intermittent support (Sideridis et al., 1997)

- Increasing the rate of active student responding and reducing competing problem behavior for students with moderate and severe disabilities and their classmates without disabilities (Arreaga-Mayer, 1998)

- Reducing the number of students in need of special education (by seventh grade) and the number of school dropouts (by eleventh grade) (Greenwood, Maheady, & Delquandri, 2002)

Other methods of peer tutoring have been effective in

- Improving reading in students with intellectual disabilities (e.g., Koury & Browder, 1986)

- Improving reading in integrated environments with students who have learning disabilities (Mathes et al., 1994) and autism (Kamps, Barbetta, Leonard, & Delquadri, 1994)

- Teaching adolescents with intellectual disabilities generalized reading of cooking product labels (Collins, Branson, & Hall, 1995)

- Improving math performace for academically at-risk fourth- and fifth-grade students (Fantuzzo, King, & Heller, 1992)

- Teaching middle school students with severe intellectual disabilities to use self-monitoring strategies to improve their classroom survival skills (e.g., getting to class on time, bringing-materials to class) (Gilberts, Agran, Hughes, & Wehmeyer, 2001)

- Teaching health and safety information to students with intellectual disabilities (Reddy et al., 1999)

Evidence of cognitive and affective benefits to the tutors indicates that

- Tutors have increased opportunity to practice learning activities

- Tutors may gain in social status (Franca, Kerr, Reitz, & Lambert, 1990)

Figure 5.8. Evidence of the effectiveness of peer tutoring.

2001). Peer tutoring programs offer a promising approach for increasing academic and social outcomes for diverse groups of learners.

Selecting Tutors

The tutor–tutee relationship must be positive in order to work well. This requires helping students accept individual differences and work cooperatively. Several authors have offered guidance for selecting tutors that is relevant to establishing positive relationships. For example, Campbell and Campbell (1995) suggested that it is important to assess and consider

1. What students know about individuals with diverse learning abilities

2. What students believe to be true about individuals with diverse learning abilities

3. How students interact with individuals who have diverse learning abilities

Based on these considerations, educators can design instruction for students to understand *real* versus *perceived* differences between themselves and their peers with diverse learning abilities.

Careful selection of tutors is likely to prevent many difficulties in implementing a peer tutoring program. Strictly speaking, peer tutors are peers of the same age, though they may be from the same or different classrooms and of the same or different abilities. Strain and Odom (1986) offered a set of guidelines that are useful for selecting peer tutors of preschool or early elementary school age: choose students who typically comply with teacher requests, have strong attendance records, have age-appropriate interests, have either a positive history or no history with the focus student, and display a willingness and ability to participate. Tutors need not always, however, be the same age as tutees.

Although peer tutoring is not known to inhibit the development of positive social relationships, given that tutors are assigned an instructional role, it is not surprising that researchers have found tutoring interactions between tutors without disabilities and tutees with disabilities to be more task-related or instructional in nature than socially related (Hughes, Carter, Hughes, Bradford, & Copeland, 2002; McMahon, Wacker, Sasso, Berg, & Newton, 1996); however, peer tutoring has been found to improve attitudes and acceptance of high school peer tutors toward students with disabilities (e.g., Clemens, 2002), and there is evidence that tutoring or helping relationships can evolve into social relationships (e.g., Staub et al., 1994). Furthermore, a meta-analysis of the effects of peer tutoring on reading outcomes found that reading gains were similar whether the students with disabilities were tutors or tutees, which indicates that students with disabilities can benefit from filling either role (Elbaum, Vaughn, Hughes, & Moody, 1999).

Nevertheless, it stands to reason that, as some have written (Van der Klift & Kunc, 1994), peer relationships that are consistently one-way teaching or helping ar-

rangements in which the tutor and tutee are classmates of the same age may sometimes work against the development of positive, reciprocal relationships. Even though the tutee may make meaningful academic skill gains when the interaction is weighted in one direction, it is less likely that mutual interactions will develop or that friendships will evolve. Clearly, there is nothing wrong with help; friends often help each other. The important things to consider are: 1) What is the purpose of the intervention? and 2) What is the overall tenor of the relationship between the focus student and his or her peers without disabilities? A well-designed plan to facilitate peer relationships will include interventions to generate support as well as interventions to promote friendships and purely sociable relationships.

Peer Tutor Training Model

Peer tutors need specific training in order to be effective. The following training components are based on guidelines outlined by Campbell and Campbell (1995):

- *Peer tutoring directions*—Peer tutoring directions consist of an instructional sequence and a script for teaching a particular task. The sequence provides the order of teaching; the tutoring script states exactly what the tutor says to the student, the reinforcement and correction methods the tutor should use, and strategies to collect data.

- *Session information*—The teacher determines the materials that will be needed, the length of time of the tutoring session, and the location where the session will be held.

Tutors are trained using five general steps

1. *Model tutoring*—The teacher models the tutoring process with the tutor.

2. *Guided practice*—The tutor practices his or her role with the teacher, who plays the tutee; the teacher then provides feedback on the tutor's performance.

3. *Supervised practice*—The tutor practices with a typically developing classmate who role-plays the tutee and gives the tutor additional practice time. The teacher observes and then provides feedback.

4. *Training*—The peer tutor conducts a session with his or her assigned tutee. The teacher observes and provides feedback following the session. The teacher conducts periodic observations to support the tutor.

5. *Evaluation*—The teacher makes follow-up observations to determine whether the tutor needs additional training or if any other changes are needed (e.g., materials, teaching method).

This approach to peer tutoring is strikingly different from merely directing two students to "take turns being the teacher." Because training and supervision are essential features of this peer tutoring approach, it may be useful for a team of teachers (e.g., two second-grade teachers, a first- and a fifth-grade teacher) to work together to establish a peer tutoring program. Once the peer tutoring process is in place and supported by a group of teachers, it should not be overwhelming and can, therefore, be maintained for years.

Designs for Peer Tutoring Programs

There are many program designs for implementing peer tutoring programs. Most tutoring programs contain six elements: 1) partner pairing strategies, 2) teaching roles for tutors, 3) regularly scheduled sessions, 4) materials adapted for tutoring,

5) frequent tests to evaluate learning, and 6) teacher monitoring of tutoring activities (Greenwood, Delquadri, & Carta, 1999). Classwide peer tutoring (CWPT) is an example of a *reciprocal approach* to tutoring, as peers alternate in their roles of tutor and tutee. Unlike reciprocal peer tutoring, other peer tutoring models utilize fixed roles, where one student always serves as the tutor, and the other always is the tutee. Fixed tutor/tutee roles are used in cross-age tutoring programs and in several incidental approaches to peer tutoring, where one student may have disabilities and the other does not.

Classwide Peer Tutoring

Juniper Gardens Children's Project first developed CWPT in the late 1970s as an intervention for improving children's learning in urban classrooms (Delquadri, Greenwood, Whorton, Carta, & Hall, 1986). Researched initially as a successful approach for building academic skills for all participants and, more recently, for building social interaction skills between students with and without disabilities, the CWPT program involves tutor–tutee pairs who work together on competing teams, with each member taking a turn as both tutor and tutee. The following are key elements of the CWPT procedure (Greenwood et al., 1999):

1. The teacher introduces or reviews material to be learned.

2. The teacher prepares the content materials that will be tutored (e.g., reading passages, spelling word lists, math fact lists).

3. New partners are assigned each week.

4. A partner pairing strategy is applied (e.g., high-performing student with low-performing student), and the class is divided into teams that are balanced in ability.

5. Reciprocal tutoring is used, during which paired students alternate roles during a session; the teacher may use a timer to indicate the end of a 10-minute period for each partner as the tutor and then as the tutee (e.g., the role of the tutor was to read a word from the week's spelling list, the role of the tutee was to spell the word out loud and write it down).

6. Teams compete for the highest team point total.

7. Individual tutees earn points contingent on their performance (e.g., two points for correct answer, one point for corrected answer).

8. Tutors provide immediate error correction to tutees.

9. Individual and team scores are posted in the classroom (e.g., individual points were added daily and logged on the team's chart, individual and team points were added at the end of the week to determine the winning team and the three best spellers of the week).

10. Social rewards are given to the winning team.

These 10 generic steps involved in CWPT can be modified to suit individual learners and classrooms. The materials used in CWPT are important. Reciprocal tutoring involves the random pairing of students, though one student should have higher academic ability. Each member of the pair alternates between being the tutor and being tutored. Therefore, for peer tutoring to work effectively, teachers must design individualized materials (e.g., spelling word lists) and ensure that tutors are adequately trained.

- The learning materials for the *partner with fewer skills* need to suit that student's ability level despite the fact that they will be relatively easy for the partner serving as tutor. Tutor training and classroom practices should emphasize an individualization philosophy: "Just because we are in the same class does not mean that we all learn the same things at the same time." Higher-ability tutors need to avoid elitist attitudes in order to fill their tutor role effectively.

- The materials for *partners with more advanced skills* must also be matched to their ability, or the tutoring will be wasted time. When their partners (with fewer skills) are in the tutor role, the materials and training must be organized so that the difficulty level of the tutoring materials does not interfere with the tutor's effectiveness.

Note that, unlike some of the cooperative approaches discussed thus far, some level of competition is encouraged with the CWPT design. Students' rewards depend not just on their own performances but also on the collective performance of their partners and team. As with cooperative learning groups in which students help each other and have interdependent roles, the CWPT approach rotates the tutor and tutee roles, though in a more structured way, with timers to signal turn taking. This feature of reciprocity (or mutual role sharing) promotes cooperative interdependence.

Peer-Assisted Learning Strategies

Peer-Assisted Learning Strategies (PALS) is another reciprocal peer tutoring program that combines CWPT with curriculum-based measurement in order to further individualize the skills targeted for each student (Fuchs, Fuchs, Hamlett, Phillips, & Bentz, 1994). PALS can be applied to reading or mathematics; it was originally designed to aid classroom teachers to differentiate instruction for students with learning disabilities.

In PALS mathematics, a computerized curriculum-based measurement system provides teachers with both group and individual reports about the specific skills students have learned (Fuchs, Fuchs, Phillips, & Karns, 1994). The program pairs students by selecting one student who knows the skills and one who doesn't; this system enables teachers to ensure that each student has a differentiated lesson. Both students fill the tutor's role during each session, which combines skill coaching and independent practice. The stronger student serves as "coach" first, presenting questions to the "player" and prompting or correcting him or her as necessary. After the coach and player roles are traded, both partners work independently on problem sheets that include a combination of new and old skills. Finally, the partners trade problem sheets, correct them, and compute their point total for the session.

PALS reading also pairs stronger and weaker readers based on curriculum-based measures. Tutoring sessions include partner reading, predictions, summarizing, and story retelling. Research has provided persuasive evidence of the effectiveness of PALS in improving reading and math achievement for students with and without learning disabilities (Baker, Gersten, Dimino, & Griffiths, 2004; Mathes et al., 1994).

Combining Peer Tutoring and Cooperative Learning Groups

Adding reciprocal peer tutoring to cooperative learning groups is an effective means for providing group members with directed practice on targeted concepts or facts; in addition to working together as a whole group to achieve a specified goal, students would pair up to briefly review the learning matter, then rotate roles. Students could start with 10 minutes of peer tutoring to review materials from the previous lesson, then add new material just prior to moving into cooperative groups. A brief tutoring session also might be placed at the end of the cooperative group activity to review or increase students' proficiency in the major concepts that the group activity addressed.

Cross-Age Tutoring Programs

There are two basic types of cross-age tutoring programs. The first type involves older students who are performing successfully at their grade level and are familiar with the subject matter tutoring younger students who are just learning the material. The age difference between the tutor and tutee facilitates a positive, mentoring relationship. These tutoring programs focus on meeting the learning needs of younger students, who may be performing below grade level in the general education curriculum or learning functional, social-communication, and other individualized skills in the context of school routines and classroom instructional activities. As with any approach, tutor training and careful planning between the students' teachers is essential for program success.

Student Snapshot

 Susan's team decided that she would benefit from having an older student tutor her rather than one of her classmates, which they thought might interfere with the development of social relationships between Susan and her peers. Once Susan agreed to the idea, her special education teacher, Ms. Bradley, worked with the seventh-grade team to identify 10 students who wanted to fulfill the middle school service requirement by learning something about teaching. These students worked with Ms. Bradley to learn the tutoring methods (see

Tutoring Guide

Subject: *Math* **When:** *11:30 to 12:00*

Skill: *Additional facts* **Where:** *Reading alcove in classroom*

Performance: *When presented with single-digit addition facts on flash cards, Susan will correctly solve 9 out of 10 facts.*

Materials: *Flashcards*   *Data collection form*   *Pencil*   *Card box*

Student to be tutored (teacher): *Susan (fifth grade, Ms. Berlier)*

Tutor/teacher: *Marie (seventh grade, Mr. Randell)*

Tutor directions:

1. *Present one flashcard at a time.*

2. *Wait 5 seconds for Susan to respond.*

3. *If response is correct, say, "Good thinking," and record a "+" next to that fact on the data form; return the card to the card box.*

4. *If no response or an incorrect response is given, record a "0" next to the fact on the data form. Then, model the correct response (e.g. say, "6 + 7 = 13; what is 6 + 7 ?"), and allow Susan to respond again following the correction.*

5. *If Susan makes a correct response following a correction, say, "You got it." If she makes an error after a correction, model the correct response and place the card at the bottom of the stack. Present this card again at the end of the session.*

6. *Present the next item.*

Reinforcement: *Praise Susan each time she responds correctly (e.g., "Good job").*

Correction procedure: *Model the correct response, and allow Susan to respond again following the correction.*

Evaluation: *Record a "+" for correct responses on the first try and a "0" for incorrect responses.*

Figure 5.9. Tutoring guide for Susan's seventh-grade tutor. (From Campbell, P.C., & Campbell, C.R. [1995]. *Building inclusive schools: Module 5. Peer involvement. Skills for involving nondisabled peers in the inclusive education school.* [p. 17]. Lawrence: University of Kansas; adapted by permission.)

Figure 5.9). Then, in cooperation with their homeroom teachers and the fourth- and fifth-grade classroom teachers who had identified 10 students (including Susan) needing tutors, they paired tutors and tutees and selected days and times for the tutors to walk to the elementary school that adjoined the middle school and work with the fourth- and fifth-grade students. Aside from meeting her academic goals, Susan also made friends in the school she would be attending the following year.

In addition to the tutees' learning the necessary information, a second model of cross-age tutoring focuses on the learning that occurs for tutors as a function of their teaching role (Gartner & Lipsky, 1990). This arrangement can be particularly useful for tutors who are performing below their grade level. These tutors are paired with younger students who are also performing at a lower grade level, allowing the tutor to benefit via the teaching process while the tutee learns the information. A variation of this procedure could institute cross-age tutoring across two entire classes, one of older students and one of younger students. Some teachers use this approach for "drop everything and read" (DEAR) time, using cross-age tutoring pairs to facilitate reading at the lower grade level.

Students with disabilities are often neglected as potential tutors because they are seen as the students who need help; however, providing these students with opportunities to serve in the tutoring role can be quite beneficial. With adequate planning and training, students with disabilities can fill the role of tutor by using the CWPT model or a cross-age tutoring program design. Gartner and Lipsky (1990) described an innovative program implemented through Brigham Young University in which children with disabilities tutored peers with and without disabilities in areas such as sign language and reading. This program demonstrated that students with disabilities could learn to perform effectively as tutors; both tutors and tutees improved academically, and many tutors also experienced increased social acceptance as a result of tutoring typically developing peers (Gartner & Lipsky, 1990).

PEER NETWORKING

Peer networking is a peer-mediated intervention model in which a small group of peers serves as tutors and social supports for a student with disabilities. This approach is typically reserved for focus students who have moderate or severe disabilities and need networks of peer support to assist them in becoming a part of the social world of their schools and classrooms. The majority of investigations of this approach to peer support have examined peer networks that were designed to improve the social and communication

skills of students with disabilities as a means of enhancing their peer interaction and acceptance.

The peers recruited for a peer network may have had prior or current contact with the focus student through a mainstreamed class, a common interest or hobby (e.g., sports, music), living in the same neighborhood, or having some other shared experience. Membership, however, should be purely voluntary; peers and focus students should be given opportunities to end their participation if desired. A group of four to five friends from an existing social network appears to be a feature that is advantageous for promoting interactions.

Peer networks have been implemented successfully for students with autism and their peers (Garrison-Harrell, Kamps, & Kravits, 1997). Fifteen first-grade students without autism were selected to form five-person peer networks for three students with autism. The typically developing peers were taught 1) how to use the focus student's augmentative communication system, and 2) social interaction skills such as initiating, responding, complimenting, and sharing during eight 30-minute training sessions implemented during a 2-week period. Focus students with autism also were taught to use their augmentative communication systems in one-to-one teaching sessions. Each peer network and a focus student with autism then participated in group activities across three settings: interactive cooperative group activities, lunchroom conversations, and either language arts or recess. The peer network intervention increased focus students' use of their communication system and the duration of their social interaction across all three settings. In addition, focus students' peer ratings by both network peers and other classmates improved, and all network peers indicated that they would be willing to be included in network activities again the following year.

Peer networking is especially well suited for middle and secondary schools, where peer groups are not so closely aligned with membership in a particular classroom group. Haring and Breen (1992) organized peer networks for two middle school teenagers, one with autism and the other with an intellectual disability. Through weekly meetings with students, adult facilitators worked to minimize their role in problem solving and encouraged peers to take control of the group.

The majority of the network members' scheduled contacts occurred during the 5-minute breaks between classes and during their half-hour lunch periods (Haring & Breen, 1992). Peers met regularly to plan and evaluate their progress; the focus student they supported was included in these meetings, which members reported as being enjoyable—a time when a group of friends could gather at school. Each of the focus students made noticeable increases in the frequency and quality of their social interactions with peers after the social network intervention was implemented.

Hughes and her collaborating researchers (2000) implemented a peer networking intervention with five students with extensive support needs and 13 general education volunteers (some of whom were enrolled in a peer buddy course). Fifty-eight other general education students also volunteered to be involved during the generalization phase of the project. Individualized communication books with line drawings representing age-appropriate topics for conversation were created for the focus students. Peer trainers were provided with a script to follow as they taught the focus students to self-prompt their use of the communication book by turning a page, pointing to the picture, and asking a question of one or more words about the picture.

The peer-mediated communication book training yielded a number of positive outcomes: increased appropriate initiations to both peer trainers and peers who had volunteered to be generalization partners; increased number of conversational topics discussed; and satisfaction from the focus students, who reported that they had more friends following the intervention (Hughes et al., 2000).

There is no single model for designing and implementing peer networks, but several general steps are followed (Haring & Breen, 1992; Hughes et al., 2000):

1. Select focus students who could benefit from improved social participation and peer support and who agree to be involved.

2. Recruit peer volunteers who share classes with or have had other contact with the focus student and/or share interests; four or five peers seems optimal.

3. Meet with peer network members to:
   - Discuss the purpose of the network and why it is needed (e.g., quality of life, teach skills through modeling).
   - Provide any necessary information about the focus student's special needs, ways of communicating, and so on.
   - Train peer network members in ways to help, communicate with, provide assistance to, and/or teach the focus student. An adult facilitator may conduct some training alone with peers, some alone with the focus student, and some during peer interactions.

4. Map the focus student's and peers' schedules to determine times to teach and/or socialize. Provide peers with an interaction schedule.

5. Establish a schedule for recording data on targeted skills/behaviors.

6. Establish a schedule for group meetings to check on progress, give feedback, gather peer suggestions, and so forth.

In addition to being an effective approach for teaching social and communication skills and building peer relationships, these social network strategies have some other advantages:

- The strategy is organized around existing peer social networks—students who know and enjoy being with each other and who offer positive peer models for social behavior.

- The focus student is matched to network members so that their interests overlap and camaraderie develops.

- Peer-centered control and problem-solving within networks is shaped; at the same time, the adult's role gradually is minimized.

CONCLUSION

Peer-mediated instructional approaches and interventions are among the most efficient and effective methods for enabling students with and without disabilities to learn alongside each other and to develop interdependent relationships. Cooperative learning classrooms are places where heterogeneous groups of students learn to work together and accept one another while also achieving positive academic and social outcomes. Peer tutoring programs facilitate cooperation among peers and can provide both tutors and tutees with academic and social benefits. Peer-networking interventions can enhance the social and communication skills of focus students, facilitate skill generalization, and increase social acceptance. Various amounts of time, professional development, and implementation support are required for a teacher to become competent in using peer-mediated instruction (King-Sears, 2001); however, teachers with experience in inclusive educational settings see these methods as worth the effort of learning them and repeatedly report satisfaction with their involvement and with the results of interventions—as do participating students with and without disabilities.

Chapter 6

Getting Started and Keeping It Going

Student Snapshot

Jennifer has intellectual disabil- ities and performs at a first- to second-grade academic level. She readily speaks, though she often uses a simpler vocabu- lary than her fifth-grade classmates; she is so- cial but not readily included in class networks. To assess issues they faced with each factor in- fluencing Jennifer's social relationships, team members used the Social Relationship Work- sheet (Figure 6.1). As they focused on each factor, they pooled what they knew and reached agreement; however, in some areas they sought additional information. After re- viewing all areas and isolating influencing fac- tors (left column of worksheet), they identified actions to be taken (right column). Using an Issue/Action Planning Form (Figure 6.2), they discussed possible actions they might take by reviewing and checking the actions listed in the Social Relationship Worksheet's right col- umn and brainstorming others. As the group made decisions about the actions they would take, they identified people responsible and set dates for when these actions would be implemented.

Jennifer's team decided to focus on several things at once. To improve Jennifer's opportu- nities for interaction with classmates, the team planned to improve her one-to-one teaching sessions by adding peers; they also decided to implement weekly cross-age tutoring for Jen- nifer using several eighth-grade students. They thought a tutor would help motivate improve- ment in reading skills and give Jennifer prac- tice with more mature interactions.

Second, they wanted to build peer support and motivate her to interact with peers in age- appropriate ways; to do this, they planned to start a PAL club. Jennifer's team identified spe- cific actions they would take in these areas, determined who would be responsible, and set dates.

For the social competence factor, the team identified issues around a general lack of co- operative skills among class members. They decided to explore classwide social skills using a skills checklist from the ACCESS Program (Walker et al., 1988; suitable for fifth-grade stu- dents and familiar to the special education teacher) and then discussed possible instruc- tion with this program and also in using coop-

erative learning groups. If these seemed needed and feasible, they would seek in- service from the elementary supervisor on co- operative groups and from the special edu- cation teacher on ASSET (Hazel et al., 1981). Jennifer's mom agreed to explore strategies in the generalization component (memberships in 4-H and scouts) and report back at the next monthly meeting.

Consistent with what is stated in previ- ous chapters, it is suggested that schools follow some general guidelines when planning, selecting, and implementing social support plans:

1. Use collaborative teams to make de- cisions and implement actions.

2. Examine the student's current social relationships as the yardstick for iden- tifying needs and judging success.

3. Involve students in the process of planning, problem solving, imple- menting, and evaluating the social support plan.

4. Seek team consensus and then take the simplest, yet still effective, actions first: This often translates into in- creasing social opportunities before undertaking more complex actions.

5. Contextualize teaching by embed- ding it in daily routines and natural social contexts.

6. Don't let supports become barriers to social interaction: Hovering adults, overzealous "helpers," stigmatizing support or instruction, and a failure to fade assistance will hinder natural peer-to-peer contact.

FACTORS INFLUENCING SOCIAL RELATIONSHIPS

Social relationships among and between children are influenced by many factors:

Social Relationship Worksheet

Classroom: *Lynn Harris, fifth grade*　　**School:** *Roundhill Elementary*　　**Date:** *10/4/05*

Focus student(s): *Jennifer*　　**Team members:** *Lynn (fifth-grade teacher), Merrill (special education teacher), Boyce (Jennifer's mom), Ed (physical education teacher), Sally (guidance counselor)*

Factors influencing social participation and relationships	Actions taken by individuals in school, classroom, and home to improve social contexts and skills
1. Opportunity: Being physically present around typically developing peers on a regular basis with routine and spontaneous occasions to interact **Issues?** (Yes) No **List priority issues:** *Too much one-to-one teaching time* **Select indicators:** ○ Percentage of school day spent in inclusive class(es) ● Number of integrated school and community settings in which the student participates ● Number of peers with whom the student has regular interactions during a day or week ○ Percentage of in-class time (or number of routines/activities) spent participating with peers	○ Assign all students to general education classes with needed supports. ○ Address architectural and physical barriers to inclusion (e.g., no ramps, elevators, or curb cuts). ○ Increase time in general education classes. ○ Increase time in other locations in the school. ○ Create during- and after-school social interaction options through friendship groups and peer support clubs. ● Fade one-to-one time with adults. ● Add in peers and increase small-group instruction. ● Integrate student seating in class, at lunch, and during in-school activities. ○ Identify and create integrated community options.
2. Atmosphere: Prevailing staff and student attitudes toward human differences and talents and related values people hold about social relationships, peer support, a competitive versus a cooperative focus, student involvement in the resolution of social concerns, regard for everyone's unique talents, and so forth **Issues?** (Yes) No **List priority issues:** 1. *Class seems less cooperative than last year.* 2. *Respect is lacking across group: respect others' abilities, value your peer groups, listen, and consider other opinions.*	○ Have staff examine values toward ability, disability, and learning. ○ Involve staff, parents, and students in creating a school mission statement. ○ Organize ability- and disability-awareness activities. ○ Organize service activities. ● Hold teacher in-service session on cooperative learning and support for its use in classrooms. ○ Explore alternatives to ability grouping and competitive activities. ○ Hold staff training on social skills and relationships and their facilitation. ● Adopt and use a social skills curriculum. ○ Train staff and students in collaborative teaming and problem solving. ● Offer student forums on social concerns such as teasing and ridicule; engage students in problem-solving school solutions. ○ Increase the number and range of extracurricular opportunities for students to develop their unique talents. *(continued)*

Figure 6.1. Social Relationship Worksheet for Jennifer. (From Breen, C.G., Haring, T.G., Weiner, J., Laitinen, R.E., & Bernstein, D.D. [1991]. Evaluating the inclusion and social competence of students with severe disabilities in community and school environments. In C.G. Breen, C.H. Kennedy, & T.G. Haring [Eds.], *Social context research project: Methods for facilitating the inclusion of students with disabilities in integrated school and community contexts* [pp. 23–53]. Santa Barbara: University of California; adapted by permission.)

Figure 6.1.　*(continued)*

Select indicators: o　Pre/post survey of knowledge of and attitudes regarding disabilities ●　Number/percentage of inclusive extracurricular activities ●　Number/percentage of classrooms with scheduled time for social skills instruction o　Number/percentage of classrooms with scheduled, structured cooperative learning groups	
3.　**Social support and motivation:** Having the needed supports and encouragement from adults and peers to interact socially and build relationships **Issues?** (Yes)　No **List priority issues:** *Jennifer seems to lack motivation for improving her interactions with peers.* **Select indicators:** o　Periodic assessment of student's peer-initiated versus adult-initiated interactions ●　Number of peer support group or peer problem-solving meetings held o　Number of people in each circle of the student's Circles of Friends o　Number of peers who list the student in their Circles of Friends	o　Explore types of adult facilitation that can encourage appropriate social interactions (e.g., modeling, backing off). ●　Explore types of peer support (e.g., peer groups using problem solving and goal setting, friendship groups, natural relationships strategies). o　Adjust and fade adult facilitation and supports. o　Identify interaction problems (e.g., aggression, excess teasing, isolation); plan and use teaching and peer supports to improve student behavior. o　Identify and resolve barriers to social interaction (e.g., schedules, student hygiene, peer network values). o　Improve communication rates by addressing student motivation, communication system, or social skill performance. ●　Involve students; examine the social contexts for interest, variety, age/ability match, cooperative features, participation, and needed modifications. ●　Use or improve peer networks.
4.　**Academic achievement:** Possessing needed academic skills (e.g., in such areas as reading, writing, math, science, social studies, vocational and community training) and the confidence that comes from having and using these skills **Issues:** (Yes)　No **List priority issues:** *Is her reading where it should be? How to improve small-group instruction?* **Select indicators:** ●　Progress data on relevant IEP goals ●　Number of peer tutoring sessions held	o　Add what is needed to enable students to succeed in learning needed skills (e.g., student choice and involvement in IEP and program, incentives for learning, accommodations, environmental changes, modifications in schoolwork that are only as special as necessary). ●　Make use of reciprocal peer tutoring and cross-age tutoring. o　Add cooperative learning methods to science, math, social studies, and literature lessons.

o Number of participatory responses from a student during a particular type of instructional activity (e.g., cooperative learning group for science, small-group reading lesson)	
5. Social competence and interaction skills: Being able to initiate interactions with peers, respond to peers' initiations, and elaborate on the initiations or responses of peers at a typical rate **Issues?** (Yes) No **List priority issues:** *Various social skills are poor across the class.* **Select indicators:** ● Number of group and/or individual social skills instructional sessions o Number of peers with whom the student interacts during a specified activity o Number or rate of peer-initiated and student-initiated interactions during a particular activity (e.g., lunch, a recreational/free time activity, teacher advisory period or class meeting) o Rate of targeted behavior problem during a specified time period	o Adopt and use a social skills curriculum. o Examine skills involved in social interactions, and identify acquisition and performance problems or competing behaviors. o Plan and use teaching methods and peer supports to improve social skill problems. ● Involve students in planning. o Identify student's communication ability; target needed skills (e.g., improve rate, expand vocabulary, improve consistency, augment with communication book/device for clarity). o Check peers' skills using alternative modes of communicating. o Determine nonstigmatizing ways to teach (format, methods) within routine contexts.
6. Maintenance and generalization of relationships: Keeping and extending social relationships as well as remembering and transferring known social skills across different people and school and nonschool settings **Issues?** (Yes) No **List priority issues:** *Improve behavior next year in middle school for Jennifer and several classmates.* **Select indicators:** ● Rate of student's success in using a self-management device/system o Number of student-initiated and/or peer-initiated interactions in a nontraining setting ● Record of number of participants at peer support group meetings over time o Number of people, places, activities, choices made by the student at different times over the course of a school year	o Contextualize any instruction. o Use adult facilitation in natural contexts. ● Fade adult facilitation to self-monitoring. o Teach students to problem-solve; encourage their independent use of these skills. o Teach students to self-manage. ● Involve family. ● Include social support in IEP. ● Plan for transition across classrooms and schools and to community and employment settings.

Issue/Action Planning Form

Student/team/group: *Jennifer and fifth-grade class*   **Date:** *10/11/05*

Team members present: *Lynn (fifth-grade teacher), Merrill (special education teacher), Boyce (Jennifer's mom), Sally (guidance counselor)*

Issue	Planned action	Person(s) responsible	By when
Too much one-to-one instruction	*Add one to two peers to J's math and reading.*	*Lynn, Merrill*	*11/5*
Little interaction with peers at lunch	*Start a PAL club that will eat once a week in old resource room; explore during peer planning.*	*Merrill*	*10/29*
Lack of motivation for improving her social skills; reading skills not progressing fast	*Contact Millie Jones in middle school; draw on her cross-age peer tutoring program for eighth graders.*	*Merrill*	*10/18*
Class social skills need improvement: Respect for different opinions, abilities, friends	*Explore ACCESS program. Use skill assessment on whole class.*	*Lynn, Merrill*	*10/18*
	Plan how to integrate fifth-grade guidance objectives with ACCESS program.	*Lynn, Sally*	*10/15*
Behavior and social group issues in middle school	*Meet with middle school special education teacher to plan spring visitation; call to set date.*	*Merrill*	*End of October*
	Visit middle school and observe lunch and in-between-class routines.	*Merrill, Boyce*	*Early November*

Figure 6.2.   Issue/Action Planning Form for Jennifer.

- Parental resources, social preferences, and values
- Family's socio-economic level
- Neighborhood density, location, and safety
- Child's temperament and emotional self-control
- Presence or absence of disabilities and any counterbalancing abilities, talents, and supports that the child has

- School and classroom a child attends, and the resulting social opportunities and instruction offered
- Student's level of achievement and success

All of these factors, and certainly others, can have an influence on a child's social activities, interaction style, and numbers and types of companions. Although some of these influences originate at the individual and family levels, others may begin within the classroom or school.

"Getting started" usually requires team members to make some *informal assessment* of each of six major factors that influence social participation:

1. Opportunity

2. Atmosphere

3. Social support and motivation

4. Academic achievement

5. Social competence and interaction skills

6. Maintenance and generalization of relationships

Assessment might be directed toward a whole classroom, a group of students who have similar social interaction opportunities, or an individual student. When a factor is found to be weak and specific issues of concern are identified, teams need to plan ways to strengthen the conditions so that supportive social relationships can develop in their school community.

The Social Relationship Worksheet (see Figure 6.1) provides the team with a format to plan school, classroom, and individual student progress. The worksheet lists the six factors that influence social participation and provides a partial list of the effective action strategies that are described in this book alongside each factor. When planning school and classroom improvements, teams should take the following steps:

1. Meet and use the worksheet to *identify any issues, problems, or barriers* that should be overcome for each of the six influencing factors

2. Decide which of the issues should become *targets for problem-solving and taking action*, taking care to address first the issues that have team consensus and a strong influence on social relationships

3. Use an *Issue/Action Planning Form* (see Figure 6.2) to list: issues that will be addressed at this time, actions that will be taken to make improvements in each issue, and who is responsible for taking action and when the action should be taken.

In selecting the issues to address and the actions to take, teams should consider the need to create a *comprehensive* and adequately *intensive* plan that will be *effective* in facilitating social interaction with peers (as well as achievement of cognitive skills and other targeted goals), but also take into account the *practicality* of the interventions (Kohler & Strain, 1999). That is, in designing an action plan for peer support, *select strategies that will be used across the day in a variety of activities, will be executed often enough to make a difference, and are realistic with respect to the degree of adult effort and involvement required.* An assessment of adult effort and involvement must take into account the amount of teacher time needed to plan activities and the amount of active adult involvement required to implement the strategy. The efficiency of teachers' efforts can be enhanced by using some strategies that are less structured and take little adult involvement once they have been initiated, some more structured and/or effortful strategies that will affect a number of students, and a few more intensive, individualized strategies for students with the greatest social needs.

Student Snapshot

 A comprehensive plan to build social competence and social relationships for Melanie, the fourth-grade student with autism, might include four components:

1. *Using naturalistic teaching to shape the use of words, gestures, and symbols to greet, request, and take turns with peers*

2. *Increasing the use of cooperative learning groups and devising ways for Melanie to learn adapted content and practice her social skills with her groupmates*

3. *Devoting class meetings to peer problem solving for all students, and occasionally addressing Melanie's social-communication, relationship, or classroom participation needs (refer to Figure 3.7).*

4. *Establishing a social-communication network of peers who are instructed in ways to initiate, respond, and take turns with Melanie and who may do additional peer problem solving on Melanie's behalf.*

Consider the adult effort and involvement that will be required to implement these strategies, and weigh them against the number of students—in addition to Melanie—who will be positively affected by the implementation of these strategies. Strategy 1, using naturalistic teaching, requires some planning to ensure that it is systematic and consistent across people and environments but is a relatively low-effort intervention.

Strategy 2, cooperative learning groups, will be implemented for the entire class; Melanie's specialized adaptations will be considered as the grade-level team (which includes Melanie's special education teacher) plans its unit activities. Once a semester, the special education teacher will write an Individual Adaptations Plan for Cooperative Learning Activities (refer to Figure 5.7), which will guide the part-time instructional assistant in Melanie's classroom in adapting materials and methods for Melanie.

Strategy 3, peer problem solving, is another global intervention for the entire class. Issues relevant to Melanie may arise spontaneously, or they may be targeted by her core team, which meets for 30 minutes once per month; this also is a relatively low-effort strategy, and, again, the fruits of this approach to peer problem solving will extend to many students.

Strategy 4, Melanie's peer social-communication network, will be the most individualized intervention for Melanie. It will require selecting students, holding several training sessions with them, doing naturalistic teaching, and monitoring the students' interactions with Melanie.

Even if they consider the amount of adult effort and involvement required to implement Melanie's peer support plan to be reasonable, some readers are likely to feel slightly (or even acutely) daunted by the task that lies before them. This can be especially true if a school has not established the *opportunities* and *atmosphere* that create schoolwide conditions that foster supportive peer relationships. Melanie attends a fully inclusive school where the membership of students with disabilities is not questioned, so her teachers and parents do not have to expend effort planning how to address some of the common barriers to social relationships that are found in schools that lack the opportunities and atmosphere to promote inclusive education.

One tactic for maintaining motivation and energy is to seek the affective and instrumental support of colleagues and parents who share an interest in the goal of socially and instructionally including all students. Apprehension also will abate if readers bear these points in mind:

- Strategies that prepare the school environment for inclusion (described in Chapter 2) establish values, attitudes, and perceptions that greatly ease the way for both natural and more highly structured facilitation of positive peer relationships.

- The vast majority of students with and without disabilities who experience difficulties with peer relationships can experience improvements by: 1) being part of a caring and accepting community; 2) participating in whole-class relationship-building activities; 3) being with adults who know how to facilitate equitable, respectful, and interdependent relationships among students; 4) participating in cooperative learning groups and other peer-mediated learning; and 5) learning social skills in natural contexts and through curriculum integration.

- Only a very small proportion of students require individualized peer support plans to address the sorts of communication, behavioral, emotional, and social needs that significantly jeopardize a student's social competence and, hence, his or her peer relationships.

The majority of strategies and methods described in this book are based on solid or very promising research. Teachers who have implemented many of these practices repeatedly report satisfaction with the results and are willing to continue their efforts because of the beneficial outcomes for themselves and their students. This is not to say that building effective peer relationships (or instituting inclusive practices in general) cannot be challenging. Learning any new skill or process can make one feel inept or frustrated; however, seeing the benefits for students can make the challenge worthwhile.

Some of the actions and changes people make in schools can improve the conditions for supportive social relationships, but other actions will make conditions less conducive to social relationships. For example, unique attendance and transportation schedules that are adopted for students with physical and intellectual disabilities could reduce interaction opportunities and complicate extracurricular activities. When teams can coordinate their planning with administrators and communicate their rationale to the larger group (administrators, parents, and peers), unexpected social barriers can often be prevented.

CLASS COMPOSITION

Sometimes, things done with good intentions in schools actually are counterproductive to the formation of positive social relationships among students. As teams complete the Social Relationship Worksheet for their students, they must also be alert to the influence of existing social networks and class distribution on their planned activities. For example, a paraprofessional could be assigned to a student with multiple disabilities in order to address the student's extra support needs; however, in doing so, the student may be hindered or even prevented from interacting with his or her classmates. Other errors that are often made include a failure to recognize the ways in which children and teenagers rapidly change during their school years, the effects these changes have on their social relationships, and the failure of teachers and school staff to make the program modifications that are needed to balance the students' development.

Social Networks within Classrooms

The composition of a classroom, which can be planned by teachers and administrators to a certain extent, can help or hinder the formation of social relationships. Class composition influences a student's social position and the networks to which the individual student belongs. The work of Farmer and Farmer (1996), which studied third- and fourth-grade classrooms; Pearl and colleagues' (1998) study of 59 elementary classrooms including students with mild disabilities; and related work with 16 mainstream elementary classrooms suggests that students with learning disabilities and emotional disturbances are not outcasts in mainstream environments. The majority of these students were members of peer groups and were well-integrated into their classroom's social structure, though not in random ways.

Some patterns and subtleties in the studied students' relationships provide clues about classroom social structures and the social positions of students with disabilities. Each classroom had three distinct clusters (social network groups)—prosocial, antisocial, and shy. The students who filled these roles were influenced by the cluster members' characteristics and the composition of the classroom. Clusters were not randomly formed but seemed to be influenced both by the class composition and the members' characteristics; members were similar to each other with regard to personal and/or social characteristics (e.g., popular girls; shy boys; aggressive, athletic boys; antisocial boys). Like their peers without disabilities, students with mild disabilities who had good social skills were members of prosocial groups or clusters, and those who had social skill impairments were members of antisocial groups. Some clusters had high centrality in the classroom's social structure; others had low. Both boys and girls filled prosocial clusters and held high to low positions within their cluster; however, some students were isolated and not associated with any cluster. There were no cross-gender clusters in these three third- and fourth-grade classrooms.

Farmer and Farmer's (1996) findings, along with the findings of other researchers, have clear implications for planning class composition in ways that will promote positive social relationships for many students.

- Special education classroom cultures were viewed as being "likely to severely constrain students' social development and impede rather than enhance the likelihood that they will learn positive social skills that generalize to other environments" (Farmer et al., 1996, p. 249).

- The behavior of mainstreamed students labeled as having emotional disturbances seemed to vary substantially depending on the availability of compatible partners, suggesting that the number of students with emotional disturbances per classroom be limited to encourage less antisocial behavior.

- Proportionally, more of the mainstreamed students with disabilities (39%) than students without disabilities (31%) held highly prominent membership in a highly prominent peer group (Farmer & Hollowell, 1994). Students with disabilities were not outcasts. Unfortunately, the students with disabilities held these positions because of, not in spite of, their problematic behavior; some teachers commented that these students were "more or less in charge of the social climate of the classroom" (Farmer et al., 1996, p. 250).

Under these circumstances, general education class membership could actually hinder the social development of students with emotional disturbances. Farmer and Hollowell's (1994) research lends support to limiting the number of students with antisocial behavior in a classroom, attending to the overall composition of each class, teaching social skills on a classwide basis, and examining the social networks within a class as part of the plan for fostering positive social relationships. These researchers advised educators to have a critical mass of boys (two or three) receiving gifted services in one general education classroom; this enabled the boys to form a core prosocial group and to support their prosocial behavior and diminish antisocial behavior.

In these classroom studies, the social integration of African American students in classrooms (regardless of whether they received special education services, gifted services, or neither) was less than ideal, particularly for girls. Additional study of larger groups is needed, but two things were found: Girls were not well integrated into the classroom's social structure, and boys were disproportionately members of antisocial clusters. Both race and gender, therefore, play a role in the social structure of a classroom and the social clusters that form; these aspects of classroom composition need to be sensitively considered when designing social support plans.

One clear conclusion is that "the composition of students in a classroom appeared to affect the possible positions any individual would hold within the structure" (Farmer & Farmer, 1996, p. 448). The ways in which teachers can influence class composition from year to year is not a simple issue. Grade-level teams and principals must work cooperatively to plan classes with a balance of students so that class composition is not a barrier to the development of positive social relationships. Although classroom planning is possible in the elementary grades, it is complicated in middle and high school by a variety of factors, including departmental organization, credits and requirements for graduation, class designations (e.g., general, advanced placement, honors), and course entry requirements.

Rule of Natural Proportions

The rule of natural proportions is an important guideline that can help teachers plan their class composition. This rule states that the percentage of students with disabilities in a given classroom should not exceed the percentage expected in the larger school population (e.g., in a school where approximately 10% of the students have IEPs, a classroom of 25 should not have more than 2 or 3 students with IEPs, only 1 of whom might have more extensive support needs). Furthermore, it would be wise to spread out students who are antisocial or who act out and provide the classes to which those students are assigned with the needed supports. This same guideline also advises teachers to avoid an imbalance in gender or racial composition.

An exception to this rule applies to students receiving gifted services; they should be assigned to classrooms in gender-matched groups of two or three students rather than being isolated by themselves. This exception may be more important for boys than for girls; it would allow boys to form a prosocial network and to avoid grouping themselves with antisocial boys or being isolated. Because girls' clusters more often accept the characteristic of "being good at schoolwork," girls getting gifted services appear to be less at risk for membership in antisocial groups or exclusion. Finally, existing supportive relationships and networks for students who have been isolated or socially needy should be maintained when possible.

Building Peer Support Networks within Classrooms

Teachers can use cooperative groups to build peer support within a classroom, particularly when the classroom contains a heterogeneous combination of students. This topic was covered in some detail in Chapter 5; however, Meyer and Henry (1993) suggested some additional ways for teachers to address the issues of isolated students and antisocial or noncooperative social networks that often exist in classrooms. They found that some students who were socially isolated fit the description of being clinically depressed; others were aggressive, engaged in acting-out behavior, and belonged to social clusters in which other students followed their lead. Some of the students had special education labels, although many did not; most were included in general education classes. All of the students disliked school.

Some of the students' peers believed that the students were treated unfairly by teachers or were treated according to a double standard; classroom rules were

General criteria for groups

Each group in the class period should be heterogeneous with respect to

- Gender
- Ethnicity (e.g., African American, Native American, European American)
- Achievement levels in the subject area
- Academic ability
- Preferred in-class activities (e.g., writing versus speaking)

Specific criteria for peer support networking

With rare exceptions, each group should contain no more than one "at-risk" student per group.

If a student receiving English as a Second Language services is in the group, try to also include another student who is bilingual (same first language) but more fluent in English.

Avoid potentially explosive or otherwise negative group combinations (e.g., two volatile students who would set one another off, a "macho" boy with "victims," too many off-task students within one group).

Try to plant one "worker" and/or a "diplomat/peacekeeper" in each of the groups.

Building specific peer supports

For each group, select at least one and possibly two students who might be a potential friend for the student at risk. These matches should

- Be good influences/models
- Have similar academic ability (although doing better academically and/or attending school more regularly)
- Seem to be a good personality match with the at-risk child (How to judge? Use your observations/best hunches.)

Figure 6.3. Criteria for constructing peer support networks. (From Meyer, L.H., & Henry, L.A. [1993]. Cooperative classroom management: Student needs and fairness in the regular classroom. In J.W. Putnam [Ed.], *Children, youth, and change series: Cooperative learning and strategies for inclusion. Celebrating diversity in the classroom* [p. 116]. Baltimore: Paul H. Brookes Publishing Co.; reprinted by permission.)

enforced when these students violated them but bent when more cooperative or more social students violated them. Teachers were not always aware of their differential rule enforcement.

In order to create a community for their students that was more supportive than that of most middle schools, teachers organized themselves into interdisciplinary teams of six to seven teachers, and each team made a 2-year commitment to a group of 135 seventh-grade students. Teams used an assessment device (School Rating Scale; Meyer & Henry, 1993) to identify students who seemed to need peer support. Teams met weekly to share their ideas and impressions and to problem-solve difficulties concerning the focus students and other specific students. Coop-

erative groups, heterogeneous in composition, were organized in each class using the criteria in Figure 6.3. These cooperative groups functioned as peer support networks with the goal of identifying potential friends for students who were at risk for being unable to gain peer support on their own.

Reconfiguring the class into cooperative groups allowed teachers to create peer support networks using criteria and information that each student reported about him- or herself after about 1 month of school; this information included the student's name, grade, gender, race, favorite activity outside school, and preferences specific to the class content (e.g., strengths and interests relating to English class). These groups functioned both as peer support networks and as cooperative learning groups in class and remained intact for a minimum of the 10-week grading period, though sometimes changes were needed. Meyer and Henry reported positive changes in academic progress during the group activities and in social connections with peers.

> Eric is a student who displays few signs of engagement during classroom instruction. During the cooperative learning structure in math class, Eric's behavior and performance changed dramatically. In other classes, Eric would slump in his seat and show all the signs of disengagement—this was most pronounced when the teacher was presenting material in a traditional lecture format. In contrast, during cooperative learning group time, he voluntarily participated and actually led his group through the assignments. He became a group leader, helping those who did not understand, encouraging peers, and keeping the group on task. (Meyer & Henry, 1993, p. 117)

Class composition can have positive or negative effects on social relationships and interactions. For this reason, teachers need to be constantly aware of the interplay between social networks and of the distribution of students by gender, race, ability level, and disability. Planning can help promote the positive effects of diversity; assigning students to cooperative learning groups can help reconfigure peer networks and create the opportunity for isolated students to be included.

SUSTAINING RELATIONSHIPS AFTER SCHOOL

Thus far, this book has focused primarily on the school environment for building social relationships among peers; however, for every school day, there is time after school; for every school week, there is a weekend; and for every school year, there is a summer. The manner in which peer supports and relationships survive vacations depends heavily on the focus student's family and the focus student; however, peer supports and relationships can be positively influenced by team planning as well. When a team is successful in fostering strong social networks for students, the positive forces of the relationships act to sustain them.

Typically, classmates who are friends will talk about one another at home, ask their parents for permission to get together, telephone or e-mail each other, and invite each other to participate in activities. When a focus student is fairly different from his or her peers with regard to ability, means of communicating, or mobility, parents of the student's peers may not be as open to sustaining the relationship; this is often due to fear, a lack of knowledge of and experience with children with disabilities, worry about liability or equipment, and even prejudice. There are several approaches schools can take to help sustain friendships during nonschool hours; however, these approaches vary according to the students' ages, social/cultural protocol in the community and within the students' families, and the schools' comfort in being involved.

Involving Parents

For students in elementary and middle school, parents typically like to know the peers with whom their children participate in after-school activities. Neighborhood schools provide greater proximity among classmates than do systems that bus students with disabilities. Proximity may mean that kids actually live in the same neighborhood, which makes after-school visiting easier. Despite proximity, many parents will be unfamiliar with the parents of their child's classmates.

Teachers can promote cross-classroom familiarity among parents in several ways. First, teachers can share, through Parent

Teacher Association (PTA) meetings and class newsletters, information about the peer support programs (name, purpose, and activities performed) or friendship programs they initiate in their classrooms. Because parental permission will be required for students to participate in these activities, parents will receive some information beforehand. Teachers can send home newsletters and use parent–teacher conferences to update parents on the progress of these groups and to keep parents informed.

Second, teachers can put together class "telephone books," though parental permission will be necessary. Even having a list of each child's name (with or without his or her address, parents' names, and telephone) can be helpful to parents of class members.

Third, family activities might be planned on a classwide, grade-level, or schoolwide basis to bring parents and classmates together more often; activities might include class plays or concerts, potluck dinners, field day events, or class trips with family support. In middle school and high school, school orientations; parent-teacher conferences; PTA-sponsored events (e.g., spaghetti dinner, spring fling, craft fair); and sports, school plays, and musical activities (e.g., band, chorus) are the primary ways families socialize with other families at school. These various activities can familiarize parents with their child's classmates and classmates' family members and may facilitate out-of-school efforts to maintain friendships.

Setting Goals

When building peer support into a student's IEP, teams should focus not only on the school day but also on the student's free time after school and during vacations. Many school systems or communities have summer recreation programs or educational or library reading programs. Teams might encourage members from peer networks to enroll in such activities together. Clubs such as Boy or Girl Scouts or 4-H and recreational sports teams such as soccer or baseball leagues for adolescents provide other opportunities for children to get together after school and during the summer. Teachers can also organize classwide or grade-level summer activities (e.g., service activities, community cleanup, school improvement efforts, reading programs) to bring students together during the summer. In some classrooms, especially in elementary schools, teachers assist parents in setting up telephone trees and car pools to facilitate student participation in class activities; if these organizational efforts are useful to families, they are often naturally maintained by parents over the summer or for weekend activities.

Addressing Physical Disabilities

If a child has special needs with regard to transportation (e.g., assistance in getting in and out of a wheelchair, adaptive equipment storage) or health or feeding concerns, the student's family members will often need to become actively involved in group activities before other parents will become comfortable with transportation or supervision of the child. When children are young, it is not unusual for their parents to accompany them to activities and take care of their needs; however, hovering parents or grandparents can be just as damaging to peer interactions as hovering teachers and teaching assistants. Finding solutions to these kinds of after-school barriers will be up to the student's team and the student him- or herself; but when approved by the focus student, the student's classmates or peers can also become involved in problem solving.

Some older students who have restricted voluntary movement will not want to share their personal needs for support (e.g., assistance with using the bathroom, getting into pajamas before a sleep over) but will want to attend the entire activity without having a parent there to help. Other students will be less aware of or concerned with receiving the physical help they need (e.g., eating) to enable their participation in an activity. The solutions to these situations will be highly individualized, although problem solvers will all focus on a common goal: to include the focus student in a way that is nonstigmatizing, allows active participation, and provides enjoyment.

Making Peer Support
Programs Permanent

Much of the work that goes into developing peer support programs occurs during the planning and initial implementation phases. Because of their broad investment and use, peer support programs are more likely to be maintained year after year when schools work together as a community to plan, pilot, and extend them. If the task is left up to several special education teachers or to an isolated classroom teacher who happens to be "good at that sort of thing," it is much more difficult to

keep social relationship support efforts active. When principals lend their support to efforts to implement a peer facilitation program and when staff members identify such an effort as a school goal, the task is legitimized and shared.

Once a program geared toward improving peer social relationships has been piloted, school staff members may want to informally evaluate its outcomes and seek ways to improve it, expand it, and make it more efficient to maintain. For example, when high school students were given credit for participating in a regular friendship activity with a student who had extensive disabilities, less effort was needed to recruit additional participants and schedule their interactions; therefore, staff members were able to spend more time preparing the participating general education student and guiding the interaction, allowing for more substantive relationships (Helmstetter et al., 1994; Keachie, 1997). When a cross-age tutoring program was judged a success for tutors and tutees, it became a regular cooperative program between the fifth- and eighth-grade students in adjoining elementary and middle schools; school resources were assigned to support the effort, and, consequently, the program recurred every year.

References

Abrey, B., Schoeller, K., Simunds, E., Gaylord, V., & Fahnestock, M. (1997). *Yes I Can Social Inclusion Curriculum*. Minneapolis: University of Minnesota, Institute on Community Integration.

Achenbach, T.M. (1991). *The Child Behavior Checklist: Manual for the teacher's report form*. Burlington: University of Vermont, Department of Psychiatry.

Adler, P.A., & Adler, P. (1996). Preadolescent clique stratification and the hierarchy of identify. *Sociological Inquiry, 66*, 111–142.

Americans with Disabilities Act (ADA) of 1990, PL 101-336, 42 U.S.C. §§ 12101 *et seq.*

Ang, R.P., & Hughes, J.N. (2002). Differential benefits of skills training with antisocial youth based on group composition: A meta-analytic investigation. *School Psychology Review, 31*(2), 164–186.

Arreaga-Mayer, C. (1998). Increasing active student responding and improving academic performance through class-wide peer tutoring. *Intervention in School and Clinic, 34*(2), 89–94.

Ayres, B., O'Brien, L., & Rogers, T. (1992). *Working together, sharing and helping each other: Cooperative learning in a first grade classroom that includes students with disabilities*. Syracuse, NY: Syracuse University, The Inclusive Education Project.

Baker, S., Gersten R., Dimino, J.A., & Griffiths, R. (2004). The sustained use of research-based instructional practice: A case study of peer-assisted learning strategies in mathematics. *Remedial and Special Education, 25*, 5–25.

Barry, L.M., & Burlew, S.B. (2004). Using social stories to teach choice and play skills to children with autism. *Focus on Autism and Other Developmental Disabilities, 19*(1), 45–52.

Barry, L.M., & Messer, J.J. (2003). A practical application of self-management for students diagnosed with attention-deficit/hyperactivity disorder. *Journal of Positive Behavior Interventions, 5*(4), 238–248.

Beck, R. (Ed.). (1997). *PROJECT RIDE: Responding to individual differences in education*. Longmont, CO: Sopris West.

Beelman, A., Pfingsten, U., & Losel, F. (1994). Effects of training social competence in children: A meta-analysis of recent evaluation studies. *Journal of Clinical Child Psychology, 21*, 260–271.

Begun, R.W. (1996). *Social skills lessons and activities for Grades 4–6*. West Nyack, NY: Center for Applied Research in Education.

Biklen, D., Corrigan, C., & Quick, D. (1989). Beyond obligation: Students' relations with each other in integrated classes. In D.K. Lipsky & A. Gartner (Eds.), *Beyond separate education: Quality education for all* (pp. 207–221). Baltimore: Paul H. Brookes Publishing Co.

Bradley, D.F., & West, J.F. (1994). Staff training for the inclusion of students with disabilities: Visions from school-based educators. *Teacher Education and Special Education, 17*(2), 117–128.

Brady, M.P., & McEvoy, M.A. (1989). Social skills training as an integration strategy. In R. Gaylord-Ross (Ed.), *Integration strategies for students with handicaps* (pp. 213–231). Baltimore: Paul H. Brookes Publishing Co.

Breen, C.G., Haring, T.G., Weiner, J., Laitinen, R.E., & Bernstein, D.D. (1991). Evaluating the inclusion and social competence of students with severe disabilities in community and school environments. In C.G. Breen, C.H. Kennedy, & T.G. Haring (Eds.), *Social context research project: Methods for facilitating the inclusion of students with disabilities in integrated school and community contexts* (pp. 23–53). Santa Barbara: University of California.

Breen, C.G., & Lovinger, L. (1991). PAL (partners at lunch) club: Evaluation of a program to support social relationships in a junior high school. In C.G. Breen, C.H. Kennedy, & T.G. Haring (Eds.), *Social context research project: Methods for facilitating the inclusion of students with disabilities in integrated school and community contexts* (pp. 106–128). Santa Barbara: University of California.

Bricker, D. (Series Ed.). (2002). *Assessment, Evaluation, and Programming System for Infants and Children (AEPS)* (2nd ed.). Baltimore: Paul H. Brookes Publishing Co.

Broer, S.M., Doyle, M.B., & Giangreco, M.F. (2005). Perspectives of students with intellectual disabilities about their experiences with paraprofessional support. *Exceptional Children, 71*(4), 415–431.

Brooks, A., Todd, A.Q., Tofflemoyer, S., & Horner, R.H. (2003). Use of functional assessment and a self-management system to increase academic engagement and work completion. *Journal of Positive Behavior Interventions, 5*(3), 144–152.

Browder, D.M., Bambara, L.M., & Belifore, P.J. (1997). Using a person-centered approach in community-based instruction for adults with developmental disabilities. *Journal of Behavioral Education, 7,* 519–528.

Brown, W.H., & Odom, S.L. (1994). Strategies and tactics for promoting generalization and maintenance of young children's social behavior. *Research in Developmental Disabilities, 15,* 99–118.

Brown, W.H., Odom, S.L., & Buysse, V. (2002). Assessment of preschool children's peer-related social competence. *Assessment for Effective Intervention, 27*(4), 61–71.

Brown, W.H., Odom, S., & Conroy, M.A. (2001). An intervention hierarchy for promoting young children's peer interactions in natural environments. *Topics in Early Childhood Special Education, 21*(3), 162–175.

Burns, M., Storey, K., & Certo, N.J. (1999). Effect of service learning on attitudes toward students with severe disabilities. *Education and Training in Mental Retardation and Developmental Disabilities, 34*(1), 58–65.

Calderella, P., & Merrell, K. (1997). Common dimensions of social skills of children and adolescents: A taxonomy of positive behaviors. *School Psychology Review, 26,* 264–278.

Callahan, K., & Rademacher, J.A. (1999). Using self-management strategies to increase the on-task behavior of a student with autism. *Journal of Positive Behavior Intervention, 1*(2), 117–122.

Campbell, P.C., & Campbell, C.R. (1995). *Building inclusive schools: Module 5. Peer involvement. Skills for involving nondisabled peers in the inclusive education school. Trainee workbook.* Lawrence: University of Kansas.

Carr, E.G., Levin, L., McConnachie, G., Carlson, J.I., Kemp, D.C., & Smith, C.E. (1994). *Communication-based intervention for problem behavior: A user's guide for producing positive change.* Baltimore: Paul H. Brookes Publishing Co.

Carr, S.C., & Punzo, R.P. (1993). The effects of self-monitoring of academic accuracy and productivity on the performance of students with behavioral disorders. *Behavioral Disorders, 18,* 241–250.

Carter, E.W., Cushing, L.S., Clark, N.M., & Kennedy, C.H. (2005). Effects of peer support interventions on students' access to the general curriculum and social interactions. *Research and Practice for Persons with Severe Disabilities, 30*(1), 15–25.

Carter, E.W., Hughes, C., Copeland, S.R., & Breen, C. (2001). Differences between high school students who do and do not volunteer to participate in a peer interaction program. *Journal of The Association for Persons with Severe Handicaps, 26*(4), 229–239.

Chadsey-Rusch, J. (1992). Toward defining and measuring social skills in employment settings. *American Journal on Mental Retardation, 96,* 405–418.

Clemenz, S.E. (2002). *The effects of peer tutoring on the attitudes of nondisabled peers.* (ERIC Document Reproduction Service No. ED467481)

Cohen, P.A., Kulik, J.A., & Kulik, C. (1982). Educational outcomes of tutoring: A meta-analysis of findings. *American Educational Research Journal, 191,* 237–248.

Cole, C.L., & Bambara, L.M. (1992). Issues surrounding the use of self-management interventions in the schools. *School Psychology Review, 21,* 193–201.

Cole, D.A., & Meyer, L.H. (1991). Social integration and severe disabilities: A longitudinal analysis of child outcomes. *Journal of Special Education, 25,* 340–351.

Collins, B.C., Branson, T.A., & Hall, M. (1995). Teaching generalized reading of cooking product labels to adolescents with mental disabilities through the use of key words taught by peer tutors. *Education and Training in Mental Retardation and Developmental Disabilities, 30,* 5–75.

Conduct Problems Prevention Research Group. (1999). Initial impact of the fast track prevention trial for conduct problems: I. The high–risk sample. *Journal of Consulting and Clinical Psychology, 67,* 631–647.

Copeland, S.R., Hughes, C., Carter, E.W., Guth, C., Presley, J., Williams, C.R., et al. (2004). Increasing access to general education: Perspectives of participants in a high school peer support program. *Remedial and Special Education, 25*(6), 342–359.

Copeland, S.R., McCall, J., Williams, C.R., Guth, C., Carter, E.W., Fowler, S.E., et al. (2002). High school peer buddies: A win-win situation. *Teaching Exceptional Children, 35*(1), 16–21.

Cosden, M.A., & Haring, T.G. (1992). Cooperative learning in the classroom: Contingencies, group interactions, and students with special needs. *Journal of Behavioral Education, 2*, 53–71.

Curran, J.M. (1999). *Changing attitudes toward people with mental retardation: Effects of extended contact within a changing social context.* (ERIC Document Reproduction Service No. ED443314)

Cushing, L.S., & Kennedy, C.H. (1997). Academic effects of providing peer support in general education classrooms on students without disabilities. *Journal of Applied Behavior Analysis, 30,* 139–151.

Davern, L., Ford, A., Erwin, E., Schnorr, R., & Rogan. P. (1993). *Working toward inclusive schools: Guidelines for developing a building-based process to create change.* Syracuse, NY: Syracuse University, Inclusive Education Project.

Davidson, N. (1985). Small-group learning and teaching in mathematics: A selective review of the research. In R. Slavin, S. Sharan, S. Kagan, R. Hertz-Lazarowitz, C. Webb, & R. Schmuch (Eds.), *Learning to cooperate, cooperating to learn* (pp. 211–229). New York: Praeger.

Delquadri, J., Greenwood, C.R., Whorton, D., Carta, J.J., & Hall, R.V. (1986). Classwide peer tutoring. *Exceptional Children, 52,* 535–542.

Derman-Sparks, L., & The Anti-Bias Curriculum Task Force. (1989). *Anti-bias Curriculum: Tools for empowering young children.* Washington, DC: National Association for the Education of Young Children.

Developmental Studies Center. (1996). *Ways we want our class to be: Class meetings that build commitment to kindness and learning.* Oakland, CA: Author.

Dobbin, J. [Producer]. (n.d.). *Shakif's MAP: Charting your journey* [Videotape]. Toronto: Inclusion Press.

Dodge, K.A. (1986). A social information processing model of social competence in childhood. In M. Perlmutter (Ed.), *Cognitive perspectives on children's social and behavioral development* (pp. 77–125). Mahwah, NJ: Lawrence Erlbaum Associates.

Dugan, E., Kamps, D., Leonard, B., Watkins, N., Rheinberger, A., & Stackhaus, J. (1995). Effects of cooperative learning groups during social studies for students with autism and fourth-grade peers. *Journal of Applied Behavior Analysis, 28,* 175–188.

Durand, V.M. (1988). The Motivation Assessment Scale. In M. Hersen & A. Bellack (Eds.), *Dictionary of behavioral assessment techniques* (pp. 309–310). Tarrytown, NY: Pergamon.

Durand. V.M., & Crimmins, D.B. (1988). *The Motivation Assessment Scale: An administration manual.* Albany: State University of New York Press.

Eichinger, J., Rizzo, T., & Sirotnik, B. (1991). Changing attitudes toward people with disabilities. *Teacher Education and Special Education, 14*(2), 121–126.

Elbaum, B., Vaughn, S., Hughes, M., & Moody, S.W. (1999). Grouping practices and reading outcomes for students with disabilities. *Exceptional Children, 65*(3), 339–415.

Elliott, S., & Gresham, F. (1991). *Social skills intervention guide.* Circle Pines, MN: American Guidance.

English, K., Shafer, K., Goldstein, H., & Kazmarek, L. (1997). *Teaching buddy skills to preschoolers.* Washington, DC: American Association on Mental Retardation.

Etscheidt, S. (1991). Reducing aggressive behavior and increasing self control: A cognitive-behavioral training program for behaviorally disordered adolescents. *Behavioral Disorders, 16,* 107–115.

Falvey, M.A., Forest, M., Pearpoint, J., & Rosenberg, R.L. (1997). *All my life's a circle: Using the tools: Circles, MAPS and PATHs* (2nd ed.). Toronto: Inclusion Press.

Fantuzzo, J.W., King, J.A., & Heller, L.R. (1992). Effects of reciprocal peer tutoring on mathematics and school adjustment: A component analysis. *Journal of Educational Psychology, 84*(3), 331–339.

Farmer, T.W., & Cadwallader, T.W. (2000). Social interactions and peer support for problem behavior. *Preventing School Failure, 44*(3), 105–114.

Farmer, T.W., & Farmer, E.M.Z. (1996). Social relationships of students with exceptionalities in mainstream classrooms: Social networks and homophily. *Exceptional Children, 62,* 431–450.

Farmer, T.W., & Hollowell, J.H. (1994). Social networks in mainstream classrooms: Social affiliations and behavioral characteristics of students with emotional and behavioral disorders. *Journal of Emotional and Behavioral Disorders, 2,* 143–155, 163.

Farmer, T.W., Pearl, R., & Van Acker, R.M. (1996). Expanding the social skills deficit framework: A developmental synthesis perspective, classroom social networks, and implications for the social growth of students with disabilities. *Journal of Special Education, 30,* 232–256.

Favazza, P.C., & Odom, S.L. (1996). Use of the Acceptance Scale to measure attitudes of kindergarten-age children. *Journal of Early Intervention, 20,* 232–249.

Favazza, P.C., & Odom, S.L. (1997). Promoting positive attitudes of kindergarten-age children toward people with disabilities. *Exceptional Children, 83,* 405–418.

Fisher, D. (1999). According to their peers: Inclusion as high school students see it. *Mental Retardation, 37,* 458–467.

Fisher, D., Pumpian, I., & Sax, C. (1998). High school students' attitudes about and recommendations for their peers with significant disabilities. *Journal of The Association for Persons with Severe Handicaps, 23,* 272–282.

Fisher, M.M., & Snell, M.E. (1999). *The use of MAPS peer support groups and teacher support in middle schools to facilitate the inclusion of students with moderate and severe disabilities.* Unpublished manuscript, Purdue University, Department of Special Education, West LaFayette, IN.

Ford, A., Messenheimer-Young, T., Toshner, J., Fitzgerald, M.A., Dyer, C., Glodoski, J., et al. (1995, July). *A team planning packet for inclusive education.* Milwaukee: Wisconsin School Inclusion Project.

Forest, M., O'Brien, J., & Pearpoint, J. (1993). *PATH: A workbook for planning positive possible futures.* Toronto: Inclusion Press.

Forness, S.R., & Kavale, K.A. (1996). Treating social skill deficits in children with learning disabilities: A meta-analysis of the research. *Learning Disabilities Quarterly, 19,* 2–13.

Franca, V.M., Kerr, M.M., Reitz, A.L., & Lambert, D. (1990). Peer tutoring among behaviorally disordered students: Academic and social benefits to tutor and tutee. *Education and Treatment of Children, 13,* 109–128.

Frea, W., Craig-Unkefer, L., Odom, S., & Johnson, D. (1999). Differential effects of structured social integration and group friendship activities for promoting social interaction with peers. *Journal of Early Intervention, 22*(3), 230–242.

Frederickson, N., & Turner, J. (2003). Utilizing the classroom peer group to address children's social needs: An evaluation of the Circle of Friends intervention approach. *Journal of Special Education, 36*(4), 234–245.

Fritz, M.F. (1990). A comparison of social interactions using a friendship awareness activity. *Education and Training in Mental Retardation, 25,* 352–359.

Fryxell, D., & Kennedy, C.H. (1995). Placement along the continuum of services and its impact on students' social relationships. *Journal of The Association for Persons with Severe Handicaps, 20,* 259–269.

Fuchs, L.S., Fuchs, D., Hamlett, C.L., Phillips, N., & Bentz, J. (1994). Classwide curriculum-based measurement: Helping general educators meet the challenge of student diversity. *Exceptional Children, 60,* 518–537.

Fuchs, L.S., Fuchs, D., Phillips, N., & Karns, K. (1994). *Peer-mediated mathematics instruction: A manual.* Nashville, TN: Vanderbilt University, Peabody College.

Furman, W., & Buhrmester, D. (1992). Age and sex differences in perceptions of networks of personal relationships. *Child Development, 63,* 103–115.

Garrison-Harrell, L., Kamps, D., & Kravits, T. (1997). The effects of peer networks on social-communicative behaviors for students with autism. *Focus on Autism and Other Developmental Disabilities, 12,* 241–254.

Gartner, A., & Lipsky, D.K. (1990). Students as instructional agents. In W. Stainback & S. Stainback (Eds.), *Support networks for inclusive schooling: Interdependent integrated education* (pp. 81–94). Baltimore: Paul H. Brookes Publishing Co.

Giangreco, M.F., Cloninger, C.J., Dennis, R.E., & Edelman, S.W. (2002). Problem-solving methods to facilitate inclusive education. In J.S. Thousand, R.A. Villa, & A.I. Nevin (Eds.), *Creativity and collaborative learning: The practical guide to empowering students, teachers, and families* (2nd ed., pp. 321–346). Baltimore: Paul H. Brookes Publishing Co.

Giangreco, M.F., Dennis, R., Cloninger, C., Edelman, S., & Schattman, R. (1993). "I've counted Jon": Transformational experiences of teachers educating students with disabilities. *Exceptional Children, 59,* 359–372.

Giangreco, M.F., Edelman, S.W., Luiselli, T.E., & MacFarland, S.Z.C. (1997). Helping or hovering? Effects of instructional assistant proximity on students with disabilities. *Exceptional Children, 64,* 7–18.

Gilberts, G.H., Agran, M., Hughes, C., & Wehmeyer, M. (2001). The effects of peer delivered self-monitoring strategies on the participation of students with severe disabilities in general education classrooms. *Journal of The Association for Persons with Severe Handicaps, 26*(1), 25–36.

Goldman, B.D., Buysse, V., & Carr, L. (1997). *Playmates and friends questionnaire for teachers.* Chapel Hill: University of North Carolina at Chapel Hill, FPG Child Development Center.

Goldstein, A. (1988). *The Prepare Curriculum: Teaching prosocial competencies.* Champaign, IL: Research Press.

Goodman, G. (1994). *Inclusive classrooms from A to Z: A handbook for educators.* Columbus, OH: Teacher's Publishing Group.

Gray, C.A. (1998). Social stories and comic strip conversations with students with Asperger syndrome and high-functioning autism. In E. Schopler & G.B. Mesibov (Eds.), *Asperger syndrome or high-functioning autism? Current issues in autism* (pp. 167–198). New York: Plenum Press.

Gray, C.A., & Garand, J.D. (1993). Social stories: Improving responses of students with autism with accurate social information. *Focus on Autistic Behavior, 8*(1), 1–10.

Greenleaf, D. (1992). The use of programmed transfer of training and structured learning therapy with disruptive adolescents in a school setting. *Journal of School Psychology, 20,* 122–130.

Greenspan, S. (1981). Defining childhood social competence: A proposed working model. In B.K. Keogh (Ed.), *Advances in special education* (Vol. 3, pp. 1–39). Greenwich, CT: JAI Press.

Greenwood, C.R., Arreaga-Mayer, C., Utley, C.A., Gaving, K.M., & Terry, B.J. (2001). Classwide peer tutoring learning management system. *Remedial and Special Education, 22,* 34–47.

Greenwood, C.R., Carta, J., & Kamps, D. (1990). Teacher-mediated versus peer-mediated instruction: A review of educational advantages and disadvantages. In H. Foot, M. Morgan, & R. Shute (Eds.), *Children helping children* (pp. 177–205). New York: John Wiley and Sons.

Greenwood, C.R., Delquadri, J., & Carta, J.J. (1999). *Classwide peer tutoring (CWPT) for teachers.* Longmont, CO: Sopris West.

Greenwood, C.R., Maheady, L., & Delquadri, J.C. (2002). Class-wide peer tutoring. In G. Stoner, M.R. Shinn, & H. Walker, (Eds.), *Interventions for achievement and behavior problems* (2nd ed., pp. 611–649). Washington, DC: National Association of School Psychologists.

Greenwood, C.R., Terry, B., Delquadri, J.C., Elliott, M., & Arreaga-Mayer, C. (1995). *Classwide peer tutoring (CWPT): Effective teaching and research review.* Kansas City: University of Kansas, Juniper Gardens Children's Project.

Gresham, F.M. (1986). Conceptual issues in the assessment of social competence in children. In P. Strain, M. Guralnick, & H. Walker (Eds.), *Children's social behavior: Development, assessment, and modifications* (pp. 143–179). San Diego: Academic Press.

Gresham, F.M. (1997). Social competence and students with behavior disorders: Where we've been, where we are, and where we should go. *Education and Treatment of Children, 20,* 233–249.

Gresham, F.M. (2000). Assessment of social skills in students with emotional and behavioral disorders. *Assessment for Effective Intervention, 26*(1), 51–58.

Gresham, F.M., & Elliott, S. (1990). *The Social Skills Rating System (SSRS).* Circle Pines, MN: American Guidance.

Gresham, F.M., Sugai, G., & Horner, R.M. (2001). Interpreting outcomes of social skills training for students with high-incidence disabilities. *Exceptional Children, 67*(3), 331–355.

Grodon, J., & LeVassuer, P. (1994). Cognitive picture rehearsal: A system to teach self-control. In K.A. Quill (Ed.), *Teaching children with autism: Strategies to enhance communication and socialization* (pp. 287–306). Albany, NY: Delmar Publishers.

Gustafson, R.N., & Haring, N.G. (1992). Social competence issues in the integration of students with handicaps. In K.A. Haring, D.L. Lovett, & N.G. Haring (Eds.), *Integrated lifestyle services for persons with disabilities* (pp. 20–58). New York: Springer-Verlag.

Hamilton, C., Fuchs, D., Fuchs, L.S., & Roberts, H. (2000). Rates of classroom participation and the validity of sociometry. *School Psychology Review, 29,* 251–266.

Hamre-Nietupski, S., Ayres, B., Nietupski, J., Savage, M., Mitchell, B., & Bramman, H. (1989). Enhancing integration of students with severe disabilities through curricular infusion: A general/special educator partnership. *Education and Training of the Mentally Retarded, 24,* 78–88.

Haring, T.G. (1992). The context of social competence: Relations, relationships, and generalization. In S.L. Odom, S.R. McConnell, & M.A. McEvoy (Eds.), *Social competence of young children with disabilities: Issues and strategies for intervention* (pp. 307–320). Baltimore: Paul H. Brookes Publishing Co.

Haring, T.G., & Breen, C.G. (1992). A peer-mediated social network intervention to enhance the social integration of persons with moderate and severe disabilities. *Journal of Applied Behavior Analysis, 25,* 319–333.

Harper, G.F., Mallette, B., & Moore, J. (1991). Peer-mediated instruction: Teaching spelling to primary school children with mild disabilities. *Journal of Reading, Writing, and Learning Disabilities International, 7*(3), 137–151.

Harper, L.V., & McCluskey, K.S. (2003). Teacher-child and child-child interactions in inclusive preschool settings: Do adults inhibit interactions? *Early Childhood Research Quarterly, 18,* 163–184.

Harris, K.R., & Pressley, M. (1991). The nature of cognitive strategy instruction: Interactive strategy construction. *Exceptional Children, 57,* 392–404.

Hartup, W.W. (1996). The company they keep: Friendships and their developmental significance. *Child Development, 67,* 1–13.

Hastings, R.P. (1996). Do special education courses have any impact on student teachers' perceptions of children with severe learning difficulties? *British Journal of Special Education, 23*(3), 139–144.

Hawkins, X. (1991). Is social validity what we are interested in? Argument for a functional approach. *Journal of Applied Behavior Analysis, 24,* 205–213.

Hazel, J., Schumaker, J., Sherman, J., & Sheldon-Wildgen, J. (1981). *ASSET: A social skills program for adolescents.* Champaign, IL: Research Press.

Helmstetter, E., Peck, C.A., & Giangreco, M. (1994). Outcomes of interactions with peers with moderate or severe disabilities: A statewide survey of high school students. *Journal of The Association for Persons with Severe Handicaps, 19,* 263–276.

Hendrickson, J.M., Shokoohi-Yekta, M., Hamre-Neitupski, S., & Gable, R.A. (1996). Middle and high school students' perceptions on being friends with peers with severe disabilities. *Exceptional Children, 63,* 19–28.

Hestenes, L., & Carroll, D.E. (2000). The play interactions of young children with and without disabilities: Individual and environmental influences. *Early Childhood Research Quarterly, 15,* 229–246.

Heyne, L.A., Schleien, S.J., & McAvoy, L.H. (1994). *Making friends: Using recreation activities to promote friendship between children with and without disabilities.* Minneapolis: University of Minnesota, Institute on Community Integration.

Holburn, S., & Vietze, P.M. (2002). *Person-centered planning: Research, practice, and future directions.* Baltimore: Paul H. Brookes Publishing Co.

Horner, R.H., & Carr, E.G. (1997). Behavioral support for students with severe disabilities: Functional assessment and comprehensive intervention. *Journal of Special Education, 31,* 84–104.

Horner, R.H., O'Neil, R.E., & Flannery, K.B. (1993). Building effective behavior support plans from functional assessment information. In M.E. Snell (Ed.), *Instruction of students with severe disabilities* (4th ed., pp. 184–214). Columbus, OH: Merrill.

Hughes, C., & Carter, E.W. (2006). *Success for all students: Promoting inclusion in secondary schools through peer buddy programs.* Boston: Allyn & Bacon.

Hughes, C., Carter, E., Brown, G., & Washington, B. (2004). A schoolwide program for promoting friendships for high school students with disabilities. *TASH Connections, 30*(1/2), 19–22.

Hughes, C., Carter, E.W., Hughes, T., Bradford, E., & Copeland, S.R. (2002). Effects of instructional versus non-instructional roles on the social interactions of high school students. *Education and Training in Mental Retardation, 37*(2), 146–162.

Hughes, C., Copeland, S.R., Agran, M., Wehmeyer, M.L., Rodi, M.S., & Presley, J.A. (2002). Using self-monitoring to improve performance in general education high school classes. *Education and Training in Mental Retardation and Developmental Disabilities, 37*(3), 262–272.

Hughes, C., Copeland, S.R., Guth, C., Rung, L.R., Hwang, B., Kleeb, G., et al. (2001). General education students' perspective on their involvement in a high school peer buddy program. *Education and Training in Mental Retardation and Developmental Disabilities, 36*(4), 343–356.

Hughes, C., Guth, C., Hall, S., Presley, J., Dye, M., & Byers, C. (1999). They are my best friends: Peer buddies promote inclusion in high school. *Teaching Exceptional Children, 31*(5), 32–37.

Hughes, C., Rung, L.L., Wehmeyer, M.L., Agran, M., Copeland, S.R., & Hwang, B. (2000). Self-prompted communication book use to increase social interaction among high school students. *Journal of The Association for Persons with Severe Handicaps, 21*(3), 153–156.

Hunt, P., Alwell, M., Farron-Davis, F., & Goetz, L. (1996). Creating socially supportive environments for fully included students who experience multiple disabilities. *Journal of The Association for Persons with Severe Handicaps, 21,* 53–71.

Hunt, P., Alwell, M., & Goetz, L. (1991). Interaction with peers through conversation turntaking with a communication book adaptation. *Augmentative and Alternative Communication, 7,* 117–126.

Hunt, P., Staub, D., Alwell, M., & Goetz, L. (1994). Achievement by all students within the context of cooperative learning groups. *Journal of The Association for Persons with Severe Handicaps, 19,* 290–301.

Hymel, S., Rubin, K., Rowden, L., & LeMare, L. (1990). Children's peer relationships: Longitudinal prediction of internalizing and externalizing problems from middle to late childhood. *Child Development, 61,* 2004–2021.

Janney, R.E., & Snell, M.E. (1996). How teachers use peer interactions to include students with moderate and severe disabilities in elementary general education classes. *Journal of The Association for Persons with Severe Handicaps, 21,* 72–80.

Janney, R., & Snell, M.E. (2000). *Teachers' guides to inclusive practices: Behavioral support.* Baltimore: Paul H. Brookes Publishing Co.

Janney, R., & Snell, M.E. (2004). *Teachers' guides to inclusive practices: Modifying schoolwork* (2nd ed.). Baltimore: Paul H. Brookes Publishing Co.

Janney, R.E., Snell, M.E., Beers, M.K., & Raynes, M. (1995). Integrating students with moderate and severe disabilities: Classroom teachers' beliefs and attitudes about implementing an educational change. *Educational Administration Quarterly, 31*(1), 86–114.

Janney, R.E., Snell, M.E., & Fisher, D. (2004, December). *Social relationships and peer support: Making inclusion work.* Presentation at the Annual Conference of TASH, Reno, NV.

Jenkins, J.R., Jewell, M., Leicester, N., Jenkins, L., & Troutner, N.M. (1991). Development of a school building model for educating students with handicaps and at-risk students in general education classrooms. *Journal of Learning Disabilities, 24,* 311–320.

Jenkins, J.R., Odom, S.L., & Speltz, M.L. (1989). Effects of social integration on preschool children with handicaps. *Exceptional Children, 55,* 420–428.

Johnson, D.W., & Johnson, R.T. (1984). Building acceptance of differences between handicapped and nonhandicapped students: The effects of cooperative and individualistic instruction. *Journal of Social Psychology, 122,* 257–267.

Johnson, D.W., & Johnson, R.T. (1989). *Cooperation and competition: Theory and research.* Edina, MN: Interaction Books.

Johnson, D.W., & Johnson, R.T. (1999). *Learning together and alone: Cooperation, competition, and individualization* (5th ed.). Boston: Allyn & Bacon.

Johnson, D.W., Johnson, R., & Holubec, E. (1993). *Circles of learning: Cooperation in the classroom* (5th ed.). Edina, MN: Interaction Book.

Johnson, D.W., Johnson, R.T., & Holubec, E.J. (1994). *Cooperative learning in the classroom.* Alexandria, VA: Association for Supervision and Curriculum Development.

Jorgensen, C. (1992). Natural supports in inclusive schools: Curricular and teaching strategies. In J. Nisbet (Ed.), *Natural supports in school, at work, and in the community for people with severe disabilities* (pp. 179–215). Baltimore: Paul H. Brookes Publishing Co.

Joseph, G.E., & Strain, P.S. (2003). Comprehensive evidence-based social-emotional curricula for young children: An analysis of efficacious adoption potential. *Topics in Early Childhood Special Education, 23*(2), 65–76.

Kagan, S. (1990). A structural approach to cooperative learning. *Educational Leadership, 47*(4), 12–15.

Kamps, D., Barbetta, P.M., Leonard, B.R., & Delquadri, J. (1994). Classwide peer tutoring: An integration strategy to improve reading skills and promote peer interactions among students with autism and general education peers. *Journal of Applied Behavior Analysis, 27,* 49–61.

Kamps, D.M., Potucek, J., Lopez, A.G., Kravits, T., & Kemmerer, K. (1997). The use of peer networks across multiple settings to improve social interaction for students with autism. *Journal of Behavioral Education, 7,* 335–357.

Kamps, D., Royer, J., Dugan, E., Kravits, T., Gonzalez-Lopez, A., Garcia, J., et al. (2002). Peer training to facilitate social interaction for elementary students with autism and their peers. *Exceptional Children, 68*(2), 173–187.

Kamps, D.M., Tankersley, M., & Ellis, C. (2000). Social skills interventions for young at-risk students: A 2-year follow-up study. *Behavioral Disorders, 25*(4), 310–324.

Kavale, K.A., & Mostert, M.P. (2004). Social skills interventions for individuals with learning disabilities. *Learning Disabilities Quarterly, 27,* 31–43.

Keachie, J. (1997, Fall). Pals, parties, and proms: The Peer Connections Program. *Impact, 10*(3), 19.

Kennedy, C.H., Cushing, L.S., & Itkonen, T. (1997). General education participation improves the social contacts and friendship networks of students with severe disabilities. *Journal of Behavioral Education, 7,* 167–189.

Kennedy, C.H., & Itkonen, T. (1994). Some effects of regular class participation on the social contacts and social networks of high school students with severe disabilities. *Journal of The Association for Persons with Severe Handicaps, 19,* 1–13.

Kennedy, C.H., Shukla, S., & Fryxell, D. (1997). Comparing the effects of educational placement on the social relationships of intermediate school students with severe disabilities. *Exceptional Children, 64,* 31–47.

Kincaid, D. (1996). Person-centered planning. In L.K. Koegel, R.L. Koegel, & G. Dunlap (Eds.), *Positive behavioral support: Including people with difficult behavior in the community* (pp. 439–465). Baltimore: Paul H. Brookes Publishing Co.

King-Sears, M.E. (2001). Institutionalizing peer-mediated instruction and interventions in schools. *Remedial and Special Education, 22*(2), 89–108.

King-Sears, M.E., & Cummings, C.S. (1996). Inclusive practices of classroom teachers. *Remedial and Special Education, 17*(4), 217–225.

Kinney, D.A. (1993). From nerds to normals: The recovery of identity among adolescents from middle school to high school. *Sociology of Education, 66,* 21–40.

Kishi, G.S., & Meyer, L.H. (1994). What children report and remember: A six-year follow-up of the effects of social contact between peers with and without severe disabilities. *Journal of The Association for Persons with Severe Handicaps, 19,* 277–289.

Knoster, T.P., Villa, R.A., & Thousand, J.S. (2000). A framework for thinking about systems change. In R.A. Villa & J.S. Thousand (Eds.), *Restructuring for caring and effective education: Piecing the puzzle together* (2nd ed.; pp. 93–128). Baltimore: Paul H. Brookes Publishing Co.

Koegel, L.K., Harrower, J.K., & Koegel, R. (1999). Support for children with developmental disabilities in full inclusion classrooms through self-management. *Journal of Positive Behavior Interventions, 1,* 26–34.

Koegel, L.K., Koegel, R.L., Hurley, C., & Frea, W.D. (1992). Improving social skills and disruptive behavior in children with autism through self-management. *Journal of Applied Behavior Analysis, 25,* 341–353.

Koegel, R.L., Koegel, L.K., & Parks, D.R. (1995). Autonomy through self-management. In R.L. Koegel & L.K. Koegel (Eds.), *Teaching children with autism: Strategies for initiating positive interactions and improving learning opportunities* (pp. 67–77). Baltimore: Paul H. Brookes Publishing Co.

Kohler, F., & Greenwood, C.R. (1990). Effects of collateral peer supportive behaviors with the classwide peer tutoring program. *Journal of Applied Behavior Analysis, 23,* 307–322.

Kohler, F.W., & Strain, P.S. (1999). Maximizing peer interactions in integrated preschool classrooms. *Topics in Early Childhood Special Education, 19*(2), 92–102.

Korinek, L., Walther-Thomas, C., McLaughlin, V.L., & Williams, B.T. (1999). Creating classroom communities and networks for student support. *Intervention in School and Clinic, 35*(1), 3–8.

Koury, M., & Browder, D. (1986). The use of delay to teach sight words by peer tutors classified as moderately mentally retarded. *Education and Training of the Mentally Retarded, 17,* 93–102.

Ladd, G.W. (1990). Having friends, keeping friends, making friends and being liked by peers in the classroom: Predictors of children's early school adjustment? *Child Development, 61,* 1081–1100.

Lorimer, P.A., Simpson, R.L., Myles, B.S., & Ganz, J.B. (2002). The use of social stories as a preventative behavioral intervention in a home setting with a child with autism. *Journal of Positive Behavior Interventions, 4*(1), 53–60.

Luria, A.R. (1961). *The role of speech in the regulation of normal and abnormal behavior.* New York: Liveright.

Maccoby, E.E. (1990). Gender and relationships. *American Psychologist, 45,* 513–520.

Maheady, L., Harper, G.F., & Mallette, B. (2001). Peer-mediated instruction and interventions and students with mild disabilities. *Remedial and Special Education, 22,* 4–14.

Mathes, P.G., Fuchs, D., Fuchs, L.S., Henley, A.M., & Sanders, A. (1994). Increasing strategic reading practice with Peabody classwide peer tutoring. *Learning Disabilities Research and Practice, 9,* 44–48.

Mathur, S.R., Kavale, K.A., Quinn, M.M., Forness, S.R., & Rutherford, R.B., Jr. (1998). Social skills interventions with students with emotional and behavioral problems: A quantitative synthesis of single-subject research. *Behavioral Disorders, 23*(3), 193–201.

McAffee, J. (2002). *Navigating the social world: A curriculum for individuals with Asperger's syndrome, high functioning autism and related disorders.* Arlington, TX: Future Horizons.

McConnell, S.R. (2002). Interventions to facilitate social interaction for young children with autism: Review of available research and recommendations for educational intervention and future research. *Journal of Autism and Developmental Disorders, 32*(5), 351–372.

McConnell, S.R., Sisson, L.A., Cort, C.A., & Strain, P.S. (1991). Effects of social skills training and contingency management on reciprocal interaction of preschool children with behavioral handicaps. *Journal of Special Education, 24,* 473–495.

McDonnell, J., Hardman, M., Hightower, J., & Kiefer-O'Donnell, R. (1991). Variables associated with in-school and after-school integration of secondary students with severe disabilities. *Education and Training in Mental Retardation, 26,* 243–257.

McDonnell, J., Mathot-Buckner, C., Thorson, N., & Fister, S. (2001). Supporting the inclusion of students with moderate and severe disabilities in junior high school general education classes: The effects of classwide peer tutoring, multi-element curriculum, and accommodations. *Education & Treatment of Children, 24*(2), 141–160.

McFall, R. (1982). A review and reformulation of the concept of social skills. *Behavioral Assessment, 4,* 1–33.

McGinnis, E., & Goldstein, A. (1990). *Skillstreaming in early childhood: Teaching prosocial skills to the preschool and kindergarten child.* Champaign, IL: Research Press.

McGinnis, E., & Goldstein, A. (1997a). *Skillstreaming the adolescent: New strategies and perspectives for teaching prosocial skills.* Champaign, IL: Research Press.

McGinnis, E., & Goldstein, A. (1997b). *Skillstreaming the elementary school child: New strategies and perspectives for teaching prosocial skills.* Champaign, IL: Research Press.

McGregor, G., & Vogelsberg, R.T. (1998). *Inclusive schooling practices: Pedagogical and research foundations.* Pittsburgh: Allegheny University of the Health Sciences.

McIntosh, R., Vaughn, S., & Zaragoza, N. (1991). A review of social interventions for students with learning disabilities. *Journal of Learning Disabilities, 24,* 451–458.

McMahon, C.M., Wacker, D.P., Sasso, G.M., Berg, W.K., & Newton, S.M., (1996). Analysis of frequency and type of interactions in a peer-mediated social skills intervention: Instructional versus social interactions. *Education and Training in Mental Retardation and Developmental Disabilities, 31,* 339–352.

McMaster, K.N., & Fuchs, D. (2002). Effects of cooperative learning on the academic achievement of students with learning disabilities: An update of Tateyama Sniezek's review. *Learning Disabilities Research and Practice, 17,* 107–117.

Meichenbaum, D.H., & Goodman, J. (1971). Training impulsive children to talk to themselves: A means of developing self-control. *Journal of Abnormal Psychology, 77*(2), 115–126.

Meyer, L.H., & Henry, L.A. (1993). Cooperative classroom management: Student needs and fairness in the regular classroom. In J.W. Putnam (Ed.), *Children, youth, and change series: Cooperative learning and strategies for inclusion. Celebrating diversity in the classroom* (pp. 93–121). Baltimore: Paul H. Brookes Publishing Co.

Meyer, L.H., Minondo, S., Fisher, M., Larson, M.J., Dunmore, S., Black, J.W., et al. (1998). Frames of friendship: Social relationships among adolescents with diverse abilities. In L.H. Meyer, H. Park, M. Grenot-Scheyer, I.S. Schwartz, & B. Harry (Eds.), *Making friends: The influences of culture and development* (pp. 189–218). Baltimore: Paul H. Brookes Publishing Co.

Miracle, S.A., Collins, B.C., Schuster, J.W., & Grisham-Brown, J. (2001). Peer versus teacher delivered instruction: Effects on acquisition and maintenance. *Education and Training in Mental Retardation and Developmental Disabilities, 36,* 375–385.

Mitchem, K.J., Young, K.R., West, R.P., & Benyo, J. (2001). CWPASM: A classwide peer-assisted self-management program for general education classrooms. *Education and Treatment of Children, 24*(2), 111–140.

Morris, D. (1997, Fall). *Invented and adapted games that allow active participation by students with severe disabilities and their peers.* Unpublished manuscript, University of Virginia, Charlottesville.

Morrison, G.M., Laughlin, J., Smith, D., Ollansky, E., & Moore, B. (1992). Preferences for sources of social support of Hispanic male adolescent with mild learning handicaps. *Education and Training in Mental Retardation and Developmental Disabilities, 27,* 132–144.

Mount, B. (2000). *Person-centered planning: Finding directions for change using personal futures planning.* New York: Graphic Futures.

Murray, C., & Greenberg, M.T. (2001). Relationships with teachers and bonds with school: Social emotional adjustment correlates for children with and without disabilities. *Psychology in the Schools, 38*(1), 25–41.

Murray-Seegert, C. (1989). *Nasty girls, thugs, and humans like us: Social relations between severely disabled and nondisabled students in high school.* Baltimore: Paul H. Brookes Publishing Co.

Myles, B.S., Simpson, R.L., Ormsbee, C.K., & Erickson, C. (1993). Integrating preschool children with autism with their normally developing peers: Research findings and best practices recommendations. *Focus on Autistic Behavior, 8,* 1–18.

Neckerman, H.J. (1996). The stability of social groups in childhood and adolescence. *Social Development, 5,* 131–145.

Nevin, A.I., Thousand, J.S., & Villa, R.A. (2002). Creative cooperative groups lesson plans. In J.S. Thousand, R.A. Villa, & A.I. Nevin (Eds.), *Creativity and collaborative learning: A practical guide to empowering students, teachers, and families* (2nd ed., pp. 129–225). Baltimore: Paul H. Brookes Publishing Co.

Newborg, J., Stock., J., Wnek, L., Guidubaldi, J., & Svinicki, J. (1988). *Battelle Developmental Inventory with recalibrated technical data and norms.* Allen, TX: DLM-Teaching Resources.

No Child Left Behind Act of 2001, PL 107-110, 115 Stat. 1425.

O'Brien, J., & Lyle, C. (2000). The five accomplishments provide a guide for the development of a personal vision. In B. Mount, *Person-centered planning: Finding directions for change using personal futures planning* (p. 25). New York: Graphic Futures.

O'Brien, J., & Lyle O'Brien, C. (1998). *A little book about person-centered planning.* Toronto: Inclusion Press

Odom, S.L., Chandler, L.K., Ostrosky, M., McConnell, S.R., & Reaney, S. (1992). Fading teacher prompts from peer-initiated interventions for young children with disabilities. *Journal of Applied Behavior Analysis, 25,* 307–315.

Odom, S.L., & McConnell, S.R. (1997). *Play time/social time: Organizing your classroom to build social interaction skills.* Minneapolis: University of Minnesota Press.

Odom, S.L., McConnell, S.R., & McEvoy, M.A. (1992). Peer-related social competence and its significance for young children with disabilities. In S.L. Odom, S.R. McConnell, & M.A. McEvoy (Eds.), *Social competence of young children with disabilities: Issues and strategies for intervention* (pp. 3–36). Baltimore: Paul H. Brookes Publishing Co.

Odom, S.L., McConnell, S.R., McEvoy, M.S., Peterson, C., Ostrosky, M., Chandler, L.K., et al. (1999). Relative effects of interventions supporting the social competence of young children with disabilities. *Topics in Early Childhood Special Education, 19*(2), 75–102.

O'Neill, R.E., Horner, R.H., Albin, R.W., Sprague, J.R., Storey, K., & Newton, J.S. (1997). *Functional assessment and program development for problem behavior: A practical handbook.* Pacific Grove, CA: Brooks/ Cole.

O'Reilly, M.F., Lancione, G.E., Sigafoos, J., O'Donoghue, D., Lacey, C., & Edrisinha, C. (2004). Teaching social skills to adults with intellectual disabilities: A comparison of external control and problem-solving interventions. *Research in Developmental Disabilities, 25,* 399–412.

Pavri, S., & Monda-Amaya, L. (2001). Social support in inclusive schools: Student and teacher perspectives. *Exceptional Children, 67*(3), 391–411.

Pearl, R., Farmer, T.W., Van Acker, R., Rodkin, P.C., Bost, K.K., Coe, M., et al. (1998). The social integration of students with mild disabilities in general education classrooms: Peer group membership and peer-assessed social behavior. *Elementary School Journal, 99*(2), 167–194.

Peck, C.A., Donaldson, J., & Pezzoli, M. (1990). Some benefits nonhandicapped adolescents perceive for themselves from their social relationships with peers who have severe handicaps. *Journal of The Association for Persons with Severe Handicaps, 15,* 241–249.

Putnam. J.W. (1997). *Cooperative learning in diverse classrooms.* Upper Saddle River, NJ: Merrill.

Putnam, J.W. (1998). *Cooperative learning and strategies for inclusion: Celebrating diversity in the classroom* (2nd ed). Baltimore: Paul H. Brookes Publishing Co.

Quill, K.A. (2000). *DO-WATCH-LISTEN-SAY: Social and communication intervention for children with autism.* Baltimore: Paul H. Brookes Publishing Co.

Reddy, S., Utley, C.A., Delquadri, J., Mortweet, S.L., Greenwood, C.R., & Bowman, V. (1999). Peer tutoring for health and safety. *Teaching Exceptional Children, 31,* 44–52.

Rimmerman, A., Hozmi, B., & Duvdevany, I. (2000). Contact and attitudes toward individuals with disabilities among students tutoring children with developmental disabilities. *Journal of Intellectual and Developmental Disability, 25*(1), 13–18.

Rizzo, T.A. (1989). *Friendship development among children in school.* Norwood, NJ: Ablex.

Roach, V. (1995, May). *Winning ways: Creating inclusive schools, classrooms, and communities.*

Alexandria, VA: National Association of State Boards of Education.

Robinson, T.R., Smith, S.W., Miller, M.D., & Brownell, M.T. (1994). Cognitive behavior modification of hyperactivity/impulsivity and aggression: A meta-analysis of school-based studies. *Journal of Educational Psychology, 91,* 195–203.

Rodifer, K., Castagnera, D., Fisher, D., & Sax, C. (1999). Kennedy High School: From case-by-case to whole-school inclusion. In D. Fisher, C. Sax., & I. Pumpian, *Inclusive high schools: Learning from contemporary classrooms* (pp. 53–74). Baltimore: Paul H. Brookes Publishing Co.

Rothman, H.R., & Cosden, M. (1995). The relationship between self-perception of a learning disability and achievement, self-concept, and social support. *Learning Disability Quarterly, 18,* 203–212.

Ryan, J.B., Reid, R., & Epstein, M.H. (2004). Peer-mediated intervention studies on academic achievement for students with EBD: A review. *Remedial and Special Education, 25*(6), 330–342.

Sale, P., & Carey, D. (1995). The sociometric status of students with disabilities in a full-inclusion school. *Exceptional Children, 62,* 6–19.

Salisbury, C.L., Evans, I.M., & Palombaro, M.M. (1997). Collaborative problem-solving to promote the inclusion of young children with significant disabilities in primary grades. *Exceptional Children, 63,* 195–209.

Salisbury, C.L., Gallucci, C., Palombaro, M.M., & Peck, C.A. (1995). Strategies that promote social relations among elementary students with and without severe disabilities in inclusive schools. *Exceptional Children, 62,* 125–137.

Salisbury, C.L., & Palombaro, M.M. (Eds.). (1997). *No problem: Working things out our way.* Pittsburgh: Allegheny Singer Research Institute, Child and Family Studies Program.

Salisbury, C.L., Palombaro, M.M., & Evans, I.M. (Eds.). (1993). *Collaborative problem solving: Instructor's manual.* Pittsburgh: Allegheny Singer Research Institute, Child and Family Studies Program.

Sasso, G.M., Meloy, K.J., & Kavale, K. (1990). Generalization, maintenance, and behavioral covariation associated with social skills training through structured learning. *Behavioral Disorders, 16,* 9–22.

Sax, C., Fisher, D., Chappell, L., & Pratt, L. (1999). John Q. Adams High School: A pilot project takes shape. In D. Fisher, C. Sax., & I. Pumpian, *Inclusive high schools:*

Learning from contemporary schools (pp. 75–101). Baltimore: Paul H. Brookes Publishing Co.

Scattone, D, Wilczynski, S.M., Edwards, R.P., & Rabian, B. (2002). Decreasing disruptive behavior of children with autism using social stories. *Journal of Autism and Developmental Disorders, 32*(6), 535–544.

Schneider, B.H. (1992). Didactic methods for enhancing children's peer relations: A qualitative review. *Clinical Psychology Review, 12,* 362–382.

Schnorr, R.F. (1997). From enrollment to membership: "Belonging" in middle and high school classes. *Journal of The Association for Persons with Severe Handicaps, 22,* 1–15.

Shade, R.A., & Stewart, R. (2001). General education and special education preservice teachers' attitudes toward inclusion. *Preventing School Failure, 46*(1), 37–41.

Sharan, S. (1994). *Handbook of cooperative learning methods.* Westport, CT: Greenwood Press.

Shukla, S., Kennedy, C.H., & Cushing, L.S. (1998). Component analysis of peer support strategies: Adult influence on the participation of peers without disabilities. *Journal of Behavioral Education, 8,* 397–413.

Shukla, S., Kennedy, C.H., & Cushing, L.S. (1999). Intermediate school students with severe disabilities: Supporting their social participation in general education classrooms. *Journal of Positive Behavior Interventions, 1,* 130–140.

Sideridis, G.D., Utley, C., Greenwood, C.R., Delquadri, J., Dawson, H., Palmer, P., et al. (1997). Classwide peer tutoring: Effects on the spelling performance and social interactions of students with mild disabilities and their typical peers in an integrated instructional setting. *Journal of Behavioral Education, 7,* 435–462.

Sigman, M., & Ruskin, E. (1999). Continuity and change in the social competence of children with autism, Down syndrome, and developmental delays. *Monographs of the Society for Research in Child Development, 64,* 1–130.

Siperstein, G.N., & Rickards, E.P. (2004). *Promoting social success: A curriculum for children with special needs.* Baltimore: Paul H. Brookes Publishing Co.

Slavin, R.E. (1990). *Cooperative learning: Theory, research and practice.* Upper Saddle River, NJ: Prentice-Hall.

Slavin, R.E. (1991). Synthesis of research on cooperative learning. *Educational Leadership, 48*(5), 71–82.

Slavin, R.E. (1995). *Cooperative learning: Theory, research and practice* (2nd ed.). Boston: Allyn & Bacon.

Slavin, R.E., Madden, N.A., & Leavey, M. (1984). Effects of team assisted individualization on the mathematics achievement of academically handicapped and nonhandicapped students. *Journal of Educational Psychology, 76*(5), 813–819.

Slavin, R., Stevens, R.J., & Madden, N.A. (1988). Cooperative integrated reading and composition (CIRC): Effective cooperative learning in reading and language arts. *Cooperative Learning, 11*(4), 16–18.

Smith, B.W., & Sugai, G. (2000). A self-management functional assessment-based behavior support plan for a middle school student with EBD. *Journal of Positive Behavior Interventions, 2*(4), 208–217.

Smith, S.W. (2002). Applying cognitive-behavioral techniques to social skills instruction. *ERIC/OSEP Digest.* (ERIC Document Reproduction Service No. ED469279)

Snell, M.E., & Janney, R. (2005). *Teachers' guides to inclusive practices: Collaborative teaming* (2nd ed.). Baltimore: Paul H. Brookes Publishing Co.

Snell, M.E., & Raynes, M. (with Byrd, J.O., Colley, K.M., Gilley, C., Pityonak, C., Stallings, M.A., Van Dyke, R., et al.). (1995). Changing roles in inclusive schools: Staff perspectives at Gilbert Linkous Elementary. *Kappa Delta Pi Record, 31,* 104–109.

Social Integration Project. (1989). *Let's be social.* Tucson, AZ: Communication Skill Builders.

Staub, D., Schwartz, I.S., Gallucci, C., & Peck, C. (1994). Four portraits of friendship at an inclusive school. *Journal of The Association for Persons with Severe Disabilities, 19,* 314–325.

Staub, D., Spaulding, M., Peck, C.A., Gallucci, C., & Schwartz, I.S. (1996). Using nondisabled peers to support the inclusion of students with disabilities. *Journal of The Association for Persons with Severe Handicaps, 21,* 194–205.

Stevens, R.J., & Slavin, R.E. (1995). Effects of a cooperative learning approach in reading and writing on academically handicapped and nonhandicapped students. *Elementary School Journal, 95*(3), 241–262.

Strain, P.S. (1991). Ensuring quality of early intervention for children with severe disabilities. In L. Meyer, C.A. Peck, & L. Brown (Eds.), *Critical issues in the lives of people with severe disabilities* (pp. 479–483). Baltimore: Paul H. Brookes Publishing Co.

Strain, P.S. (2001). Empirically based social skill intervention: A case for quality-of-life improvement. *Behavioral Disorders, 27*(1), 30–36.

Strain, P.S., Kohler, F.W., Storey, K., & Danko, C.D. (1994). Teaching preschoolers with autism to self-monitor their social interactions: An analysis of results in home and school settings. *Journal of Emotional and Behavioral Disorders, 2,* 78–88.

Strain, P.S., & Odom, S.L. (1986). Peer social initiations: Effective intervention for social skills development of exceptional children. *Exceptional Children, 52,* 543–551.

Strain, P.S., & Schwartz, I. (2001). ABA and the development of meaningful social relations for young children with autism. *Focus on Autism and Other Developmental Disorders, 16*(2), 120–144.

Strain, P.S., Storey, K., & Smith, D. (1991). Quality of life outcomes for young special needs children. *Early Education and Development, 2,* 40–53.

Sugai, G., & Lewis, T.J. (1996). Preferred and promising practices for social skills instruction. *Focus on Exceptional Children, 29*(4), 1–16.

U.S. Department of Education. (2002). *Twenty-fourth annual report to congress on the implementation of the Individuals with Disabilities Education Act.* Jessup, MD: Author.

Utley, C.A., Mortweek, S.L., & Greenwood, C.R. (1997). Peer-mediated instruction and interventions. *Focus on Exceptional Children, 29*(5), 1–23.

Van der Klift, E., & Kunc, N. (1994). Beyond benevolence: Friendship and the politics of help. In J.S. Thousand, R.A. Villa, & A.I. Nevin (Eds.), *Creativity and collaborative learning: The practical guide to empowering students and teachers* (2nd ed., pp. 391–401). Baltimore: Paul H. Brookes Publishing Co.

Vance, E., & Weaver, P.J. (2002). *Class meetings: Young children solving problems together.* Washington, DC: National Association for the Education of Young Children.

Vandercook, T., York, J., & Forest, M. (1989). The McGill Action Planning System (MAPS): A strategy for building the vision. *Journal of The Association for Persons with Severe Handicaps, 14,* 205–215.

Vaughn, S., Elbaum, B.E., & Schumm, J.S. (1996). The effects of inclusion on the social functioning of students with learning disabilities. *Learning Disability Quarterly, 29,* 598–608.

Vaughn, S., & Haager, A. (1990). Social competence and learning disabilities: A prospective study. In H.L. Swanson & B.K. Keogh (Eds.), *Learning disabilities: Theoreti-*

cal and research issues (pp. 175–191). Mahwah, NJ: Lawrence Erlbaum Associates.

Vaughn, S., Kim, A., Morris, C.V., Sloan, M., Hughes, M.T., Elbaum, B., & Sridhar, D. (2003). Social skills interventions for young children with disabilities: A synthesis of group design studies. *Remedial and Special Education, 24*(1), 2–15.

Vaughn, S., Levine, L., & Ridley, C.A. (1986). *PALS: Problem-solving and affective learning strategies.* Chicago: Science Research Associates.

Villa, R.A., & Thousand, J.S. (2002). One divided by two or more. In J.S. Thousand, R.A. Villa, & A.I. Nevin (Eds.), *Creativity and collaborative learning: A practical guide to empowering students and teachers* (2nd ed., pp. 79–101). Baltimore: Paul H. Brookes Publishing Co.

Villa, R.A., & Thousand, J.S. (2005). *Creating an inclusive school* (2nd ed). Alexandria, VA: Association for Supervision and Curriculum Development.

Vogtle, L.K. (1996). Friendship between children with and without disabilities. *Dissertation Abstracts International, 57/01,* AAC9421262.

Wagner, M., Cadwallader, T.W., Marder, C., Newman, L., Garza, N., & Blackorby, J. (2002). *The other 80% of their time: The experiences of elementary and middle school students with disabilities in their nonschool hours.* Menlo Park, CA: SRI International.

Walker, H.M., Colvin, G., & Ramsey, E. (1995). *Antisocial behavior in school: Strategies and best practices.* Pacific Grove, CA: Brooks/Cole.

Walker, H.M., Hops, H., & Greenwood, C.R. (1993). *RECESS: A program for reducing negative-aggressive behavior.* Seattle: Educational Achievement Systems.

Walker, H.M., & McConnell, S.R. (1995). *The Walker-McConnell Scale of Social Competence and School Adjustment* (Rev. ed.). San Diego: Singular Publishing.

Walker, H.M., McConnell, S.R., Holmes, D., Todis, B., Walker, J., & Golden, N. (1983). *The Walker Social Skills Curriculum: The ACCEPTS program. A curriculum for children's effective peer and teacher skills.* Austin, TX: PRO-ED.

Walker, H.M., Ramsey, E., & Gresham, F.M. (2004). *Antisocial behavior in schools: Evidence-based practices* (2nd ed.). Pacific Grove, CA: Brooks/Cole.

Walker, H.M., Schwarz, I.E., Nippold, M., Irvin, L.K., & Noell, J. (1994). Social skills in school-age children and youth: Issues and best practices in assessment and intervention. *Topics in Language Disorders: Pragmatics and Social Skills in School-Age Children and Adolescents, 14*(3), 70–82.

Walker, H.M., & Severson, H.H. (1992). *Systematic Screening for Behavior Disorders (SSBD): User's guide and technical manual.* Longmont, CO: Sopris West.

Walker, H.M., Severson, H.H., & Feil, E.G. (1995). *The Early Screening Project: A proven child-find process.* Longmont, CO: Sopris West.

Walker, H.M., Stiller, B., Golly, A., Kavanagh, K., Severson, H.H., & Feil, E.G. (1997). *First step to success.* Longmont, CO: Sopris West.

Walker, H., Todis, B., Holmes, D., & Horton, G. (1988). *The Walker Social Skills Curriculum: The ACCESS program. Adolescent curriculum for communication and effective social skills.* Austin, TX: PRO-ED.

Watson, S.M.R., & Keith, K.D. (2002). Comparing the quality of life of school-age children with and without disabilities. *Mental Retardation, 40*(4), 304–312.

Williams, G.A., & Asher, S.R. (1992). Assessment of loneliness at school among children with mild mental retardation. *American Journal on Mental Retardation, 96,* 373–385.

Williams, G.J., & Reisberg, L. (2003). Successful inclusion: Teaching social skills through curriculum integration. *Intervention in School and Clinic, 38*(4), 205–210.

Wittmer, D., Doll, B., & Strain, P. (1996). Social and emotional development in early childhood: The identification of competence and disabilities. *Journal of Early Intervention, 20,* 299–318.

York-Barr, J., Doyle, M.B., & Kronberg, R.M. (Eds.). (1996). *Creating inclusive school communities: A staff development series for general and special educators: Module 3a. Curriculum as everything students learn in school. Planning for transitions. Facilitator's guide.* Baltimore: Paul H. Brookes Publishing Co.

Young, B., Simpson, R.L., Smith-Myles, B., & Kamps, D.M. (1996). An examination of paraprofessional involvement in supporting inclusion of students with autism. *Focus on Autism and Other Developmental Disabilities, 12*(1), 31–38, 48.

Zaragoza, N., Vaughn, S., & McIntosh, R. (1991). Social skills interventions and children with behavior problems: A review. *Behavioral Disorders, 16*(4), 260–275.

Appendix A

Blank Forms

Rating Scale to Assess a Student's Relationships

School: _____   Date: _____

Classroom: _____   Focus student(s): _____

Ratings: Frequently   Sometimes   Never   No opportunity to observe (NO)

Assessment question	Rating	Ideas for improvement
Ghost/guest: Does the focus child frequently get "passed over" as if he or she were not there (ghost)? Do staff members talk about another placement as soon as there is a problem (guest)?	Frequently Sometimes Never NO	
Inclusion child: Does the teacher say, "I have 27 students plus 2 included students"?	Frequently Sometimes Never NO	
I'll help: Do classmates use the words *work with* or *help* whenever they refer to times spent with the focus child?	Frequently Sometimes Never NO	
Just another child: Is the focus child expected to participate in class activities along with everyone else?	Frequently Sometimes Never NO	
Regular friend: Has the focus child ever been invited to a party by a classmate?	Frequently Sometimes Never NO	
Best friend: Does the focus child have one or more friends who call him or her on the telephone at home and/or who visit him or her after school or on weekends?	Frequently Sometimes Never NO	

From Meyer, L.H., Minondo, S., Fisher, M., Larson, M.J., Dunmore, S., Black, J.W., et al. (1998). Frames of friendship: Social relationships among adolescents with diverse abilities. In L.H. Meyer, H. Park, M. Grenot-Scheyer, I.S. Schwartz, & B. Harry (Eds.), *Making friends: The influences of culture and development* (pp. 189–218). Baltimore: Paul H. Brookes Publishing Co.; adapted by permission.)

ABC Recording Form

Student: Observer: Dates:

Class/routine: Location:

Behavior(s):   Possible setting event:

Antecedents	Behavior	Consequences
What happened before?	What is the problem behavior?	What happened afterward?

Cooperative Learning Lesson Plan

Content area: **Date:**

Grade: **Teacher:**

Lesson objectives:

1. Group lesson objective(s):

2. Cooperative skill objective(s):

Adaptations/accommodations for individual learning needs:

Student   Adaptations/accommodation(s)

Materials:

For lesson introduction/review, directions, and closure:

For each group:

Lesson steps:

(continued)

Lesson steps *(continued)*

Summary/closure:

Group members with individual goals:

Comments:

Cooperative Learning Group Agenda

Activity:

Date: **Time:**

Task:

Members and jobs:

Facilitator: Reporter:

Scout: Timekeeper

Recorder: Materials:

Check off each step as you complete it.

☐ 1.

☐ 2.

☐ 3.

☐ 4.

☐ 5.

☐ 6.

☐ 7.

☐ 8.

☐ 9.

☐ 10.

Individual Adaptations Plan for Cooperative Learning Activities

Student: School year/semester:

Teacher(s):   Grade:

Individualized education program goals:

Objectives for participation:

Cooperative learning group assignment:

Role assignment:

Positioning and environmental considerations:

Peer supports during cooperative learning activities:

Training/supervision needed by classmates:

Adult supports during cooperative learning activities:

Social Relationship Worksheet

Classroom: School: Date:

Focus student(s):   Team members:

Factors influencing social participation and relationships	Actions taken by individuals in school, classroom, and home to improve social contexts and skills
1. **Opportunity:** Being physically present around typically developing peers on a regular basis with routine and spontaneous occasions to interact **Issues?** Yes No **List priority issues:** **Select indicators:** o Percentage of school day spent in inclusive class(es) o Number of integrated school and community settings in which the student participates o Number of peers with whom the student has regular interactions during a day or week o Percentage of in-class time (or number of routines/activities) spent participating with peers	o Assign all students to general education classes with needed supports. o Address architectural and physical barriers to inclusion (e.g., no ramps, elevators, or curb cuts). o Increase time in general education classes. o Increase time in other locations in the school. o Create during- and after-school social interaction options through friendship groups and peer support clubs. o Fade one-to-one time with adults. o Add in peers and increase small-group instruction. o Integrate student seating in class, at lunch, and during in-school activities. o Identify and create integrated community options.
2. **Atmosphere:** Prevailing staff and student attitudes toward human differences and talents and related values people hold about social relationships, peer support, a competitive versus a cooperative focus, student involvement in the resolution of social concerns, regard for everyone's unique talents, and so forth **Issues?** Yes No **List priority issues:** **Select indicators:** o Pre/post survey of knowledge of and attitudes regarding disabilities o Number/percentage of inclusive extracurricular activities o Number/percentage of classrooms with scheduled time for social skills instruction o Number/percentage of classrooms with scheduled, structured cooperative learning groups	o Have staff examine values toward ability, disability, and learning. o Involve staff, parents, and students in creating a school mission statement. o Organize ability- and disability-awareness activities. o Organize service activities. o Hold teacher in-service session on cooperative learning and support for its use in classrooms. o Explore alternatives to ability grouping and competitive activities. o Hold staff training on social skills and relationships and their facilitation. o Adopt and use a social skills curriculum. o Train staff and students in collaborative teaming and problem solving. o Offer student forums on social concerns such as teasing and ridicule; engage students in problem-solving school solutions. o Increase the number and range of extracurricular opportunities for students to develop their unique talents.

(continued)

3. **Social support and motivation:** Having the needed supports and encouragement from adults and peers to interact socially and build relationships **Issues?** Yes No **List priority issues:** **Select indicators:** o Periodic assessment of student's peer-initiated versus adult-initiated interactions o Number of peer support group or peer problem-solving meetings held o Number of people in each circle of the student's Circles of Friends o Number of peers who list the student in their Circles of Friends	o Explore types of adult facilitation that can encourage appropriate social interactions (e.g., modeling, backing off). o Explore types of peer support (e.g., peer groups using problem solving and goal setting, friendship groups, natural relationships strategies). o Adjust and fade adult facilitation and supports. o Identify interaction problems (e.g., aggression, excess teasing, isolation); plan and use teaching and peer supports to improve student behavior. o Identify and resolve barriers to social interaction (e.g., schedules, student hygiene, peer network values). o Improve communication rates by addressing student motivation, communication system, or social skill performance. o Involve students; examine the social contexts for interest, variety, age/ability match, cooperative features, participation, and needed modifications. o Use or improve peer networks.
4. **Academic achievement:** Possessing needed academic skills (e.g., in such areas as reading, writing, math, science, social studies, vocational and community training) and the confidence that comes from having and using these skills **Issues:** Yes No **List priority issues:** **Select indicators:** o Progress data on relevant IEP goals o Number of peer tutoring sessions held o Number of participatory responses from a student during a particular type of instructional activity (e.g., cooperative learning group for science, small-group reading lesson)	o Add what is needed to enable students to succeed in learning needed skills (e.g., student choice and involvement in IEP and program, incentives for learning, accommodations, environmental changes, modifications in schoolwork that are only as special as necessary). o Make use of reciprocal peer tutoring and cross-age tutoring. o Add cooperative learning methods to science, math, social studies, and literature lessons.

(continued)

5. **Social competence and interaction skills:** Being able to initiate interactions with peers, respond to peers' initiations, and elaborate on the initiations or responses of peers at a typical rate **Issues?** Yes No **List priority issues:** **Select indicators:** o Number of group and/or individual social skills instructional sessions o Number of peers with whom the student interacts during a specified activity o Number or rate of peer-initiated and student-initiated interactions during a particular activity (e.g., lunch, a recreational/free time activity, teacher advisory period or class meeting) o Rate of targeted behavior problem during a specified time period	o Adopt and use a social skills curriculum. o Examine skills involved in social interactions, and identify acquisition and performance problems or competing behaviors. o Plan and use teaching methods and peer supports to improve social skill problems. o Involve students in planning. o Identify student's communication ability; target needed skills (e.g., improve rate, expand vocabulary, improve consistency, augment with communication book/device for clarity). o Check peers' skills using alternative modes of communicating. o Determine nonstigmatizing ways to teach (format, methods) within routine contexts.
6. **Maintenance and generalization of relationships:** Keeping and extending social relationships as well as remembering and transferring known social skills across different people and school and nonschool settings **Issues?** Yes No **List priority issues:** **Select indicators:** o Rate of student's success in using a self-management device/system o Number of student-initiated and/or peer-initiated interactions in a nontraining setting o Record of number of participants at peer support group meetings over time o Number of people, places, activities, choices made by the student at different times over the course of a school year	o Contextualize any instruction. o Use adult facilitation in natural contexts. o Fade adult facilitation to self-monitoring. o Teach students to problem-solve; encourage their independent use of these skills. o Teach students to self-manage. o Involve family. o Include social support in IEP. o Plan for transition across classrooms and schools and to community and employment settings.

From Breen, C.G., Haring, T.G., Weiner, J., Laitinen, R.E., & Bernstein, D.D. (1991). Evaluating the inclusion and social competence of students with severe disabilities in community and school environments. In C.G. Breen, C.H. Kennedy, & T.G. Haring (Eds.), *Social context research project: Methods for facilitating the inclusion of students with disabilities in integrated school and community contexts* (pp. 23–53). Santa Barbara: University of California; adapted by permission.

Issue/Action Planning Form

Student/team/group: Date:

Team members present:

Issue	Planned action	Person(s) responsible	By when

Appendix B

Resources on
Social Relationships and Peer Support

COOPERATIVE LEARNING GROUPS

Cosden, M.A., & Haring, T.G. (1992). Cooperative learning in the classroom: Contingencies, group interactions, and students with special needs. *Journal of Behavioral Education, 2,* 53–71.

Hunt, P., Staub, D., Alwell, M., & Goetz, L. (1994). Achievement by all students within the context of cooperative learning groups. *Journal of The Association for Persons with Severe Handicaps, 19,* 290–301.

Johnson, D.W., & Johnson, R.T. (1999). *Learning together and alone: Cooperation, competition, and individualization* (5th ed.). Boston: Allyn & Bacon.

Johnson, D.W., Johnson, R.T., & Holubec, E.J. (1993). *Circles of learning: Cooperation in the classroom* (5th ed.). Edina, MN: Interaction Book Co.

Johnson, D.W., Johnson, R.T., & Holubec, E.J. (1994). *Cooperative learning in the classroom.* Alexandria, VA: Association for Supervision and Curriculum Development.

Putnam, J.W. (1997). *Cooperative learning in diverse classrooms.* Upper Saddle River, NJ: Merrill.

Putnam, J.W. (Ed.). (1998). *Cooperative learning and strategies for inclusion: Celebrating diversity in the classroom* (2nd ed.). Baltimore: Paul H. Brookes Publishing Co.

Sharan, S. (1994). *Handbook of cooperative learning methods.* Westport, CT: Greenwood Press.

Slavin, R.E. (1995). *Cooperative learning: Theory, research and practice* (2nd ed.). Boston: Allyn & Bacon.

FRIENDSHIPS

Amando, A.N. (Ed.). (1993). *Friendships and community connections between people with and without developmental disabilities.* Baltimore: Paul H. Brookes Publishing Co.

Falvey, M., Forest, M., Pearpoint, J., & Rosenberg, R. (1997). *All my life's a circle: Using the tools—Circles, MAPS and PATHs* (2nd ed.). Toronto: Inclusion Press.

Heyne, L.A., Schleien, S.J., & McAvoy, L.H. (1993). *Making friends: Using recreation activities to promote friendship between children with and without disabilities.* Minneapolis: University of Minnesota, Institute on Community Integration.

Institute on Community Integration, University of Minnesota. (n.d.). *Yes I Can Social Inclusion Program for Middle and High School Students.* Available at http://www.ici.umn.edu/yesican/

Meyer, L.H., Park, H.-S., Grenot-Scheyer, M., Schwartz, I.S., & Harry, B. (Eds.). (1998). *Making friends: The influences of culture and development.* Baltimore: Paul H. Brookes Publishing Co.

O'Brien, J., & Lyle O'Brien, C. (1998). *A little book about person-centered planning.* Toronto: Inclusion Press.

Pearpoint, J., O'Brien, J., & Forest, M. (1993). *PATH: A workbook for planning positive possible futures.* Toronto: Inclusion Press.

Schaffner, B., & Buswell, B. (1992). *Connecting students: A guide to thoughtful friendship facilitation for educators and families.* Colorado Springs, CO: Peak Parent Center.

Staub, D. (1998). *Delicate threads: Friendships between children with and without special needs in inclusive settings.* Bethesda, MD: Woodbine House.

Tashie, C., & Rossetti, Z. (2002). Quick-guide #13: Supporting friendships for all students. In M.F. Giangreco (Ed.), *Quick-guides to inclusion 3: Ideas for educating students with disabilities* (pp. 57–83). Baltimore: Paul H. Brookes Publishing Co.

IMPROVING ATTITUDES AND THE SCHOOL SOCIAL ENVIRONMENT

Benton, H. (1996). *Whoa, Nellie!* Columbus, OH: Open Minds.

Blaska, J.K., & Lynch, E.C. (1998). Is everyone included? Using children's literature to facilitate the understanding of disabilities. *Young Children, 53*(2), 36–38.

Bodine, R.J., Crawford, D.K., & Schrumpf, F. (2003). *Creating the peaceable school: A comprehensive program for teaching conflict resolution.* Champaign, IL: Research Press.

Bunch, G. (n.d.). *Kids, disabilities and regular classrooms: An annotated bibliography of selected children's literature on disability.* Toronto: Inclusion Press.

Derman-Sparks, L., & The Anti-Bias Curriculum Task Force. (1989). *Anti-bias Curriculum: Tools for empowering young children.* Washington, DC: National Association for the Education of Young Children.

Developmental Studies Center. (1996). *Ways we want our class to be: Class meetings that build commitment to kindness and learning.* Oakland, CA: Author.

Dyches, T.T., & Prater, M.A. (2000). Developmental disability in children's literature: Issues and annotated bibliography. *MRDD Prism Series, 3.* Arlington, VA: Council for Exceptional Children.

Elias, M.J., Zins, J.E., Weissberg, R.P., Frey, K.S., Greenberg, M.T., Haynes, N.M., et al. (1997). *Promoting social and emotional learning: Guidelines for educators.* Alexandria, VA: Association for Supervision and Curriculum Development.

National Information Center for Children and Youth with Disabilities. (NICHCY). (2001, June). *Children's literature and disability: Resources you can use* (2nd ed.). Washington, DC: Author.

National Information Center for Children and Youth with Disabilities. (NICHCY). (2003, March). *Resource lists: Disability awareness* (2nd ed.). Washington, DC: Author.

Prater, M.A. (2000). Using juvenile literature with portrayals of disabilities in your classroom. *Intervention in School and Clinic, 35*(3), 167–176.

Salend, S.J. (1999). Facilitating friendships among diverse students. *Intervention in School and Clinic, 35*(1), 9–15.

Sax, C., Fisher, D., Chappell, L., & Pratt, L. (1999). John Q. Adams High School: A pilot project takes shape. In D. Fisher, C. Sax., & I. Pumpian, *Inclusive high schools: Learning from contemporary classrooms* (pp. 75–101). Baltimore: Paul H. Brookes Publishing Co.

Schrumpf, F., Crawford, D.K., & Bodine, R.J. (1997). *Peer mediation: Conflict resolution in schools* (Rev. ed.). Champaign, IL: Research Press.

Vaughn, S., & Rothlein, L. (1994). *Read it again! Books to prepare children for inclusion (Grades K–3).* Glenview, IL: GoodYear Books/Scott, Foresman.

Institute on Disability, University of New Hampshire. (n.d.). *Petroglyphs: We used to think, now we know* [Videotape]. Durham, NH: Author.

Karten, T.J. (2005). *Inclusion strategies that work! Research-based methods for the classroom.* Thousand Oaks, CA: Corwin Press.

McGregor, G., & Vogelsberg, R.T. (1998). *Inclusive schooling practices: Pedagogical and research foundations. A synthesis of the literature that informs best practices about inclusive schooling.* Baltimore: Paul H. Brookes Publishing Co.

National Center for Children and Youth with Disabilities. (NICHCY). (1995, July). Planning for inclusion. *NICHCY News Digest, 5*(1), 1–31.

Odom, S.L. (Ed.). (2002). *Widening the circle: Including children with disabilities in preschool programs.* Williston, VT: Teachers College Press.

Philipsen, M. (Ed.). (2000, July). *Hot topics series: Assessing inclusion. Strategies for success.* Bloomington, IN: Phil Delta Kappa, Center on Evaluation, Development, and Research.

Roach, V. (1995, May). *Winning ways: Creating inclusive schools, classrooms, and communities.* Alexandria, VA: National Association of State Boards of Education.

Villa, R.A., & Thousand, J.S. (2000). *Creating an inclusive school* (2nd ed). Alexandria, VA: Association for Supervision and Curriculum Development.

Villa, R.A., & Thousand, J.S. (Eds.). (2000). *Restructuring for caring and effective education: Piecing the puzzle together* (2nd ed.). Baltimore: Paul H. Brookes Publishing Co.

York-Barr, J. (Series Ed.). (1996). *Creating inclusive school communities: A staff development series for general and special educators* (Modules 1–5). Baltimore: Paul H. Brookes Publishing Co.

INCLUSIVE SCHOOLS

Bunch, G.O. (1998). *Inclusion: How to. Essential classroom strategies.* Toronto: Inclusion Press.

Fisher, D., Sax, C., & Pumpian, I. (1999). *Inclusive high schools: Learning from contemporary classrooms.* Baltimore: Paul H. Brookes Publishing Co.

Fryxell, D., & Kennedy, C.H. (1995). Placement along the continuum of services and its impact on students' social relationships. *Journal of The Association for Persons with Severe Handicaps, 20,* 259–269.

PEER PROBLEM-SOLVING

Giangreco, M.F., Cloninger, C.J., Dennis, R.E., & Edelman, S.W. (2002). Problem-solving methods to facilitate inclusive education. In J.S. Thousand, R.A. Villa, & A.I. Nevin (Eds.), *Creativity and collaborative learning: The practical guide to empowering students, teachers, and families* (2nd ed., pp. 111–134). Baltimore: Paul H. Brookes Publishing Co.

Salisbury, C.L., & Palombaro, M.M. (Eds.). (1993). *No problem: Working things out our way.*

Pittsburgh: Allegheny Singer Research Institute, Child and Family Studies Program.

Salisbury, C.L., Palombaro, M.M., & Evans, I.M. (Eds.). (1993). *Collaborative problem solving: Instructor's manual.* Pittsburgh: Allegheny Singer Research Institute, Child and Family Studies Program.

PEER RELATIONSHIPS THROUGH PEER SUPPORT

Dobbin, J. [Producer]. (n.d.). *MAPS step by step: John O'Brien facilitating Shakif Asante's MAP* [Videotape]. Toronto: Inclusion Press.

English, K., Shafer, K., Goldstein, H., & Kazmarek, L. (1997). *Teaching buddy skills to preschoolers.* Washington, DC: American Association on Mental Retardation.

Forest, M., & Pearpoint, J. (1997). *All means all: An introduction to Circles, MAPs, and PATHs* [Videotape]. Toronto: Inclusion Press.

Forest, M., & Pearpoint, J. (1997). *All means all: An introduction to Circles, MAPS, and PATHs Program II: Moving students form isolation into action* [Videotape]. Toronto: Inclusion Press.

Garrison-Harrell, L., Kamps, D., & Kravits, T. (1997). The effects of peer networks on social-communicative behaviors for students with autism. *Focus on Autism and Other Developmental Disabilities, 12,* 241–254.

Haring, T.G., & Breen, C.G. (1992). A peer-mediated social network intervention to enhance the social integration of persons with moderate and severe disabilities. *Journal of Applied Behavior Analysis, 25,* 319–333.

Hendrickson, J.M., Shokoohi-Yekta, M., Hamre-Nietupski, S., & Gable, R.A. (1996). Middle and high school students' perceptions on being friends with peers with severe disabilities. *Exceptional Children, 63,* 19–28.

Holburn, S., & Vietze, P.M. (Eds.). (2002). *Person-centered planning: Research, practice, and future directions.* Baltimore: Paul H. Brookes Publishing Co.

Hughes, C., & Carter, E.W. (2006). *Success for all students: Promoting inclusion in secondary schools through peer buddy programs.* Boston: Allyn & Bacon.

Hunt, P., Alwell, M., Farron-Davis, F., & Goetz, L. (1996). Creating socially supportive environments for fully included students who experience multiple disabilities. *Journal of*

The Association for Persons with Severe Handicaps, 21, 53–71.

Janney, R.E., & Snell, M.E. (1996). How teachers use peer interactions to include students with moderate and severe disabilities in elementary general education classes. *Journal of The Association for Persons with Severe Handicaps, 21,* 72–80.

Kamps, D.M., Potucek, J., Lopez, A.G., Kravits, T., & Kemmerer, K. (1997). The use of peer networks across multiple settings to improve social interaction for students with autism. *Journal of Behavioral Education, 7,* 335–357.

Kohler, F.W., & Strain, P.S. (1999). Maximizing peer-mediated resources in integrated preschool classrooms. *Topics in Early Childhood Education, 19*(2), 92–110.

Metropolitan Nashville Peer Buddy Program. Information available at http://www.ed.uiuc.edu/sped/tri/peerbuddy.htm

Perske, R. (1988). *Circles of Friends: People with disabilities and their friends enrich the lives of one another.* Nashville: Abingdon Press.

Salisbury, C.L., Gallucci, C., Palombaro, M.M., & Peck, C.A. (1995). Strategies that promote social relations among elementary students with and without severe disabilities in inclusive schools. *Exceptional Children, 62,* 125–137.

Schaffner, B., & Buswell, B.E. (1992). *Connecting students: A guide to thoughtful friendship facilitation for educators and families.* Colorado Springs, CO: PEAK Parent Center.

Staub, D., Spaulding, M., Peck, C.A., Gallucci, C., & Schwatz, I.S. (1996). Using non-disabled peers to support the inclusion of students with disabilities. *Journal of The Association for Persons with Severe Handicaps, 21,* 194–205.

PEER TUTORING AND CROSS-AGE TUTORING

Greenwood, C.R., Delquadri, J., & Carta, J. (1997). *Together we can! Classwide peer tutoring to improve basic academic skills.* Longmont, CO: Sopris West.

Greenwood, C.R., Delquadri, J., & Carta, J.J. (1999). *ClassWide Peer Tutoring (CWPT) for teachers.* Longmont, CO: Sopris West.

Greenwood, C.R., Terry, B., Delquadri, J.C., Elliott, M., & Arreaga-Mayer, C. (1995). *Classwide peer tutoring (CWPT): Effective teaching and research review.* Kansas City: University of Kansas, Juniper Gardens Children's Project.

Kamps, D., Barbetta, P.M., Leonard, B.R., & Delquadri, J. (1994). Classwide peer tutoring: An integration strategy to improve reading skills and promote peer interactions among students with autism and general education peers. *Journal of Applied Behavior Analysis, 27*, 49–61.

PROBLEM BEHAVIOR

Carr, E.G., Levin, L., McConnachie, G., Carlson, J.I., Kemp, D.C., & Smith, C.E. (1997). *Communication-based intervention for problem behavior: A user's guide for producing positive change.* Baltimore: Paul H. Brookes Publishing Co.

Janney, R.E., & Snell, M.E. (2000). *Teachers' guides to inclusive practices: Behavioral support.* Baltimore: Paul H. Brookes Publishing Co.

Koegel, R.L., Koegel, L.K., & Parks, D.R. (1995). "Teach the individual" model of generalization: Autonomy through self-management. In R.L. Koegel & L.K. Koegel (Eds.), *Teaching children with autism: Strategies for initiating positive interactions and improving learning opportunities* (pp. 67–77). Baltimore: Paul H. Brookes Publishing Co.

O'Neill, R.E., Horner, R.H., Albin, R.W., Storey, K., & Sprague, J.R. (1990). *Functional analysis of problem behavior: A practical assessment guide.* Pacific Grove, CA: Brooks/Cole.

Walker, H.M., Colvin, G., & Ramsey, E. (1995). *Antisocial behavior in school: Strategies and best practices.* Pacific Grove, CA: Brooks/Cole.

SOCIAL COMPETENCE

Brown, W.H., Odom, S.L., & Buysse, V. (2002). Assessment of preschool children's peer-related social competence. *Assessment for Effective Intervention, 27*(4), 61–71.

Gresham, F.M. (1997). Social competence and students with behavior disorders: Where we've been, where we are, and where we should go. *Education and Treatment of Children, 20*, 233–249.

Gustafson, R.N., & Haring, N.G. (1992). Social competence issues in the integration of students with handicaps. In K.A. Haring, D.L. Lovett, & N.G. Haring (Eds.), *Integrated lifestysle services for persons with disabilities* (pp. 20–58). New York: Springer-Verlag.

Odom, S.L., McConnell, S.R., & McEvoy, M.A. (1992). Peer-related social competence and its significance for young children with disabilities. In S.L. Odom, S.R. McConnell, & M.A. McEvoy (Eds.), *Social competence of young children with disabilities: Issues and strategies for intervention* (pp. 3–36). Baltimore: Paul H. Brookes Publishing Co.

SOCIAL RELATIONSHIPS

Haring, T.G. (1991). Social relationships. In L.H. Meyer, C.A. Peck, & L. Brown (Eds.), *Critical issues in the lives of people with severe disabilities* (pp. 195–217). Baltimore: Paul H. Brookes Publishing Co.

Meyer, L.H., Park, H.-S., Grenot-Scheyer, M., Schwartz, I.S., & Harry, B. (Eds.). (1998). *Making friends: The influences of culture and development.* Baltimore: Paul H. Brookes Publishing Co.

Odom, S.L., McConnell, S.R., McEvoy, M.S., Peterson, C., Ostrosky, M., Chandler, L.K., et al. (1999). Relative effects of interventions supporting the social competence of young children with disabilities. *Topics in Early Childhood Special Education, 19*(2), 75–102.

Pianta, R.C., & Walsh, D.J. (1996). *High-risk children in schools: Constructing sustaining relationships.* New York: Routledge.

Snell, M.E., & Vogtle, L.K. (1996). Interpersonal relationships of school-aged children and adolescents with mental retardation. In R.L. Schalock (Ed.), *Quality of life: Its application to persons with disabilities* (Vol. 2, pp. 43–61). Washington, DC: American Association on Mental Retardation.

TEACHING SOCIAL SKILLS AND SELF-CONTROL

Brown, W.H., & Odom, S.L. (1994). Strategies and tactics for promoting generalization and maintenance of young children's social behavior. *Research in Developmental Disabilities, 15*, 99–118.

Chandler, L.K. (1992). Promoting children's social/survival skills as a strategy for transition to mainstreamed kindergarten programs. In S.L. Odom, S.R. McConnell, & M.A. McEvoy (Eds.), *Social competence of young children with disabilities: Issues and strategies for intervention* (pp. 245–276). Baltimore: Paul H. Brookes Publishing Co.

English, K., Shafer, K., Goldstein, H., & Kaczmarek, L. (1997). *Teaching buddy skills to preschoolers.* Washington, DC: American Association on Mental Retardation.

Forness, S.R., & Kavale, K.A. (1996). Treating social skill deficits in children with learning disabilities: A meta-analysis of the research. *Learning Disabilities Quarterly, 19,* 2–13.

Gray, C.A. (1998). Social stories and comic strip conversations with students with Asperger syndrome and high-functioning autism. In E. Schopler & G.B. Mesibov (Eds.), *Asperger syndrome or high-functioning autism? Current issues in autism* (pp. 167–198). New York: Plenum Press.

Gray, C.A., & Garand, J.D. (1993). Social stories: Improving responses of students with autism with accurate social information. *Focus on Autistic Behavior, 8*(1), 1–10.

Hodgdon, L.Q. (1994). Solving social-behavioral problems through the use of visually supported communication. In K.A. Quill (Ed.), *Teaching children with autism: Strategies to enhance communication and socialization* (pp. 265–286). New York: Delmar.

Porro, B. (2002). *Teaching conflict resolution with the Rainbow Kids Program.* Alexandria, VA: Association for Supervision and Curriculum Development.

Smith, S.W. (2002). Applying cognitive-behavioral techniques to social skills instruction. *ERIC/OSEP Digest.* (ERIC Reproduction Services No. ED469279)

Walker, H.M., Colvin, G., & Ramsey, E. (1995). *Antisocial behavior in school: Strategies and best practices.* Pacific Grove, CA: Brooks/Cole.

Walker, H.M., Schwarz, I.E., Nippold, M., Irwin, L.K., & Noell, J. (1994). Social skills in school-age children and youth: Issues and best practices in assessment and intervention. *Topics in Language Disorders: Pragmatics and Social Skills in School age Children and Adolescents, 14*(3), 70–82.

TEAM PLANNING

Giangreco, M.F., Cloninger, C.J., Dennis, R.E., & Edelman, S.W. (2002). Problem-solving methods to facilitate inclusive education. In J.S. Thousand, R.A. Villa, & A.I. Nevin (Eds.), *Creativity and collaborative learning: The practical guide to empowering students, teachers, and families* (2nd ed., pp. 111–134). Baltimore: Paul H. Brookes Publishing Co.

Snell, M.E., & Janney, R.E. (2005). *Teachers' guides to inclusive practices: Collaborative teaming* (2nd ed). Baltimore: Paul H. Brookes Publishing Co.

Index

Page numbers followed by *f* indicate figures.